STRANGE HORIZONS

BOOKS BY SAM MOSKOWITZ

The Immortal Storm: A History of Science Fiction Fandom

Explorers of the Infinite: Shapers of Science Fiction

Seekers of Tomorrow: Masters of Modern Science Fiction

Science Fiction by Gaslight: A History and Anthology of Science Fiction in the Popular Magazines, 1891–1911

Under the Moons of Mars: A History and Anthology of "The Scientific Romance" in the Munsey Magazines, 1912–1920

EDITED BY SAM MOSKOWITZ

Masterpieces of Science Fiction

Modern Masterpieces of Science Fiction

The Man Who Called Himself Poe

The Crystal Man by Edward Page Mitchell

Three Stories by Murray Leinster, Jack Williamson and John Wyndham

Life Everlasting, and Other Tales of Science, Fantasy and Horror by David H. Keller, M.D.

Out of the Storm by William Hope Hodgson

Strange Signposts (with Roger Elwood)

Exploring Other Worlds

The Coming of the Robots

Editor's Choice in Science Fiction

Futures to Infinity

Horrors Unknown

Horrors Unseen

When Women Rule

Great Railroad Stories of the World

STRANGE HORIZONS

THE SPECTRUM OF SCIENCE FICTION

SAMUEL

SAM MOSKOWITZ

CHARLES SCRIBNER'S SONS / NEW YORK

Library of Congress Cataloging in Publication Data
Moskowitz, Samuel.
    Strange horizons.
    1. Science fiction—History and criticism. I. Title.
PN3448.S45M665   809.3'876   76–17088
ISBN 0-684-14774-2

Space, God, and Science Fiction appeared in a briefer version as *Religion in Science Fiction: God, Space & Faith* in AMAZING STORIES, copyright © 1965 Ziff-Davis Publishing Company.

The Day of the Messiah appeared in a briefer version as *The Jew in Science Fiction* in WORLDS OF TOMORROW, copyright © 1966 The Galaxy Publishing Company.

Rockets to Green Pastures appeared in a briefer version as *The Negro in Science Fiction* in WORLDS OF TOMORROW, copyright © 1967 The Galaxy Publishing Corporation.

When Women Rule appeared in a briefer version in IF SCIENCE FICTION, copyright © 1967 The Galaxy Publishing Corporation, copyright © 1972 Sam Moskowitz.

Better the World Below Than the World Above appeared as *S. Fowler Wright: The Devil's Disciple?* in AMAZING STORIES, copyright © 1964 Ziff-Davis Publishing Company.

The Invasion of the Incredible Headshrinkers appeared as *The Psychiatric Syndrome in Science Fiction* in WORLDS OF TOMORROW, copyright © 1966 The Galaxy Publishing Corporation.

From Sherlock to Spaceships appeared in a briefer version as *The Sleuth in Science Fiction* in WORLDS OF TOMORROW, copyright © 1966 The Galaxy Publishing Corporation.

Tom Swift and the Syndicate appeared in a briefer version in WORLDS OF TOMORROW, copyright © 1966 The Galaxy Publishing Corporation.

Warriors of If, copyright © 1975 Sam Moskowitz.

Lo! The Poor Forteans appeared in a briefer version in AMAZING STORIES, copyright © 1965 The Ziff-Davis Publishing Company.

Portraitist of Prescience appeared in a briefer version as *Virgil Finlay* in WORLDS OF TOMORROW, copyright © 1965 The Galaxy Publishing Corporation, copyright © 1971 Sam Moskowitz.

CONTENTS

INTRODUCTION

Science fiction now enjoys the respect of the world. Its deserved recognition is based primarily on the incredible accuracy of its scientific prophecy. But the content of science fiction today, as in the past, has always been a much richer mixture than technical predictions. My definition of the genre gives some idea of its scope: "Science fiction is a branch of fantasy identifiable by the fact that it eases the 'willing suspension of disbelief' on the part of its readers by utilizing an atmosphere of scientific credibility for its imaginative speculations in physical science, space, time, social science, and philosophy."

For hundreds of years what we today call science fiction has provided a wide latitude for the expression of ideas, controversial or otherwise, on every conceivable subject. That is why the famed utopians Sir Thomas More, Francis Bacon, Louis Sébastian Mercier, Edward Bulwer Lytton, and Edward Bellamy—to name a few—were so absorbed with it. This leads us to the question whether the prognostications of science fiction writers were as good for great social, religious, and psychological changes as they have proven to be on technical invention. The purpose of this volume is to investigate and, if possible, to answer that question.

To accomplish that objective, this book must serve a double purpose. It must not only be an analysis and commentary on subjects as timely as religion, anti-Semitism, civil rights, crime, women's liberation, birth control, war, teen-agers, psychiatry, and unexplained phenomena, but also a history and reference of the larger part of the topics covered, as they have appeared in science fiction. Most of the material presented and the background research appears for the first time anywhere, in this book.

The results are sometimes dramatic. A number of the great literary figures of science fiction lose a bit of luster from the glowing beacon of their vaunted humanitarianism when their racist attitudes are uncovered. Science fiction as a barometer of man's subconscious *desire* for war is raised most provocatively. The acceptance of science fiction as a means of promoting faith

1

by religious groups seems at odds with the ancient debate of science versus religion. The substantial incorporation of science fiction elements into crime fiction, even to the extent of an occasional successful marriage of the two, provides a new literary perspective. Science fiction's obsession with Freud and other schools of psychiatry in the fifties adds an entirely new dimension to the literature. Juvenile science fiction as a positive influence on the attitudes of teen-agers is well worth evaluating. These are but a few aspects of science fiction to come out of the research upon which this book is based. The material presented here is but the beginning, as the barriers are broken for new areas of inquiry.

Interwoven with this are biographical backgrounds of previously little-known prime movers in the field of science fiction —authors like Arthur B. Reeve, S. Fowler Wright, David H. Keller, M.D., Howard R. Garis, Edward Stratemeyer, George Griffith, and artist Virgil Finlay—whose lives and careers involve fascinating new material on the history of the publishing industry itself and how integral a part science fiction has played in its growth. John W. Campbell, one of the great editors of science fiction, once stated, "Science fiction is a field, not a path." It is one of the purposes of this book to take a giant step toward validating that statement.

This volume is a further effort in a continuing investigation of the ramifications of science fiction to fill in the historical gaps in the framework provided by the author's previous histories: *Explorers of the Infinite, Seekers of Tomorrow, Science Fiction by Gaslight, Under the Moons of Mars,* and *The Crystal Man.*

While, like the others, it has great appeal to the science fiction reader, student, scholar, and collector, it also has a great deal to offer those whose primary interest is in the timely subjects discussed. This wider group may learn that science fiction, while immediately fine entertainment and prediction, also addresses itself seriously to many other facets of the human social condition.

RELIGION:

Space, God, and Science Fiction

The element of religious thought in science fiction might never have rated more significance than a student's term paper had it not been for the advent of space rocketry and the theological exercises of "reformed" atheist Clive Staples Lewis. Opponents of Christianity gleefully pointed out that none of its gospels made allowances for other physical worlds and most certainly, not even by indirection, for intelligent aliens in *non-human* forms. They reminded that strict adherence to the teachings of Christianity indicated that all such hypothetical multitudes were doomed to limbo or worse, and this, despite the conceivable possibility that *they may never have fallen from grace.*

Until recent years, the clergy could relegate such questions to the same order of urgency as that of Talmudic scholars debating how many angels could dance on the head of a pin. Now that men have landed on the moon's surface, the necessity for reinterpretation of the Scriptures was obviously becoming not merely desirable but actually essential.

Science fiction had frequently been used as a propagandizing and proselytizing medium, as a means for reinforcing the will of those of little faith, or for seducing the undecided into the fold. Richard Marsh, who scored a greatly popular success with his mystical novel *The Beetle* in 1897, told the story of *A Second Coming* in 1900 (John Lane). Christ returns to perform a succession of miracles and departs as enigmatically as he came. Robert Hugh Benson reached best-seller status with *Lord of the World* (Dodd, Mead, 1908), in which he warned of the victory of socialistic humanism by the year 2000 and the decline of other religions, particularly Catholicism, if the then-current trends continued. A companion book, *The Dawn of All* (Herder, 1911), was equally popular and portrayed the world of 1973 where Catholics have virtually converted everyone except for isolated dissidents.

Long before there were science fiction magazines, the genre had been used to promulgate mystical beliefs and theories. The spirits of the dead are discovered on other planets, as in John Jacob Astor's *A Journey in Other Worlds* (1894); an interstellar ship, which has outraced light, captures the events of the Crucifixion by long-range observation in *Around a Distant Star* by Jean Delaire (1904); a Venusian named Manrolin appears as the "Angel of the Lord" to the Virgin Mary, carrying with him a concentrated ray of creative energy which brings about the Immaculate Conception resulting in the birth of Christ in *Loma, a Citizen of Venus* (1897); and there is the evangelistic message of *Life in a Thousand Worlds* by the Reverend W. S. Harris (1905), where, after exploring all the worlds of our solar system, traversing out into the galaxy, and finally reaching Heaven, the author poetically summarizes:

> *There are saints from unnumbered planets,*
> *Where they live in a million ways*
> *Now they mingle in perfect glory*
> *Through the length of eternal days.*

Not every cleric was so presumptuous, for in prefacing *Aleriel, or A Voyage to Other Worlds* (1886), the Reverend W. S. Lach-Szyrma, vicar of Newlyn St. Peter, England, and a frequent science fiction writer, stated: "As to the theological question of God's dealings with the inhabitants of other worlds, I have hardly presumed to touch the subject. These things we can only know when we see no more as 'in a glass darkly, but face to face'; and it seems to me that those who have ventured to speculate on it, as Kircher or Swedenborg, have exceeded propriety."

For the most part, when science fiction became part of the periodical world, editors had been content to subscribe to Lach-Szyrma's philosophy. If you didn't find very much religion in science fiction, you didn't run across very much sin either, so there was little cause for complaint.

A short story that might have been a landmark if it had appeared in a less obscure publication was William Hope Hodgson's chilling science fiction–horror tale of the scientist who succeeded in duplicating the darkening effect that occurred while Christ was dying on the cross. Entitled "The Baumoff Explosive," it appeared in England's *Nash's Weekly* for September 7, 1919.

Baumoff, a religious fanatic, was convinced that the passage in St. Matthew, "Now from the sixth hour there was a darkness over the land unto the ninth hour," was literally true. It was his belief that at a moment approaching death, or of great stress or anguish, the vibrations that conveyed light were disturbed by any living being, but in most cases the effect was imperceptible.

With Stafford, a member of British Intelligence, present, Baumoff ingests some of his mixture, and then drives sterilized spikes into his feet and hands to produce a stress situation such as Christ would have suffered.

In scenes of great power and mounting horror, Stafford finds the room beginning to darken and Baumoff relives the Crucifixion.

The moment arrives when the room is almost completely dark and finally the blackness is pierced by the words "Eloi Eloi lama sobochthani" (Hebrew for "My God! My God! Why hast thou forsaken me!"). But they are not delivered in the tones of Baumoff. "It was not a voice of despair," Stafford related, "but a voice sneering in an incredible, bestial, monstrous fashion."

Baumoff's heart gives out, but Stafford believes that he was " 'entered' by some Christ-aping monster of the Void." He also offers rational alternatives, but so superbly has Hodgson wrought his effects that they strengthen the more fantastic theory.

In 1966 Michael Moorcock, editor of *New Worlds,* the British magazine devoted to avant-garde science fiction, published a long novelette *Behold the Man* which he had written on the theme. Karl Glogauer, an amateur psychiatrist, travels in a time device back to the era of Christ. He meets John the Baptist, and gradually, through circumstances and events, realizes that he is Christ! Moorcock shows that the *idea* of Christ preceded the *actuality:* that when people need a great religion, they'll create one from the materials at hand.

Two approaches to the use of religion in modern science fiction became popular at roughly the same time: one in hardcover mainstream writing, when The Bodley Head, London, issued C. S. Lewis's *Out of the Silent Planet* in 1938; the other in the science fiction magazines, when serialization of Robert A. Heinlein's *If This Goes On—* was begun in the February 1940 *Astounding Science-Fiction.*

Among modern works of science fiction, only Aldous Huxley's *Brave New World* (1933) and George Orwell's *1984* (1949) have received as extensive critical recognition as *Out of the Silent Planet* by C. S. Lewis. Lewis takes theology to the planets, unabashedly carrying with him the materials that religious opponents said would be exposed and discredited as a result of the first space voyage, and utilizes them as unalterable laws of the universe. It was a modern milestone in the spotlighting of religious themes in space fiction.

On the Mars of *Out of the Silent Planet,* our kidnapped hero, a Cambridge philologist named Ransom, escapes from his captors to discover a world in which Paradise has never been lost and whose intelligent inhabitants have never fallen from that high state. It is ruled over by an angel, a creature of light and energy. Three diverse life-forms exist there: a race of seven-foot-long otterlike creatures proficient at fishing and poetry; large frog-bodied animals that are miners and artisans; and immense eighteen-foot-tall avian intelligences, who delight in astronomy and history. All three races are "human," all three have *souls,* and all three dwell in perfect harmony and cooperation.

"The Silent Planet" is Earth, whose angel is "bent" (the Devil), and nothing has been heard from that world by the other planets since before the creation of man. Only the Earth is no longer a member of the solar unity.

In recent times, apologists for Christianity have tended to explain certain background aspects of their faith as allegorical messages not intended to be accepted literally. Lewis would have none of that. At the time he wrote his book, he subscribed to the literal interpretation. There is not only a God, but there was an Eden and man was tempted and did fall from his high estate, even as described in Milton's *Paradise Lost;* angels *did* exist and do *now* exist and the battle between the Hosts of Heaven and Satan did most certainly occur and Satan was defeated and is held incommunicado with his evil minions on the planet Earth.

What made such a premise acceptable at all to many readers was Lewis's superior feel for the language, an immense sincerity, and most especially an obvious love for the format of the space story. A prefatory note in *Out of the Silent Planet* states, "The author would be sorry if any reader supposed he was too stupid to have enjoyed Mr. H. G. Wells's fantasies or too ungrateful to acknowledge his debt to them."

There were numerous other fantasies which Lewis doted upon, very definitely those of George MacDonald and Charles Williams (who popularized the device of taking the supernatural for granted and placing it into the context of a detective story), as well as *The Worm Ouroboros* by E. R. Eddison. Most specifically Lewis cited Olaf Stapledon's *Last and First Men* (1930) and "an essay in J. B. S. Haldane's *Possible Worlds,*" both of which he regarded as an immoral view of man's outlook on space travel, as the inspiration for *Out of the Silent Planet.* He was to a degree impressed by William Hope Hodgson's apocalyptic novel of the last epoch of man, *The Night Land* (1912).

Stapledon's volume, which chronicled the history of man through the next two billion years, including migrations to Venus and Neptune, supplied intensive detail on the religions which symbolized each period of the development of humanity, telling, for example, of the rise of the cult of the Divine Boy in the Patogonian culture, which held that God was the fruit of man's endeavor and whose Golden Rule was "Remain young in spirit." The rise of "The Third Men" in Stapledon's work brought into being a prophet who proclaimed music as the ultimate religion, and the monarch of the land assumed the title of Supreme Melody, and so was founded the Universal Church of Harmony, which held that "every human being was a melody, demanding completion within a greater musical theme of society." There were other religions through the eons leading to the final one, "The Soul of All," where the Last Men now living on the planet Neptune explore the past so that members of the human race would find rapport not only with all others living, but with all others who had ever lived.

This seemingly heretical picture of ages of men wearing out and casting off old beliefs even as they designed new ones for their times was anathema to Lewis. In his youth, he lapsed into atheism as a result of wide reading and study of the classics which outlined a variety of religious beliefs having presumably as great a logic as Christianity, coupled with the harshness of some of the precepts of Christianity. An entire book, *Surprised by Joy* (1955), is devoted to this story, relating the bits and pieces of realization which saw him voluntarily return to the faith at the age of thirty-one. Then, in the manner of many difficult converts, he set about making the justification of his decision the be-all and end-all of his life.

It appears very probable that Stapledon secured the design for *Last and First Men* from Haldane's *The Last Judgement* (1927), subtitled "A Scientist's Vision of the Future of Man," which was a chronological presentation of the next forty million years of man, written as an essay. What undoubtedly riled Lewis about Haldane, a scientist who became a Marxist, was that he began and ended his presentation with disdainful references to the shortcomings of Christianity when faced by scientific facts. In this context Haldane said: "But the more serious objection (to Christianity) is perhaps to the scale of magnitudes employed. The misbehaviors of the human race might induce their creator to wipe out their planet, but hardly the entire stellar system. We may be bad, but I cannot believe that we are as bad as all that. *At worst our earth is only a very small septic area in the universe, which could be sterilized without very great trouble, and conceivably is not even worth sterilizing.*"

Those very closing lines provide the entire thesis of *Out of the Silent Planet*, where Earth is ostracized by the rest of the solar system. Lewis had replied to Haldane in effect, "I do believe you are right," and based his story on that premise. What Lewis had also done was to resume the battle of religion against science, with science the villain.

The battleground moved from Mars to Venus in *Perelandra* (Bodley Head, 1943), with the same set of human characters as *Out of the Silent Planet*. Venus, a younger world, is in the precise state of development as the Earth was at the time of Adam and Eve. Satan, who may not leave Earth himself, sends the scientist Weston by spaceship to seduce the Eve of the Evening Star and create another Fallen World.

In plot it is cosmic cloak-and-dagger, but the critical reception it received when issued in 1944 was overwhelming. A sample is provided in the review by the Pulitzer Prize–winning poet and satirical critic Leonard Bacon, writing the cover piece for the April 8, 1944, issue of *The Saturday Review of Litera-*

8

ture: "One reads with every kind of excitement. One's own fancy, one's own thought, leap after the writer's. Agreement, dissent, analogy wake in the lethargic mind. The gleams of satire, the strokes of illumination, leave very little to be desired. . . . It has been impossible to give a notion of the freshness and clearness, the unpretentious nobility of the fable and the thought. . . ."

The third book in the trilogy, *That Hideous Strength* (J. Lane, 1945), finds the Devil prompting the misguided men behind National Institute for Co-ordinated Experiments to use science to "take over the human race and recondition it: make man a really efficient animal." In prefacing *That Hideous Strength,* C. S. Lewis again bows in the direction of Olaf Stapledon, of whom he says, ". . . I admire his invention (though not his philosophy) so much that I should feel no shame to borrow."

But Lewis borrows *much more* than superficial plot from Stapledon; he borrows from Stapledon, an agnostic, *an entire religious philosophy as it applied to the space age.* Stapledon expressed the philosophy that man might be "the spark destined to revitalize the cosmos." Lewis embraces with fervor that view in "Will We Lose God in Outer Space" (*Christian Herald,* April 1958) in wrestling with the problem of why the Earth was singled out for the appearance of Christ: *"It may be that redemption, starting with us, is to work from us and through us."*

It is almost as though he had answered "Yes" to the challenging question posed by Olaf Stapledon in his last book, *The Opening of the Eyes* (1954):

Tell me, Christians. Is it that in each world of all the myriad Earth-like worlds blossoming throughout the galaxy and the whole cosmos of galaxies, God incarnates himself as a local Jesus, to save his erring creatures? Or is it that once only, and on our unique planet, the supreme miracle happens; *and that from this chosen world alone the gospel must radiate throughout the cosmos?* By rocket spaceship, traveling at half the speed of light shall some future Paul spread the good news among the Transgalactic gentiles? It is not inconceivable. For those who need Jesus to be God, either possibility is believable.

The other major approach to theology in science fiction was popularized by Robert A. Heinlein with his two-part serial, *If*

This Goes On— (*Astounding Science-Fiction*, February and March 1940). There was a prelude to that story that was never written. It was to have been called *The Sound of His Wings* and "it would have recounted the early life, rise as a television evangelist, and subsequent political career of the Reverend Nehemiah Scudder, the First Prophet, President of the United States and destroyer of its Constitution, founder of the theocracy."

In *If This Goes On*—, all of the United States is ruled by a government set up as a religion and guards for the "Angels of the Lord" are graduated from West Point. Heinlein underscores the ultimate potential of a state religion and by indirection offers a scathing indictment of the manner by which faith has been used as a means of enslaving and exploiting man.

Heinlein sincerely believed that "we could lose our freedom by succumbing to a wave of religious hysteria, I am sorry to say that I consider it possible. I hope that it is not probable. But there is a latent deep strain of religious fanaticism in this our culture; it is rooted in our history and it has broken out many times in the past."

Religion had only been gingerly touched upon in magazine science fiction of the past. About as candid as anyone cared to get was John Beynon Harris (John Wyndham) in his remarkable story "The Venus Adventure" (*Wonder Stories*, May 1932), which showed how a primitivist religion, based upon the beliefs of a fanatical space pioneer, led a Venusian sect down the road to degeneracy and cannibalism. Contrasting it with the progress of another group free of superstition and with the same start, Harris left no question as to where he stood on the subject of mystical belief.

The true godfather of the incorporation of religion into the modern science fiction magazines was John W. Campbell. An early intimation of his interest in the subject was expressed in "The Machine" (*Astounding Stories*, February 1935) wherein human sacrifices are thrown into the moving gears of a gigantic thinking machine which runs the world, by a race of humans that have forgotten not only their own history but the reason the machine was built. The idea for the second novel dealing with a religious topic that Robert Heinlein wrote, *Sixth Column* (under the pen name of Anson MacDonald), was suggested by Campbell. A three-part story beginning in the January 1941

Astounding Science-Fiction, it told of an America conquered by Asiatics, which forms a new religion in whose temples it trains the cadre of an army of liberation. Its relationship to Campbell's "Out of Night" (*Astounding Science-Fiction,* October 1937) is trademarked by the giant image of blackness in the shape of a man that appears at the end of each story.

The real moral problem posed in *Sixth Column* is the necessity for Americans to perform devotedly the ritual and follow the dogma of a religion that they know to be *false,* for the salvation of the nation.

Heinlein's most inspired use of religion was in "Universe" (*Astounding Science-Fiction,* May 1941), a story which has as its locale a gargantuan spaceship that has been traveling for thousands of years through space toward a forgotten destination. A radiation accident has produced a group of mutations, some with two heads. Through the centuries, new generations have evolved the belief that the ship is the entire universe. The concept of sin arises to explain the appearance of mutations who occupy a different portion of the ship. The faith of the people is superbly delineated, even complete to an epic poem concerning its origin.

Clifford D. Simak took up Heinlein's idea and developed the intricacies of a religion that might be essential for survival on a 1,000-year space journey in "Spacebred Generations" (*Science-Fiction Plus,* August 1953), down to ceremony, ritual, symbol, and the implications of the procedures. Simak was no Johnny-come-lately to the use of religion in science fiction. He had preceded Heinlein and was the father of the *sacrilegious* story in science fiction, which would find at least one adherent, Lester Del Rey. Simak's first story in that vein was "The Voice in the Void" (*Wonder Stories Quarterly,* Spring 1932), where the messiah of the Martian religion, after his death, is revealed to have been an Earthman who landed on that planet. More daring was "The Creator," rejected by every magazine of the period and finally published in the March-April 1935 issue of a semiprofessional magazine, *Marvel Tales.* Carried out of space by a time machine, the characters discover that the Earth was not created by God but is actually the laboratory experiment of a macrocosmic being.

Simak's supercharged novel *Cosmic Engineers* has as a special character an insane entity, too ancient to be responsible, who parallels God on his world in a manner that is no endorsement of established religion. Simak evidently welcomed Heinlein's precedent in breaking a controversial taboo; his novelette *Hunch* (*Astounding Science-Fiction*, July 1943) is a highly sophisticated blow at the religious claims of a hereafter, particularly the concept of heaven which he disguises under the term "Sanctuary," a future haven in the stars for those burdened by earthly woes.

Simak's novel *Time Quarry*, serialized in *Galaxy Science Fiction* starting with the October 1950 issue and issued in hardcover as *Time and Again* (Simon & Schuster, 1951), was a *tour de force* utilizing the webwork technique in science fiction, several plots alternating and finally meshing, involving a man who is killed in space, is reconstructed, and returns to Earth to read a copy of a book he will write in the *future* that will start a new religion. The details of that religion are inspired by Olaf Stapledon, and its premise is that "nothing walks alone," that all intelligence, regardless of its form, is brought into awareness through a symbiosis with an intangible, universal energizer. Like Stapledon, Simak opposes the vestments of worship, believing that the ultimate salvation of the race rests in the unity of man.

In *Universe*, Heinlein indicated that the "devils" of that spaceship—the mutated creatures—actually represented the brightest hope of the "normal" humans aboard. Fritz Leiber, writing in *Gather, Darkness!* (*Astounding Science-Fiction*, May-June-July 1943), set up a situation where a cult under the guise of devil worshipers is set up to overthrow a religious dictatorship obviously inspired by Heinlein's *If This Goes On—*.

Though it did not serve to spark Leiber's work, David H. Keller's book *The Devil and the Doctor* (Simon & Schuster, 1940) contained the basic elements of the plot of *Gather, Darkness!* and, to a degree, could be offered as a science fiction counter to C. S. Lewis's *Screwtape Letters* (Geoffrey Bles, 1942), where the Devil discourses on the various methods of tempting a human to his damnation. *The Devil and the Doctor* is the story of Robin Goodfellow (the Devil) who comes to tea with a middle-aged physician (Jacob Hubler) and proceeds to tell his side of Creation, the War in Heaven, and the Fall. From his earliest days "exploring the dead craters of the moon, or canoeing on the canals of Mars," the Devil proves to be a much more decent sort than his "brother" angel. It has been the Devil who has taught men all concepts of progress and imparted learning while his brother angel wanted only unquestioning superstitious worship.

There was virtually a moratorium on significant science fiction involving religion during World War II. The one figure to emerge, who for a brief time wrote science fiction with a moral tone strong enough to be termed religious, was H. F. Heard (Gerald Heard), whose three books *The Great Fog* (1944), *The Doppelgangers* (1947), and *The Lost Cavern* (1948) contained fantastic detective stories with a religious theme after the manner of Charles Williams, as well as science fiction which championed the moral values and the positive philosophies of religion without exposing unquestioning acceptance of rituals or dogma. Heard's viewpoint concerning spiritual values became a campaign in contrast to Lewis's crusade which more nearly resembled a vice.

The man who finally carried the torch of C. S. Lewis into the science fiction magazines was Ray Bradbury. Experimenting with offbeat *subject matter* as well as style, Bradbury had been bombarding the slicks with his stories and had already sold to *Collier's, Charm, Mademoiselle,* and *The New Yorker.* "The Man" (*Thrilling Wonder Stories,* February 1949) was quite evidently something aimed at a better market and rejected. Readers scarcely credited their eyes as they read the situation of the first ship of an earth fleet which lands on another world, ignored because something more important happened only the day before—the coming of Christ.

But Ray Bradbury was not the first to suggest the provocative theology of a Christ who travels from planet to planet dispensing his philosophy. Charles Napier Richards in his novel *Atalanta, or Twelve Months in the Evening Star* (Simpkin Marshall, Hamilton, Kent & Co. Ltd., 1909) included as a member of the crew of the antigravity spaceship *Asteroid,* about to make the first trip to Venus, the Reverend Clarence Radcliffe. His avowed aim is to convert whatever Venusians he may find to Christianity. He feels he has fertile ground when the Venusians turn out to be sun worshipers. His preachments are cut short when he is informed that a man came long ago to Venus who claimed "He was the son of the mighty God." They had listened

13

at first, but finally found him so exasperating that they arrested him and sentenced him to build a road. When the road was finished they ordered him to leave. He told them that he was going to Karamandra (Earth), which world was far more in need of his teachings than they, but would someday send his messengers back to show them the light.

When the minister seizes on their rejection of Christ as proof that they need the teachings of his world, he is asked the question, "And how did your world act towards Him when He came to them?"

A similar approach is found in Bradbury's "In This Sign" (*Imagination,* April 1951) published in his collection *The Illustrated Man* (1951) as "The Fire Balloons." It involves two Episcopalian fathers, one of whom has written a book titled *The Problem of Sin on Other Worlds.* They set off for Mars to establish a church to redeem Martians from their weaknesses. Their intent is "to leave old sins here. And on to Mars to find *new* sins."

Their confidence is sublime. "I will recognize sin," one states, *"even* on Mars."

They learn of blue globes of sheer energy in the Martian highlands, which give every indication of intelligence. A church is built in this area and then the strains of their organ draw the Martian globes to them.

The Martians telepathically transmit the message that they were once physical entities but now are energy creatures, casting off all desires of the flesh, owning no property, subscribing to no arrogance, living eternally, and doing no harm. "We have left sin behind," they say, "and it is gone like the soiled snow of an evil winter, and it is gone like the panting nights of hottest summer, and our season is temperate and our clime is rich in thought."

The Fathers, thoroughly chastened, ask to learn from them.

The related plot line was utilized by James Blish for "A Case of Conscience" in *If,* September 1953, and made the cover story. The protagonist, Father Ramon Ruiz-Sanchez, lands with a space expedition upon the planet Lithia, fifty light-years from Earth, to establish its suitability as a port-of-call for spaceships. They discover an intelligent reptilian race free of the acquisitive and emotional faults of man.

The priest decides that this world is too perfect for the laws

14

of probability and therefore may be an illusionary trap baited by the Powers of Darkness. He leaves, unable to find any flaw in the presentment, with the gift of a vase containing a Lithian fertilized egg. If everything on this planet is as it seems, he is carrying back to Earth a bizarre, scaled new "Christ," created after the manner of this race, without original sin.

The fate of the transplanted Lithian on Earth is chronicled in a lengthened version of *A Case of Conscience* (Ballantine Books, 1958). Its behavior is antipodal to that of its forebears. The priest is excommunicated from the church for his attitudes concerning Lithia, with the admonition by the hierarchy that if the "unfallen" world were truly the work of the Devil, exorcism might have proved effective.

Earthmen begin building a fusion-bomb plant on Lithia, disturbing the idyllic situation. Then the news arrives that the Earth-raised Lithian is on his way to the planet of his genesis, to figuratively assume the role of the snake in the Garden of Eden. Rising before a device that *instantaneously* transmits pictures and sounds over fifty light-years, as they occur, the priest exorcises Satan from the planet. As he concludes his rites, the entire world of Lithia blooms into a nova. The scientists believe that an accident at the fusion-bomb plant has destroyed the planet, but the priest is convinced that he has sprung the theological trap and saved the faith.

The lengthened version won the Hugo award as the best science fiction novel of 1958 at the Seventeenth Annual World Science Fiction Convention in Pittsburgh, 1959.

Three years earlier, the Fourteenth Annual World Science Fiction Convention in New York selected Arthur C. Clarke's short story "The Star" (*Infinity Science Fiction,* November 1955) for an award. A group of astronomers, light-years from Earth, explore the remnants of a supernova that exploded with inconceivable fury 6,000 years earlier. On a single seared planet, too far out to be dissolved in the disaster, they discover a vault containing the record of a humanoid race. It had flourished on one of the worlds that once swung about this burned-out star, and had built a civilization whose beauty and worthiness was admirable. The impending disaster was known to them but they had not yet developed interstellar travel. This record was their own epitaph.

The story is told by the chief astrophysicist, who is also a

15

Jesuit. His report ends in the tortured lines, "There can be no reasonable doubt: The ancient mystery is solved at last. Yet— O, God, there were so many stars you *could* have used.

"What was the need to give these people to the fire, that the symbol of their passing might shine above Bethlehem?"

This was not Clarke's first venture into religion. "The Nine Billion Names of God" (*Star Science Fiction Stories,* Ballantine Books, 1953) told of a Tibetan lamasery which installs an automatic sequence computer which is given the problem of determining and collating all the secret names of God. The monks believe that when they have found every conceivable variation of the name of God, man's purpose on Earth will have been achieved. The American technicians know that the monks have reached their goal when they see that "overhead, without any fuss, the stars were going out."

At the Nineteenth Annual World Science Fiction Convention in Seattle in 1961, another theosophical science fiction novel, *A Canticle for Leibowitz* by Walter M. Miller, Jr., won the Hugo as the best science fiction novel of 1960. The impact of theology as a force in the plotting of science fiction was an undeniable reality.

The series of stories from which *A Canticle for Leibowitz* was expanded appeared as a trilogy in *The Magazine of Fantasy and Science Fiction* during 1955, 1956, and 1957. The whole proved infinitely better than any of the parts. Atomic disaster has destroyed most of civilization and spread cannibalistic mutations across the countryside. The repository of knowledge is the Albertian Order of St. Leibowitz, named after a Jewish physicist who was strangled after the blowup. The story ranges across thousands of years, in which the disciples of St. Leibowitz spark a renaissance and start the world on the path of progress again.

Though this novel is one of the most favorable pictures of the Catholic church ever set down on paper, it follows Heinlein rather than Lewis. Miller thumbs his nose at most supernaturalism and mocks ritual and dogma even as he seeks to justify its necessity in an ignorant world. Heinlein showed religious charlatanism as a cover for evil; Miller displays it as a justifiable means for a demonstrable good.

A Canticle for Leibowitz is the finest work of religious science fiction written to date. The presentation is direct, yet its message eloquent. The characterization is magnificent, particularly the device of the ageless Wandering Jew, who serves to unify the events that span the centuries. The story is absorbing and only a weak ending, where the monks leave a devastated earth for a sanctuary in space, mars one of the most mature and satisfying efforts to come from the ranks of science fiction writers.

Lester del Rey also took a cue from *A Cancticle for Leibowitz*, that the rigmarole of the Church might cloak ultimate good. *The Eleventh Commandment* (Regency Books, January 1962) told of a postatomic world ruled by the Church. Anyone from other planets is welcomed (after spirits are exorcised from their spaceships), but no one is permitted to emigrate. An ever-spiraling population reduces people to misery sanctioned because of the attitude of the Church against birth control. It is revealed that the Church is implementing a necessary plan to stabilize a viable human species from a catastrophic welter of mutations.

This was not del Rey's first venture in religion. His "If Ye Have Faith . . ." (*Other Worlds*, May 1951) utilized God as a character in the story. He appears in the Gobi Desert, conveyed by a glowing spacecraft under the television cameras of the world. Only one believer really gets his message, which is confirmed when the sun goes out!

Far more sacrilegious in the Simak vein, yet accepting the Lewis precept that every word of the gospel is literally true, was *For I Am a Jealous God* (*Star Short Novels*, 1954) in which God turns against the human race and swings over to the side of aliens invading from another world.

Stories like *For I Am a Jealous God* are merely clever plays on religious belief, if not deliberate satire. This is without question true of *A Case of Conscience* by James Blish, who extended the success of that story into a trilogy. *Faust Aleph Null*, serialized in *If* (August–October 1967), tells of the future when the spells of black magic seem to have resumed their potency and are even used in business. The pattern of life changes as the influence of a new generation of warlocks and wizards becomes manifest. It is all scientifically bewildering until the last lines where it is revealed that God is dead and Satan now comes into his own. With additional material the work appeared as *Black Easter* (Doubleday, 1968).

Blish completed the trilogy with *The Day After Judgment*, a short novel in the August-September 1970 *Galaxy*. It commences as a tightly written replay of the final atomic war, but carries on as a sequel to *Black Easter*. Satan appears in a fortress in Death Valley, but far from being elated at his victory, he is sickened by the foulness of mankind, which far exceeds his own wickedness. He makes the point that evil is senseless if there is no good, and there is no joy in it. He cannot bear to play God to such as man. He begs mankind to aspire to become God so that he can be relieved of the intolerable burden.

Undoubtedly one of the most skillful and ingenious science fiction stories involving theology ever written was "The Quest for Saint Aquin" by Anthony Boucher (*New Tales of Space and Time*, edited by Raymond J. Healy, 1951). The impoverished pope of the postatomic war world, where few believers exist, orders one of his holy men, Thomas, to seek the remains of Saint Aquin, a good man who before his death led many people back to the Church. Mounted on a robot ass, Thomas engages in a dialogue with the machine which cynically challenges his faith. The discovery that Saint Aquin was actually a robot, *who nevertheless must be canonized if the Church is ever to attract adherents,* is almost more than the good Thomas can bear.

Not all attempts at religion in science fiction intellectually dealt with high-level theosophical problems. Paul Lawrence Payne, one-time editor of *Planet Stories*, wrote "Fool's Errand" for the October 1952 *Thrilling Wonder Stories*. The story relates a running argument on religion by crew members of a space vessel all the way to Mars and ends when a cross is planted in the sand to be found by one of the more devout religionists, a Jew, in hope of shaking his faith. Evangelistic was Richard H. Nelson's "Patrol" (*Imagination,* October 1952), where a group of spacemen land on a small planet where all their equipment ceases to function and the broken arm of one of their party refuses to respond to pain killer. After a thorough fright at their dilemma, they accept the existence of God and pray to Him. Instantly all their equipment again functions and the man's arm is healed.

It is perhaps significant that the author who broke the taboos against sex in science fiction with *The Lovers* (*Startling Stories,* August 1952), Philip José Farmer, should also be most fascinated by religion. That novel and its sequel, *Moth and Rust* (*Startling Stories,* June 1953), not only incorporate as background a variety of new religions that have replaced Christianity, but interpenetrate the effect of religion on the actions, speech, and outlook of the people in the stories. Religion becomes an important element—but merely one element—in his stories.

The Lovers weaves into the fabric of its plot a state church (the Sturch) that is not averse to dominating and destroying cultures found on other planets to make room for Earthmen. Its founder is Isaac Sigmen, author of *The Western Talmud,* and he holds the same divinity in the Sturch as Jesus does for Christians. The harsh attitudes of this religion towards marriage and sex play a vital part in delineating the tragic consequences of a love affair the protagonist is involved in with a nonhuman creature. *Moth and Rust* has one dramatic sequence that implies that God may be black.

Farmer plays with religion as a child with a new toy. He is neither for it nor against it. His tales of Father Carmody, a world-hopping Roman Catholic priest, bring this rotund and impious cleric into a series of confrontations with faith-testing problems, of which the most soul-searching is contained in "Father" (*The Magazine of Fantasy and Science Fiction,* July 1955). Here, in company with a bishop, he lands on a world where a single manlike giant is in rapport with every living thing on the planet, who resurrects the dead creatures by a chemical process when they die. The bishop is offered the supreme temptation: to take over "temporarily" while the God of this world enjoys a vacation.

The men who prompted the revolutionary reevaluation of the role of religion in science fiction, Olaf Stapledon and C. S. Lewis, are both dead. The man who personally introduced it into the science fiction magazines, Robert A. Heinlein, has created a popular success in his novel *Stranger in a Strange Land* (Putnam, 1961) by making religion a pivotal premise of his work. Valentine Michael Smith, an Earthman raised by Martians, returns to Earth to dispense their religious philosophy. By satiric intent and ingenious logic, murder, sexual permissiveness, and even cannibalism are permissible in this religion. There is no one God, but every living, reasoning person in composite makes up the structure of the Supreme Being, with the catchphrase "*Thou* art God" encapsulating its meaning.

As might be expected, Valentine Michael Smith is eventually

stoned, shot, and burned by a mob in front of the TV camera. As this carnage is perpetrated on his person, Smith beatifically preaches, "Oh my brothers, I love you so!" And finally, "Thou art God. Know that and the way is opened."

All the foregoing is obviously pretty provocative stuff. Has it shocked the clergy? Are religionists rising in wrath against it? They were willing to accept C. S. Lewis's expositions, but he was unquestionably on the side of the angels. The same could certainly not be said of Ray Bradbury, James Blish, Lester del Rey, Arthur C. Clarke, or Robert A. Heinlein.

All sects have not been heard from but *The Episcopalian* for January 1966 gave its answer when it carried Betty T. Balke's story "Apostle to Alpha," wherein 95 million American Christian believers combine resources to send the first Space Apostle to a planet around Alpha, where an intelligent race is known to live. The government cooperates and religious compromises are made where the messenger of "Christ" is "to be baptized again—all the way *under* the water, to please 30 million churchmen who hold no belief for 'sprinkling.' Remember when the Salvation Army waived its musical requirements after Oates [the proselytizing astronaut] satisfied them that he played a passable clarinet? Oates also promised, at least on Alpha, to give up dancing and card-playing, for the sake of those who disapproved of both."

The years pass, and communications from Oates prove disturbingly vague. Particularly inexplicable is his apparent lack of desire to have shipped to him 256,000 Holy Bibles to hasten the progress of his task. Upon his return, Oates reports that the mission is a complete success, despite the fact that all his film is overexposed and scientific samples lost.

Then the truth comes out. The project was an utter flop. Nothing of any consequence was accomplished. All data were lost and the natives found are scarcely worth the effort of a second attempt. Oates resigns and seeks missionary assignment in Central America.

The inside story?

The race of Alphans are actually superbly intelligent birds: "They live in perfect harmony, have never fallen from grace, never touched the apple."

Their world is an unbelievable treasure trove of precious metals and gems. "Against even the mildest human, these Alphans would be . . . utterly defenseless." Oates and the heads of his missionary project have deliberately framed a false story and destroyed all evidence "so millions of God's gentlest, unfallen creatures have been protected from *us.*"

In view of the foregoing, it would appear that not only is the clergy unlikely to be upset by any speculations that may appear in the science fiction magazines, but they are already psychologically ready for anything the space age may bring.

ANTI-SEMITISM:

The Day of the Messiah

Saint Isaac Edward Leibowitz, canonized as the Patron of the Albertian Order of St. Leibowitz, a Catholic institution that strives to keep the light of knowledge alive after the first atomic war, is virtually a latter-day Christ. Like Christ, Leibowitz, a scientist, was betrayed to the mob—hungering for the lives of all men who had played some role in bringing about the world holocaust—by an associate, a fellow technician. He was strangled and roasted simultaneously, becoming a martyr to the cause of preserving knowledge under the cloak of religion.

Quite appropriately, he was a Jew, and if there was the slightest doubt about the matter, it was confirmed by the discovery of scribbled notes in his handwriting which read: "Pound pastrami . . . can kraut, six bagels—bring home for Emma." The utterly remarkable and fascinating account of the consequences of his heroism are chronicled in *A Canticle for Leibowitz* by Walter M. Miller, Jr. (Lippincott, 1960), one of the landmarks in modern science fiction.

Leibowitz is not the only Jew in the novel. The other is Benjamin Eleazer, *the* Wandering Jew, eternally aged and immortal, confidant of the priestly hierarchy, who serves to unify the episodic character of the novel. The Wandering Jew is a common figure in the literature of the past 300 years; he first appeared in *Flores Historiarum,* a manuscript written by the monk Roger Wendover in 1235, who may be truthfully said to have fathered the immortality concept in science fiction.

The Jews are directly responsible for popularizing two major themes in science fiction: the robot, descendant of the legends of the Golem (and simultaneously the notion of artificial creation of life), and the physical superman from the story of Samson from Judges in the Old Testament.

The Jew is treated sympathetically in *A Canticle for Leibo-*

witz. The "Saint" himself nobly tried to preserve the science which would constitute the basis for rehabilitation of mankind. His hopeless search for his wife Emily is noted. While decimated mankind seeks to destroy every remnant of the knowledge which brought them to disaster, Leibowitz organizes "booklegging" groups to smuggle out valuable references wherever they may be found and to bury them in kegs against future usefulness.

Symbolically, Miller has again made the Jews the People of the Book, the apostles of enlightenment. During the long period following the Diaspora (the dispersion of the Jews after their conquest by the Romans between 100 A.D. and 200 A.D.), first the Palestinian and then the Babylonian Talmud were compiled. These volumes contained the basic "laws" and philosophy, together with commentaries, which were the guide to Jewish life. Great campaigns by enemies were conducted in which these volumes were gathered and burned. The knowledge was saved by Talmudic scholars (common in Czarist Russia), who memorized all or parts of the Talmud. Such men frequently did not work, were often supported by their wives, were accorded great respect, and spent all their lives in perusing the Talmud. The Jews could be driven from place to place, but the entire structure of their way of life went with them, regardless of how many books were burned.

Leibowitz, similarly, had staffs of "memorizers," who committed key books to memory so that they could later be written down again. Drawing a parallel to the method of the Jews before him, Leibowitz saw to it that only paper—and not knowledge—was destroyed.

Because of its faith in the future of science and its remarkable record of accurate technological predictions, science fiction has gained a reputation as a literature of enlightenment and progressiveness. Although the overall effect of *A Canticle for Leibowitz* is a warm affection for the Catholic church and a good-natured wink at its defects, Walter Miller's attitude towards the Jews can also be said to be one of tolerance and good feeling.

Have the Jews in the past found the science fiction writers to be as understanding as Miller? Have they discovered champions against the inequities which have traditionally been their lot? Do stories concerning them project a liberal, forward-looking view, as might be expected from a seer of science?

If we are to shunt aside the involvement of the Wandering Jew in literature (a subject large enough for a separate tract by itself), one of the early appearances of a Jewish character in an important work of science fiction is that of Jules Simon in Fitz-James O'Brien's landmark "The Diamond Lens" (*Atlantic Monthly,* January 1858). The story deals with a young man who seeks to grind the ultimate microscope. He finds, through a medium, that he needs a diamond of extraordinary size to make the proper lens. In his boardinghouse he makes the acquaintance of Jules Simon, who owns a diamond of the size he needs to build his microscope, and determines to kill him for it. "After all, what was the life of a little peddling Jew, in comparison with the interests of science? Human beings are taken every day from the condemned prisons to be experimented on by surgeons. This man, Simon, was by his own confession a criminal, a robber, and I believed on my soul a murderer."

He stabs Simon to death, steals the diamond, and builds the microscope he has planned. The famed story of the beautiful girl, Animula, that he sees in a drop of water, has become a literary classic. Watching her die when the water dissolves results in his breakdown.

What reflects interestingly upon O'Brien's attitude toward Jews is that his hero is not punished for his murder. His inability to function is treated as a poignant tragedy and the murder of Jules Simon is justified on the basis that the man is a Jew (yet earlier he said he only "thinks" he is a Jew). In the story, Simon has never done an unkind thing to the hero, to the contrary has assisted him in numerous ways, yet the implication is made that because the man is a Jew, he is probably also a murderer.

One other episode in another of O'Brien's fantasies reveals his feelings toward Jews. In the opening pages of "The Wonder-Smith" (*Atlantic Monthly,* October 1859), he describes a Golosh Street on the East Side of New York as follows: "It has never been able to shake off the Hebraic taint of filth which it inherits from the ancestral thoroughfare. It is slushy and greasy, as if it were twin brother of the Roman ghetto."

The Jewish "taint" gives the street the ominous evil to support the foul machinations of Herr Hippe, a man who makes manikins, instinct with fiendish life, to commit foul, senseless killings.

New York of that period had a relatively small Jewish population of German Jews, noted for their self-help and philanthrophy. A Jew to seek public assistance, regardless of how impoverished, was virtually unknown. No Jew had ever been buried in Potter's Field. O'Brien's association with the Jewish population could have at best been marginal, confined to boardinghouse landlords and pawn shop owners. His attitude would seem to have reflected stereotyped prejudice.

Such an assumption seems buttressed by his biographer Francis Wolle in his book *Fitz-James O'Brien* (University of Colorado, 1944) when he quotes the doctor who treated O'Brien's battered visage after an unfortunate encounter with a barkeeper as saying: "I remember that nose particularly on account of his urgent solicitude that I should make it slightly aquiline, but avoid the Israelitish extreme. *Romans* rather than *Hebrews* furnished the text."

A far more startling anti-Semitic attitude appeared in a major novel of Jules Verne, *Hector Servadac, or The Career of a Comet* (1877). A near-collision with a comet appears to have torn a section off the earth, including part of the seacoast, and plastered it around the sphere of a comet, though this is so unclear as to utterly defy rationalization or scientific explanation. The "heroes" of the novel are Captain Hector Servadac, an officer stationed in Mostaganem, Algeria, and his orderly, Ben Zoof. They find a number of other humans stranded on this runaway comet with them, including the crews of two ships.

One of the ships is owned by Isaac Hakkabut, a native of Cologne, and is stocked with quantities of food and other supplies which will form the margin of survival for all the "castaways." When Servadac and Zoof first encounter Hakkabut, four Spaniards are forcing him to dance to the point of exhaustion. When he appeals to the newcomers for help, Zoof "ordered the Jew to hold his tongue at once."

Zoof's appraisal of the man follows: "Small and skinny, with eyes bright and cunning, a hooked nose, a short yellow beard, unkempt hair, huge feet, and long bony hands, he presented all the typical characteristics of the German Jew, the heartless, wily usurer, the hardened miser and skinflint. As iron is attracted by the magnet, so was this Shylock attracted by the sight of gold, nor would he have hesitated to draw the life-blood of his creditors, if by such means he could secure his claims." This incredible analysis is made even though this is the first time Zoof has set eyes on Hakkabut.

The venom against the hapless Jew is augmented by the fact that he is a *German* Jew and the author, Jules Verne, is French. They talk of appropriating his merchandise, but then decide they will "pay" him on their own terms for what they need, since the money is useless to anyone.

The baiting of Hakkabut provides the diversion of the *entire* novel and is the major subtheme of the book. Verne makes Hakkabut out to be a contemptible miser, an opportunist, a cheat with dishonest scales, but for the first half of the book's considerable length offers no tangible evidence of these charges except precognition.

When Hakkabut disbelieves his "companions'" story that they have been carried off on a comet and in an attempt to verify it speaks to various members present in four different languages, Servadac's reaction is "but whether he speaks French, Russian, Spanish, German, or Italian, he is neither more nor less than a Jew."

As the book proceeds the Jew-baiting mounts to such an intensity that one is ashamed and embarrassed for Jules Verne. Again and again lines throughout the book read, "vicious . . . greed and avarice of the miserable Jew," or "His oaths [Hakkabut's] were simply dreadful; his imprecations on the accursed race were full of wrath"; or "His uncomely figure and repulsive countenance . . ."

When the group is making its escape from the comet to return to Earth, they note Hakkabut has the money they have paid him for his goods (plus his previous wealth) strapped around his body. They force him to discard it at the threat of being left behind to die. The truth is that anti-Semitism was part of Jules Verne and his writings from the beginning of his career. It was blatant as early as 1852 in his novelette *Martin Paz* (also called *The Pearl of Lima*) which first appeared in the July and August issues of *Musée des Familles*. His use of Samuel, a Peruvian Jew, as an amoral father, ready to sell his daughter to a wealthy half-breed in marriage for 100,000 piasters, might be excused as a stereotype except for other elements in the story. One finds a Spanish Don feeling a sense of "abhorrence" at the idea of even an Indian stooping so low as to fall in love with a *Jewess*, and he hopes to disenchant him of the idea. When he sees the attractive girl he exclaims, *"That* the daughter of a Jew!"* The half-breed suitor, who engages in a dirk battle with the Indian for the girl's favors, is himself repelled at the thought that the girl he is planning to marry has been known to pray in a synagogue.

It might be asked if Verne represented a European view, whereas the United States, which was built by the labor and genius of the oppressed foreign-born, undoubtedly had a more enlightened attitude. A reply may be offered in the text of one of the landmarks of American nineteenth-century science fiction, *Caesar's Column: A Story of the Twentieth Century,* written by Ignatius Donnelly, the vacillating and bombastic Republican politician, and published in 1890 under the pen name Edmund Boisgilbert, M.D. The book sold extremely well, over a quarter of a million copies, and is a "dystopia," spotlighting the world of 1988, where despite such scientific progress as international air travel, white light, wire transmission of newspapers, pushbutton meals, air conditioning, heat from the depths of the earth, legalized euthanasia, and an instrument for judging the health of the body through its electrical emanations, the masses are oppressed and kept in poverty by a wealthy oligarchy of capitalists.

The ruler of the land is Prince Cabano, whose real name is Jacob Isaacs. "Isaacs," repeats the visitor, "is a Jewish name."

> "Yes, the aristocracy of the world is now almost altogether of Hebrew origin."
>
> "Indeed, how does that happen?"
>
> "Well," is the reply, "it was the old question of the survival of the fittest. Christianity fell upon the Jews, originally a race of agriculturists and shepherds, and forced them, for many centuries, through the most terrible ordeal of persecution the history of mankind bears any record of. Only the strong of body, the cunning of brain, the long-headed, the persistent, the men with capacity to live where a dog would starve, survived the awful trial. Like breeds like; and now the Christian world is paying, in tears and blood, for the sufferings inflicted by their bigoted and ignorant ancestors upon a noble race. When the time came for liberty and fair play the Jew was master in the contest with the Gentile, who hated and feared him."

"The world is to-day Semitized," the Ugandian is told. "The children of Japeth lie prostrate slaves at the feet of the children of Shem; and the sons of Ham bow humbly before their August Domain."

The title, *Caesar's Column*, is derived from the gigantic cement monument built over the bodies of 250,000 of the dead upper class—almost entirely Jews—after a revolution of the masses.

Donnelly's attitude reflected the amazement of the times, that the pack pedlars, junk dealers, ragpickers, and sweatshop workers were able to produce men of achievement not only in business, but in other fields as well.

It can be said that in popular fiction for the masses, Donnelly's view of the Jew was not a majority view. Prentiss Ingraham, one of the most capable of the dime novelists, wrote *The Jew Detective; or The Beautiful Convict* for *Beadle's New York Dime Library*, July 1, 1891. The detective here is a Jew who heroically clears a non-Jewish woman who has been falsely sent to jail for murder. When he asks her hand, she replies, " 'You say you are known as Judah the Jew. Well, I have been called Cora the Convict, and though I am not a Jewess, my Christian friends deserted me in my anguish and danger, and you have been my truest, best friend through all, and to you I now turn for happiness in life, for your people shall be my people, your creed my creed, and your God my God.' "

When the Russian government officially embarked on an intensified anti-Semitic policy after the murder of Alexander II in 1881, Jews frantically tried to escape westward as once they had been driven eastward. In Germany, Austria, and France they were met with the most extraordinary viciousness. Seventy thousand Jews flooded into London, Manchester, and Leeds between 1888 and 1891; over a million emigrated to the United States between 1881 and 1905. While at first the British were fearful that cheap labor would cost them their jobs, there were no anti-Semitic outbreaks such as in Russia, Germany, and France, but the Jew did become a frequent subject in the literature of the period, both positively and negatively.

The Russian treatment of the Jews plays a leading role in *The Angel of the Revolution* by George Griffith (Tower Publishing, London, 1893), an author who today ranks high on the list of forgotten creators of science fiction, but whose book was one of the best-selling future-war stories of all time. Major protagonists of the novel are Natas, a Jew who married a Christian woman in England, and his courageous fighting daughter, Natasha. The commonly held belief at the time that Jews had strange powers was expressed in the device of making Natas an accomplished hypnotist, who can use this power to influence men. Nevertheless, George Griffith's presentation of the horrors the Jews were suffering in Russia is not only sympathetic, but so graphic that coupled with the wide popularity of the book, may very well have had a positive effect on the attitude of the British toward the Jews.

There is also a strong possibility that George L. Du Maurier for his famed novel *Trilby* (Osgood, McIlvaine, London, 1894) took Svengali, his Jew with hypnotic powers, from *Angel of the Revolution*. The major difference between the two was that George Du Maurier had strong prejudices against the Jews and preferred to cast them in villainous roles. These prejudices were apparent even in his first book, *Peter Ibbetson* (Harper & Brothers, 1891), the writing of which was commenced the night Henry James complimented George Du Maurier on his ability to plot. This semiautobiographical novel is a fantasy of a man who lives another life while dreaming in the companionship of another dreamer, a woman. They not only range the earth but travel in time as far back as the age of the Mammoth.

A passage in the book accuses the Jew of corrupting the entire intent of prayer and reads: "To pray for any personal boon or remission of evil—to bend the knee, or lift one's voice in praise or thanksgiving for any earthly good that had befallen one, either through inheritance, or chance, or one's own successful endeavor—was in my eyes simply futile; but, putting its futility aside, it was an act of servile presumption, of wheedling impertinence, not without suspicion of a lively sense of favors to come.

"It seemed to me as though the Jews—a superstitious and businesslike people, who know what they want and do not care how they get it—must have taught us to pray like that."

H. G. Wells claimed the Jewish Problem had no right to exist, and pretended impatience with his Jewish friend and business partner Walter Low, who disagreed, and with whom he jointly published *The University Correspondent* (1893). Yet he was not unaffected by the buildup of Jews in England, especially with the fact that as Jews saved their money they tended to buy up the wretched tenements of their area of the city and became landlords. *The Invisible Man* (C. A. Pearson, 1897) clearly reflects this fact when Griffin, the Invisible Man, seeking a spot to continue his experiments rents "a large unfurnished room in a big ill-managed lodging-house in a slum near Great Portland Street."

When Griffin succeeds in making a cat invisible, its wailings arouse the neighborhood. In telling his friend of the incident he states, "And there was some one rapping at the door. It was my landlord with threats and inquiries, an old Polish Jew in a long grey coat and greasy slippers."

The landlord suspects him of being a vivisectionist and begins questioning Griffin, who throws him from the room. The landlord returns with an eviction notice. Assuming invisibility, Griffin leaves after burning the house to cover his trail.

In this portion of the story Wells has deliberately utilized a Jew as the sort of person who would readily evict a tenant from his premises, to make a necessary sequence credible. He also implies that setting fire to the home of a *Jew* would not be considered enough of a crime to turn his hero into a villain, and he has Griffin add, "—and no doubt it was insured."

Wells's most unbelievable anti-Semitic passages contained in *The War of the Worlds* are little known, because they appeared only in the original magazine publications (*Pearson's Magazine*, April–December 1897, in England; *The Cosmopolitan*, May–December 1897, in the United States). Hordes are streaming out of doomed London before the deadly rays of the invading Martians. Among them is a "bearded, eagle-faced man lugging a small handbag which split even as my brother's eyes rested on it and disgorged a mass of sovereigns that seemed to break up into separate coins as it struck the ground. . . . The Jew stopped and looked stupidly at the heap, and the shaft of a cab struck his shoulder and sent him reeling." He dashes to the center of the road to pick up his coins, and as he rises a horse bears him down and the wheels of a wagon ride over him, breaking his back.

". . . Clutching the Jew's collar with his free hand, my brother lugged him sideways, but he still clung to his money, and regarded my brother fiercely, hammering at his arm with a handful of gold. . . . My brother looked up, and the man with the gold twisted his head round and bit the wrist that held his collar."

It is hard to imagine a more cruel image than that of Wells's Jew in *War of the Worlds;* back broken, paralyzed from the waist down, clinging to his gold and in his efforts to retain his "wealth" literally biting the wrist of the arm that is trying to pull him out of harm's way. The word "Jew" was changed to "man" in the first American hardcover edition by Harper's in 1898 and has remained that way since.

Applauding all the persecutions against Jews by the Continental nations was M. P. Shiel, an author born in Montserrat, British West Indies, in 1865. His anti-Semitism was among the most extreme of any known science fiction writer, and his books lacking some direct or implied slur at the Jews are in the minority. The most vicious of his novels was *The Lord of the Sea* (1901).

Shiel saw the buying of land by Jews in England as an ominous thing. He showed almost half of England's land bought up by Jews and decrees going forth to the oppressed British farmers that they must wear a *fez with tassel* as the symbol of their peonage. Jews control Parliament, and lecherous Jews grasp for lovely Christian girls without bothering to remove vestments of their prayer. Fiendish knife-brandishing Jewish guards are everywhere.

The "hero" of the story, Richard Hogarth, made wealthy by finding a great diamond from a meteor, builds floating metal forts which command the seas and bring England to her knees. He proclaims himself king of England and almost his first act is a manifesto which will forbid Jews to own any land, to work on any land, to teach in any school (even their own), to attend any public school or university or sign any legal contract, preside at any official ceremony, and rules out conversion as a salvation.

He buys Palestine for the Jews, divests them of their property, and ships them all out "so that the return to simplicity and honesty was quickly accomplished." When his rule is overthrown by a coup, Hogarth learns that he was actually born a Jew, though raised by an Irish father, and is also shipped off to Palestine.

Shiel is apparently one of those writers who is frequently talked about but rarely read. If he has been read, a gentleman's silence has been maintained about the contents of his novels. Shiel early formed an *Übermensch* (superman) philosophy, out-

lined in his novels, which not only includes views that foreshadowed Nazi dogma but quite obviously deals with "a final solution to the Jewish problem."

Shiel was also strongly anti-Negro, anti-Oriental, anti-Chris-
tian, and prowar. One London rumor said he was part Negro,
but a facsimile of his birth certificate neither confirms nor dis-
proves it. An early photo shows negroid features.

A rather unique novel with a Jewish central character was
*Pharaoh's Broker, Being the Very Remarkable Experiences in
Another World of Isador Werner* by Ellsworth Douglass, the
pen name of American writer Elmer Dwiggins. The book was
first published by C. Arthur Peason Limited, London, in 1899.
Isador Werner, a youthful and successful Jewish speculator on
wheat in the Chicago Exchange, finances the building of an
antigravity spaceship which takes him and several companions
to Mars. His knowledge of Hebrew proves invaluable when it
is found that a young Martian government overseer speaks Hebrew! Werner slowly realizes that each planet goes through
parallel development in which the same incidents occur. Mars
is developing at a slower rate than Earth, and is in the period
now when a Jewish "Joseph" has come into Egypt and is storing
away wheat during the seven fat years to take care of the seven
lean years.

Werner sees a chance to change the history of this world,
because if it follows as on Earth, the Martian Jews in a few years
will go into bondage as slaves of the Egyptians. Utilizing his
knowledge that the Martians are in the last of the fat years, he
corners the market on wheat and feeds the poor so they will not
have to accept slavery in exchange for food.

In a sense, *Pharaoh's Broker* was an exception, for to slur and
malign the Jew appeared so integral a part of the literary world
before World War I that the element of logic and rationality
departed. Again and again, the vile charges which might have
gained weight through repetition were rendered fraudulent by
the author's own words. An obvious but rather typical example
was contained in Andrée Hope's two-part novelette of horror
and human degradation in *Russia Beneath the Dark Shadow*
which ran in the August and September 1885 issues of the
eminently respected *The English Illustrated Magazine*. The
heroine, entering a small community, says, "There are many

dirty towns in the eastern portion of Europe, but for supremacy in dirt B— will carry off the palm. Inhabited almost exclusively by Jews of a low class, each street presents an aspect of squalor and filth unequalled probably in the so-called civilized world." Then follows the statement: ". ...ckening combination of *pigs' styes* and train oil filled the air."

Just why would a Jewish community in old Russia raise pigs?

Some of the science fiction published in England shortly after the turn of the century was so overtly anti-Semitic that if it truly represented the mood of the populace, it seems almost a miracle that the Jews were able to survive. Max Pemberton, the initial editor of the famed boy's magazine *Chums* and for which he wrote his first science fiction novel *The Iron Pirate* in 1892, was typical. He became editor of the influential *Cassell's Magazine* in 1896, which ranked not far below *The Strand, Pearson's,* and *Pall Mall* in its day. Among the novels he contributed to its pages was *The Giant's Gate* (December 1900 to November 1901). The science fiction aspect is the invention of a highly advanced submarine, based in France, which can be steered with fingertip control through the underwater defenses of the Thames—through "the gate of England"—from which the book's title is derived.

The long novel is set against a background of France "when no man dared to say aloud that Dreyfus was innocent," and the hero, Jules Davignon, who seeks to overthrow the government of France and come into power, "did not love the Jews." Max Pemberton wrote adventure and intrigue with skill and some sophistication: "Paris took down the shutters of the Jews and broke their windows. All said and done the Jews were rich, and glass was cheap."

Davignon "cursed the Jews," because the pogrom was delaying his progress towards dinner and he was hungry. If there were no Jews, there would be no disturbance and he would not be held up.

This and scores of other references of an uncomplimentary nature appear to be little more than character delineation, until the long novel reaches its climax with Davignon saving himself from a charge of treason with an impassioned and inspired burst of oratory, and becomes the personification of the noble and martyred spirit of patriotism. Only then is the fact subtly brought home to the perceptive reader that Max Pemberton, later knighted, was not writing as the Devil's advocate, but from conviction.

Probably the single novel that is most unbelievable for the amount of vitriol and venom poured on the Jews was *Ichabod* (James Milne, 1910), written by James Blyth, a regular contributor to *Cassell's Magazine*. His specialty was fiction and articles of the sea and ships, with occasional historical pieces, but he had written *The Aerial Burglars* (Ward, Lock, 1906), a science fiction novel which involved the use of a singular aircraft with flapping wings, capable of hovering and used for the purpose of accomplishing a major jewel theft. The ruthlessness of the "heroes," who are thieves, murderers, kidnappers, spies, employing not only scientific invention but astrology and hypnotism to achieve their ends indicates a sense of morality on the part of the author warped beyond salvage. Among the characters in the book is a Jewish jewel dealer, described as an "oily Hebrew," whose name is Hyman Alterschwein. (Alterschwein literally means "old pig.")

Ichabod told of a plot by Germany to conquer England from within, assisted by the finances of the wealthy Jews of that country and the recruiting of hundreds of thousands of Jewish immigrants as troops. His reasoning: the Jews "were the enemies of the English, because they despised the foolish generosity which the English had shown them, and because they envied the riches which the English had still managed to save from Semitic clutches."

Aware of this plot, patriotic Englishmen rally to thwart it, including an old colonel who will do "anything honourable . . . to cleanse this country of the poisonous fungus of those alien Jews, of the cancerous growth which has eaten farther into England than the East-End, the growth which has city men, lawyers, merchants, aye, and politicians, as the tentacles of its vile body."

When any page can be opened at random and anti-Semitic passages found, it seems almost as though the author took page proofs and wrote smears against the Jews on every page that was missing them.

Filthy Jewish children transmit the eye disease trachoma to clean, innocent gentile schoolmates. The author does not believe that Jews steal male babies for blood sacrifices on the holidays, but they *do* snatch Christian tots and sell them to the blood worshipers for the rites of Satanism. It was noted that "certain colleges had become so lost to all sense of decency that they catered for the abominable thing, and advertised kosher halls, and kept a tame rabbi. . . . the millionaire Jews . . . shied at the name of kosher . . . But their 'satyr snouts' betrayed them." When a wealthy Jew dies leaving his money to enable Continental Jews to escape the persecution of the continent and migrate to England, the author says, "There could be no doubt that the recent vast bequest would bring twenty or thirty thousand Semitic aliens, reeking of filth, covered with vermin, tainted with trachoma, and, in some cases, even leprosy, over to this unhappy country." The foregoing is but a tiny fraction of the charges made.

It all ends happily enough with the Jewish plot foiled, Germany humbled, and though the protagonist Noel Pettigrew, the architect of the counterattack against the Jews, does not live to see it, he is honored for having "cleared our shores of the blight, the poisoning aphids, which sucked our blood."

It might be said that this was the sort of extreme reaction that might appear in a hardcover, and that no popular periodical would dare countenance anything as rabid. This, unfortunately, was not the case. One of the most respected publications of its day, *The Idler,* edited by the famed Jerome K. Jerome and his able partner Robert Barr, and truly a more literary prototype of today's *New Yorker,* had no such element in its frequent science fiction, but "Talks with a Nurse," a first-person anonymous documentary written by G. G. Burgin (a specialist in the interview) published in the November 1895 issue, certainly must have raised an eyebrow even in its day.

"But the Jews are really the worst of all," Burgin quotes a nameless nurse. "You don't know what lying is until you encounter a few representative Whitechapel Jews." She notes that while Jewish parents are fond of their children in "an animal sort of way," they contribute to the mortality rate in the hospitals by feeding them rotten strawberries under the bedclothes when the nurse's back is turned (a sketch of an ugly, hook-nosed crone spooning the deadly stuff to a bed-ridden child graphically illustrates the text), sneaking up fried fish and pastry to children suffering from internal inflammation, and "as to keeping it covered with a blanket, that is, apparently, beyond her [a Jewish mother's] intelligence."

Spiritually as well as physically, the Jews were feared. The coming of the long-heralded Messiah could endanger the religious community of England, as in *The Flight of Icarus* by Henry Byatt (Sisley's Ltd., 1907), which was popular enough to go into several printings. From Germany to England comes Michael the Cohen, a man who apparently cannot be stopped by guards, who inspires instant faith among the Jews and seems capable of minor miracles. He cures the sick in the hospitals and appears to hopelessly trapped miners underground and leads them to safety. He rallies not only the Jews to his side but the Christians, who begin to convert to Judaism by the thousands. The British government is powerless against him, for if expelled, one-third of the country would follow, with resultant economic ruin, or even conceivably civil war.

A "Delilah" is introduced to this "Samson" to discover the secret of his powers so that it can be shorn from him. They fall madly in love, but she still persists in trying to determine the source of his miracles. Finally, following the defeat of an attempted coup, he reveals to her that he is the "Apostate Thief, Michael, the accursed despoiler of the Holy of Holies." He had stolen the secrets of the Ark of the Covenant centuries past and has the power to rule the world. She curses him and leaves him. He intercepts and tries to dissuade her, but she will not hear. Suddenly, in the emotional stress, his powers desert him. He flees from his White Temple and his followers return the government to its rightful rulers. His love goes to a convent, and after an ordeal of imprisonment and wandering, he dies in her arms.

What the novel actually says is that no Jew, no matter how humanitarian his contribution, no matter how godlike his bearing, can derive his substance from other than an evil source because he has denied his Redeemer. He therefore cannot be trusted to run a government or provide a philosophy of life to live by.

Where the anti-Semitic line became less frequent as the main thrust of the story, it still persisted in character delineation. A not unusual example is to be found in *World of Women* (also reprinted as *The Goslings*) by J. D. Beresford (Collins, London,

1913, and issued in America by Macauley the same year). Beresford had scored an unlikely dual hit in 1911 with the first of a realistic trilogy of the British lower middle class, *The History of Jacob Stahl,* and had also published the same year one of the finest examples of the superman novel ever written, *The Hampdenshire Wonder* (Sidgwick & Jackson). *World of Women* deals with a strange malady that kills all but an infinitessimal group of men, and the women of England form their own communes to survive.

During the initial exodus from the cities, one of the women who leaves London is a Jewess who has married for money and now has "cooked and eaten the absurdly expensive but diminutive dog upon which she had lavished the only love of which she had been capable. She had wept continuously as she ate her idol, but for the first time she had regretted his littleness." There is no water with which to wash, "and in any case she did not feel inclined to wash."

Gangs of women are breaking into homes, killing and being killed to take food, but the Jewess, Mrs. Isaacson, is held to be loathsome, because she tried to *buy* food with valuable jewels and money. When she offers to help one family group push an old grandmother in a "trolley" up and down hills, and actually keeps her end of the bargain, she is "suspected"—and rightly —of having as an *ulterior* motive, the desire to *earn* some food. When finally, after hours of pushing in the heat, and with all nearly faint with hunger, they stop to rest and share some of their food: "Mrs. Isaacson strove desperately and with some success to control the greed that showed in the concentrated eagerness of her eyes and the grasping crook of her fingers."

Mrs. Isaacson joins a farm commune of women, but though she at first works, her genetic taint shortly interferes and she complains of heart trouble and finally is accused of burglarizing the room where the preciously limited commodities of tea, coffee, sugar, soap, and other things are stored. She is caught one night drinking out of a whiskey bottle by a lighted candle. "The thought of witchcraft intruded itself" to the women who discover the crime. Mrs. Isaacson with seventeen others (non-Jews) who think like her leave the main commune.

The Jews today have one of the lowest alcoholism rates in the Western world. In 1913, when this book was published, alcoholism was virtually nonexistent among Jewish men and it has always been lower among Jewish women. With Mrs. Isaacson's choice of foods to steal, why whiskey? If anyone else had a bottle of whiskey, she could just drink, but if a Jew has one, witchcraft is involved!

The man who had the most fun with the idea of a Jewish Messiah was Guillaume Apollinaire, the famed avant gardist, proponent of the Cubist movement and a superb writer. A collection of short stories of his published under the title *L'Hérésiarque et Cie* in Paris in 1910 contained "Remote Projection," of a man named Aldavid who has invented a device for duplicating himself and appears to the Jews as a Messiah in many cities throughout the world simultaneously. Jewish bankers are arrested to keep them from leaving the country to go to Palestine and precipitating a financial crisis!

Beyond indicating that the status of the Jews as late as 1910 was none too good in France or in most other nations of the world, Apollinaire's short story was avant-garde for the period and a minor masterpiece of science fiction. He wrote a number of superior science fiction short stories, some of which were initially published in the same collection as *Space Projection*.

When Theodore Roosevelt admitted a Jew, Oscar Strauss, to his cabinet in 1906, he defended his choice with the statement: "Any discrimination for or against a man because of his creed or nativity strikes me as infamy." James Creelman, in agreement with Roosevelt, departed from his muckraking articles of the period and wrote for *Pearson's Magazine* a two-part series titled *Israel Unbound* (February-March 1907). He itemized the many prominent Jews who had contributed to the growth of the United States and predicted emancipation of the Jews from the Ghetto, which he described as "a square mile with Jewish tenements . . . and it contains more than 300,000 Jews."

Few were as sanguine as Creelman at the time. To most, this utterly foreign mass of impoverished Jews, speaking a strange language, could not possibly make the adjustments to modern American society. To a degree this view was reflected by Harris Merton Lyon, talented pre-World War I short-story writer, in his fantasy "The 2000th Christmas," which appeared in *Hampton's Magazine* for January 1910. It opened with the lines: "It was eleven o'clock of a cold Christmas Eve in the year 1999. In the little old tumbledown carpenter shop of meek old Meyer

Abrams, back in a ramshackle courtyard of the Ghetto, sat the strange young Jew, alone."

In the years between 1910 and 1999, nothing has changed, except for the worse. Hundreds of thousands of Jews, half-frozen for lack of fuel, almost starved for lack of food, inhabit the East Side of New York in utter hopelessness. The young Jew is an immigrant carpenter from Europe, who apprises a world where all opportunity has fled, and where a few wealthy men control the riches of the country. On Christmas Eve, this strange young Jew, Josephson, leaves the Ghetto and travels to the home of the richest man in the nation, who is old and alone. With inspired zeal he convinces the man to set up schools to train deprived youth of the country in skills that will lift them above their condition; to set up special agencies to see that all men are employed, a task at which the government has failed. When convinced he has succeeded in goading the wealthy man into action, he leaves. The next morning he is found frozen to death in one of the mangers in the estate's stables.

The Argosy and other all-fiction magazines published by Frank A. Munsey became the standard-bearers for science fiction in the United States before World War I, and one of the early more popular authors was a prolific dime-novel writer who sold prodigally to the pulp magazines under the name of William Wallace Cook. Five of his science fiction novels which originally were serialized in *The Argosy* were reprinted in paperback in 1925 and included *A Round Trip to the Year 2000, Marooned in 1492, Castaway at the Pole, Adrift in the Unknown,* and *The Eighth Wonder.* The last was originally run in *The Argosy* in four monthly installments, November 1906 to February 1907, and featured the inventive genius of Copernicus Jones, an eccentric scientist who builds a gigantic electromagnet in North Dakota, which will siphon off the electrical energy of the North American continent and give him a power monopoly. In order to finance his scheme, he throws in with Ira Perk, a thirty-seven-year-old ex-bicycle salesman who has obtained, on a swap from a Mexican, a Honduran lottery ticket which is now worth $50,000. To raise the cash to travel to Honduras to collect on his ticket, Perk convinces Solomon Levi, a local money lender, to give him an advance. Levi attaches the condition that his son Moses must accompany him, expenses paid, to see that he does not abscond.

When the electromagnet is built, it draws loose metal for twenty-five miles around, causing considerable damage, but produces no electricity. Levi, who suspects what is going on, demands payment for several threshing machines he held claim to which were destroyed by the device.

The electromagnet slows down the rotation of the earth sixteen minutes a day, changing the seasons and forcing government action to halt it. The professor who has failed in an attempt to hold the world up for $1 billion ransom and caused untold catastrophic damage is pictured as eccentric but noble, but the Jew who has loaned big money on a lottery ticket when no one else would to make the venture possible is felt to be not entitled to interest on the loan and is a "leech" when he seeks to be repaid for the destruction of a piece of equipment he legitimately owns.

One of the most unflattering uses of the Jew as a character in science fiction published in the Munsey magazines was George Allan England's *The Golden Blight* which ran in six weekly installments in *The Cavalier* beginning May 18, 1912. England was a rabid socialist and a good part of the book was a diatribe against capitalism. Young scientist John Storm invents a ray which will turn gold into worthless white ash. He systematically employs it to destroy the gold reserves of the world and bring an end to capitalism. The Jewish financier Maximilian Braunschweig buys up almost the entire world's supply of gold ash with silver and stores it in a single vault in the United States and invites the primary capitalists of the world to view it.

When they are assembled he informs them that it will revert to pure gold and he will control the world's supply. Braunschweig, after being cursed by those who have been fooled by him, is described by the author: "His eyes, half-seen and cavernous, glowered like those of Lucifer surveying the lost souls which all had fallen that *he* might rise to evil power.

" 'Behold' cried he in a loud voice, the hidden fanaticism of his soul suddenly bursting forth, 'Behold this shall be the true Zionism! A Jew shall enslave you all, you pagans and you Gentiles! Behold, my race comes to its own, again! Vengeance is mine, saith the Lord; I will repay! . . . all governments, all great men, pagan or *goy*, no matter . . . *Rache!* Revenge! Praised be Jehovah, *Gott* in Israel!' "

As the gold ash converts to gold, the friction causes it to

become molten and it flows over the group of capitalists destroying them all. Last to die is Braunschweig: *"All mine—mine! All—"* he exults as the molten tide inundates him. This dramatic scene was depicted by renowned socialist illustrator John Sloan, one of five drawings in the hardcover edition published by The H. K. Fly Company, New York, in 1916.

The latent prejudice displayed by England's depiction of the Jew as the personification of capitalism was ironic, for even as he wrote, the labor unions had been welded into a strong force by a Jew, Samuel Gompers, and the leading socialist drive of the nation emanated from the Jewish Lower East Side of New York. If to be a socialist was a sign of human nobility, the Jews were to receive no credit for it in England's book. When the novel was reprinted in the March 1949 issue of *Fantastic Novels,* some of the passages quoted were excised.

Was there deliberate anti-Semitism in the Munsey publications? The late playwright George S. Kaufman makes a point of citing in his memoirs that when Frank A. Munsey spotted him on the magazine's premises he ordered: "Get that Jew out of here!" However, Robert Davis, Munsey's editor, did buy stories from Jewish authors including Ludwig Lewisohn, Fannie Hurst, E. J. Rath, and Victor Rousseau, and he did hire Leo Margulies as an assistant in a literary agency he formed in 1920.

Jewish characters play a significant role in two stories by Edgar Rice Burroughs. The most prominent was Adolph Bluber, the fat German Jew involved with an unsavory group who plan to steal gold from the decaying city of Opar, the last outpost of the vanished Atlantean empire. He is a rather insipid villain, heavy with accent, providing comic relief in *Tarzan and the Golden Lion,* the cover story of the fortieth-anniversary December 9, 1922, issue of *Argosy All-Story Weekly,* which ran for seven installments through to the January 20, 1923, issue.

In this novel, Edgar Rice Burroughs has a glorious array of villains, including a Spaniard who is a double for Tarzan, Arabs, Negroes, Englishmen, a Russian, Oparians, and even a woman. The bad guys refer to "dirty Jew," "niggers," "dago," and "limeys," but Tarzan is always strictly correct. The Jew evinces cowardice but does actually very little of a mean or vicious nature, and suffers no unusual punishment.

An entirely different kind of Jew appears in his novel *The Moon Men* serialized in *Argosy All-Story Weekly,* February 21,

1925, to March 14, 1925. Destroyed from within by promises of a communistic form of government, the earth falls under the rule of the Kalkars, men from the moon, and reverts to primitivism. Written as a warning story against communist subversion in 1919, *The Moon Men* was originally titled *Under the Red Flag* and rejected by every magazine it was submitted to including Edgar Rice Burroughs's regular markets, *All-Story Weekly* and *The Blue Book Magazine*. The success of his scientific romance *The Moon Maid* (*Argosy All-Story Magazine*, May 5, 1923, to June 2, 1923) gave Burroughs the idea of reshaping *Under the Red Flag* as a sequel. This very serious, well-written novel has as a character an aged Jewish tanner, Moses Samuels, friend of the hero, Julian 8th. Samuels is sketched with an empathy and tenderness which makes the reader feel that Burroughs had a real person in mind and the characterization contains no false notes. The bitter pill of unreasoning anti-Semitism is found in the next century as Samuels, speaking of the Moon masters, states: "Sometimes they are liberal—as they can afford to be with the property of others; but if he is a half-breed, as I hear he is, he will hate a Jew, and I shall get nothing. However, if he is pure Kalkar it may be different—the pure Kalkars do not hate a Jew more than they hate other Earthmen, though there is one Jew who hates a Kalkar."

The non-Jews of the world who yearn for religion have forgotten the tenets of their fragmentary belief, but symbolically Burroughs has Samuels return it to them in the form of a carving in ivory of Christ on the cross which he gives his friend, Julian 8th. It has been passed down in Samuels's family for generations since it was given to one of his ancestors by a nun.

Religion is forbidden in the world of the future and the Kalkars, suspecting Samuels, find the image of Christ on Julian 8th's person. Accused, Samuels mocks them with the words: "Who ever heard of a Jew worshipping Christ?"

They torture him, but he will not reveal the names of other religionists. He dies in the arms of his young friend Julian, who relates: "Tears came to my eyes in spite of all that I could do, for friends are few, and I had loved this old Jew, as we all did who knew him. He had been a gentle character, loyal to his friends and inclined to be a little too forgiving to his enemies —even the Kalkars. That he was courageous his death proved."

Most of the segment about Samuels is excised from the hardcover version included in *The Moon Maid* and published by McClurg in 1926. Burroughs's biographer Irwin Porges claims that a villainous Jew appears in the unpublished novel *Marcia of the Doorsteps.*

When World War I ended, many of the European nations were economically prostrate. To take their minds off their troubles, politicians blamed the Jews. Quickly, the fulcrum of hatreds that would lead to Hitler and end with Auschwitz began to seethe. In Austria, author Hugo Bettauer produced a satirical book, *The City Without Jews,* which analyzed the role of the Jews in his country and what would happen if they were all driven out.

In his novel, the chancellor of Austria convinces the League of Nations that if he is not permitted to expel the Jews, the only alternative is for his nation to join in a union with Germany. Even those citizens with a small amount of Jewish blood are to be expelled. The chancellor lauds the Jews' "extraordinary intelligence, their strivings for higher things, their model family life," but states, "The trouble is simply that we Austrian Aryans are no match for the Jews . . . because this minority possesses qualities which we lack."

Eventually one of the major supporters of the original movement to drive the Jews from the country states: "Yes, it seems that a very delicate mechanism has been interfered with too abruptly! There are some Jewish qualities that are not to be underestimated, and which we miss badly."

It is remembered that the rich Jews usually spent their money as fast as they made it, to the benefit of all and that their banking advice, due to their international connections, was sound. A "League of True Christians" arises and campaigns to repeal the anti-Jewish laws. This is done and the book ends with the mayor of Vienna greeting the first Son of Israel back with the words: "My beloved Jew."

Published in early 1925, the novel sold a quarter of a million copies in Europe in less than a year, but Bettauer did not live to see it. He was killed in March 1925 "by a zealous twenty year-old 'Nordic.' " At the trial, "the murderer declared himself content with his deed, as he had resolved to save German *Kultur* from degeneration, and believed that Bettauer was a menace to this *Kultur.*"

Strangest of all, Hugo Bettauer was *not* a Jew. Salomea Neumark Brainin, who translated the novel for publication by the Bloch Publishing Co., New York, in 1926, said in her introduction that he was "a good Christian, the scion of a Protestant Viennese merchant family. Not a Jew—not an interested propagandist! A talented journalist of the Danube City, whose versatile pen mastered the novel as well as the *feuilleton.*"

When the main body of science fiction and fantasy magazines came into existence in the twenties, a parade of new writers turned to the writing of this type of material, creating a vast field for examination. Yet, until almost 1950, the number of Jewish characters to appear in literally thousands of stories was inconsequential. This was to a large extent due to the cautious policies of the pulp magazines, which were predominantly slanted at a teenage audience; very little of religion, sex, or other subjects that might have proven socially questionable was allowed.

To a degree it may have been influenced by the fact that the publisher of the first American all-fantasy magazine *Weird Tales* in 1923, Jacob Clark Henneberger, was Jewish, as was Hugo Gernsback, publisher of *Amazing Stories*, the first science fiction magazine, in 1926 (and later seven other titles). Jews who edited large-circulation periodicals in that time tended to abstain almost entirely from matter in any way involving the Jews. Yet Hugo Gernsback permitted the publication of Jules Verne's *Hector Servadac* as *Off on a Comet*, complete in the first two issues of *Amazing Stories*, and also ran "The Diamond Lens" by Fitz-James O'Brien, neither banning nor censoring the authors.

While it is extremely difficult to positively identify those publishers, editors, and writers of science fiction who are Jews, a substantial number are known. Among the publishers are Ned Pines, publisher of *Thrilling Wonder Stories, Startling Stories, Captain Future, Fantastic Story Magazine,* and *Strange Stories;* Louis Silberkliet, publisher *of Science Fiction, Future Fiction, Science Fiction Quarterly,* and *Dynamic Science Fiction;* Bernard Ziff, publisher from 1938 of *Amazing Stories* and *Fantastic Adventures;* Sol Cohen, who carried on those magazines from 1965; Joseph Ferman, publisher of *The Magazine of Fantasy and Science Fiction* and *Venture Science Fiction;* Leo Margulies, publisher of *Fantastic Universe, Satellite Science Fiction,* and *Weird Tales;* Irwin Stein, publisher of *Infinity Science Fiction* and *Science Fiction Adventures;* Abraham Goodman, publisher of *Marvel Science Stories* and *Dynamic Science Stories;* Arnold E. Abramson, publisher of *Galaxy;* as well as several others.

Jewish magazine editors include Horace L. Gold, first editor of *Galaxy Science Fiction;* David Lasser, first editor of *Wonder Stories;* Mort Weisinger, editor of *Thrilling Wonder Stories* and *Startling Stories* and later editor of *Superman Comics;* Samuel Mines, one of the last editors of *Thrilling Wonder Stories* and *Startling Stories;* Norman Lobsenz and Cele Lolli, editors of *Amazing Stories* and *Fantastic;* Judy Lynn del Rey, editor of *Galaxy* and *If,* and now Ballantine's science fiction paperbacks; and Donald A. Wollheim, editor of the *Avon Fantasy Reader, Avon Science Fiction Reader,* and today publisher and editor of DAW Pocketbooks, a science fiction specialty line.

Some Jewish science fiction writers are Isaac Asimov, Alfred Bester, Henry Kuttner, Robert Bloch, William Tenn, Stanley G. Weinbaum, Harry Harrison, Robert Silverberg, Avram Davidson, Harlan Ellison, Cyril Kornbluth, Judith Merril, Nat Schachner, Arthur Leo Zaget, John Christopher (Christopher Samuel Youd), Robert Sheckley, Curt Siodmak, Norman Spinrad, Howard Fast, Gertrude Friedberg, Mirra Ginsburg, Lawrence M. Janifer, Herbert Kastle, Ward Moore, David V. Reed, Mordecai Roshwald, Raymond Z. Gallun, Victor Rousseau (Emanuel), Isaac R. Nathanson, and Arthur Porges. Of special historical interest, Harry Enton, who wrote the first four of the Frank Reade dime-novel series, the first and most famous of the science fiction dime novels for *Boys of New York* beginning in 1876, was a pen name for Harry Cohen, who also wrote under the pen name of Harry Harrison.

With so large a contribution to the field of science fiction by only 3 percent of the U.S. population, it would seem in order to ask if science fiction is producing a body of literature derived from Jewish life and experience. Is there anything comparable to what is being produced in the mainstream by Saul Bellow, Bernard Malamud, Philip Roth, or even Herman Wouk?

Scarcely a semblance. When Jack Dann put together *Wandering Stars,* intended to be an anthology of Jewish science fiction in 1974, he was forced to commission new stories to fill the book.

One of the very few he found of merit was "The Golem" by Avram Davidson (*The Magazine of Fantasy and Science Fic-*

tion, March 1955), which tells, in the Yiddish idiom, of the encounter of a robot with an old Jewish couple and how their traditional knowledge of the Golem does him in.

During the twenties and the thirties, the Jew as a part of a science fiction story appeared more significantly outside of the magazine field than within it.

Olaf Stapledon, whose *Last and First Men* (1930) is one of the classics of modern science fiction, had a very distinct opinion to express about the Jews in that book. At a period in the future about 4,000 years from now, when an Americanized world civilization has collapsed because of exhaustion of fuel supplies:

> The Jews had made themselves invaluable in the financial organizations of the world state, having far outstripped the other races because they alone had preserved a furtive respect for pure intelligence . . . Thus in time the Jews had made something like a "corner" in intelligence. This precious commodity they used largely for their own purposes; for two thousand years of persecution had long ago rendered them permanently tribalistic . . . In them intelligence had become utterly subservient to tribalism. There was thus some excuse for the universal hate and even physical repulsion with which they were regarded; for they alone had failed to make the one great advance from tribalism to cosmopolitanism.

If Jewish science fiction writers were not dealing with Jewish problems in the magazines, they were, to some extent, doing so in books. A volume that was first considered to be the vanity publishing venture of a crank, *The Last of the Japs and the Jews* by Solomon Cruso, issued under the imprint of Herman W. Lefkowitz, Inc., in 1933, appears anything but that today. The story is told in flashbacks from the year 2390 A.D., when a "mighty army of Indian warriors stood ready to expel the invasion of the White enemy."

Prime mover of "history" was Chang Kochubey, half Chinese, one-quarter Russian, one-quarter Jewish. Caucasian-looking in appearance, he is stung by racial prejudice in several forms, including denial of a Mexican woman he loves. The book is a blatantly obvious but nevertheless powerfully plotted warning against the consequences of racial intolerance. Japan is destroyed in an earthquake but the portion of Tokyo with the nation's treasury rises above water and is discovered by Kochubey. He also discovers secret plans for a far-ranging submarine and a near-indestructible aircraft.

With these weapons, he leads China, India, and Turkey in a war against the white races, eventually subduing them. He turns the United States back to the Indians, who carry on the legend that someday the white men will return to conquer them again.

In broad generalities, the author makes many predictions that now strike close to home. He foresees the total destruction of the Jews in Europe: "But who will weep over the terrible calamities and disasters, which befell the Jewish nation all over Europe, where they were massacred and slaughtered by the Christian population of every nation, before the arrival of the Indo-China-Turkish armies?

"Who will weep for the additional *six million* murdered Jews making a total of eleven million Jews killed in Europe, Asia, Africa, Australia and New Zealand?"

Solomon Cruso wrote a sequel to *The Last of the Japs and the Jews*, which provided considerable detailed background to its strange events, titled *Messiah on the Horizon* (Audubon Publishing Company, New York, 1940). The story tells of how Japan was prepared to accept the Jews before sinking beneath the seas, of the discovery of counterinventions to the ones utilized by China, India, and Turkey in their conquest of the white race by the Europeans who now set out to reconquer Asia. At that point an erratically behaving Halley's Comet appears, and just when it seems that the Asian army will be destroyed, Europe is torn from the earth and becomes a second moon 120,000 miles away.

There is a guiding intelligence behind this and he is Jehovah, the original God of the Universe and the God who tried unsuccessfully to make the Jews his proselytizers. It seems that the reason the world has been in such a fearful state is that God has been taking his Sabbath, his day of rest, and permitted events to take their own course. His "day" was of considerable length, but now he is back on the job.

The arctic regions are turned tropical and all the races of the world convert to Judaism, his religion. He denies that Christ was his son, or that Mohammed was his prophet.

Like *The Last of the Japs and the Jews* this would normally be regarded as a rather frenetic vanity volume except that there is enough truth and ingenious imagination to command respect. Like the first volume, the crude overly forthright style has sufficient narrative drive to retain attention. When it was written the idea of even suggesting a semiscientific rational God like this one being considered within bounds for science fiction was highly questionable. Since that time, authors like Lester del Rey, James Blish, and Ray Bradbury have contributed effective stories with similar elements. If their contributions have any legitimacy, then *Messiah on the Horizon* must be granted pioneer status.

Robert Nathan in *Road of Ages* (Knopf, 1935) saw the same hell ahead for Jews as Solomon Cruso. His book opens: "The Jews were going into exile. Eastward across Europe the great columns moved slowly and with difficulty toward the deserts of Asia, where these unhappy people, driven from all the countries of the world, and for the last time in retreat, had been offered a haven by the Mongols. At night their fires burned along the Danube or lighted the dark Bakony forests; while the wood reaches of Tisza echoed with the tramp of feet, the creak of carts, the purring of motors, and conversation in all the languages of the world."

We follow the travelers across the great Asian wastes as they fight off peasant raids. Nathan shows that, set upon by the world, far from being a tribal united group, differences of opinion reach the point where actual violence occurs. His tale is an allegorical minature of the Jewish situation, culminating when the Mongolian hills are in sight.

Until recently, Robert Nathan's tragic vision seemed at most symbolic. The idea of tens of thousands of Jews trekking across the Asian wilderness toward Mongolia was unbelievable at best. But the death of Lieutenant General Kichiro Higuchi of the Imperial Japanese Army in December 1970 presented a stunning epilogue to Nathan's "allegory." It was revealed that 20,000 Jews had made their way across Russia to the Siberian-Manchurian border in 1938 to escape Nazi persecution and were gathered in the town of Otpor. They were dying of cold and the vicissitudes of their journey. They were refused asylum by both Joseph Stalin and Japan. An appeal by the Jewish Club of Harbin, the largest city in Manchuria, to Lieutenant General Higuchi moved him so that he sent twelve trains to Otpor and transported the Jews to safety, 5,000 of them remaining in Manchuria. The story is little known, but Lieutenant General Higuchi was appointed a trustee of Japan's Israel Association in honor of his humanitarian achievement.

In modern science fiction, the existence of Israel has made itself felt. Philip José Farmer in *The Lovers* (*Startling Stories*, August 1952) and its sequel *Moth and Rust* (*Startling Stories*, June 1953) finds the Israel of the future one of the dominant world powers and a new religion ostensibly derived from a Jew named Sigmen and codified in a book called *The Western Talmud* holding sway. John Christopher in *The Year of the Comet* (Michael Joseph, 1955) ends with Israel's preparing to take over a disorganized world with flying infantrymen and a heat ray.

What does all this add up to?

Simply, that for all its justified claims to inspired scientific and technological prophecy, the science fiction writers, including the very greatest, have struck out when it came to any enlightened handling of the Jew as a people or as an individual. In almost every case, except for a Jewish author writing on Jewish problems, even in those in which the hero was Jewish, the science fiction writer from Fitz-James O'Brien up to the moderns has mirrored the common prejudices and situations of his period.

The fear seems to be that it is dangerous to give the Jew equality and fair play—not because he isn't ready for it but because he might do too well. It is safer to keep him out of the picture.

If anything, where they have used Jewish characters, science fiction writers appear to be more reactionary and intolerant than mainstream writers. A reading of *The Jew in the Literature of England* by Montagu Frank Modder (The Jewish Publication Society of America, 1939) reveals that even in the nineteenth century there were some kindly, understanding, and balanced views of the Jews in the literature of that period to offset the works of the merciless bigot. They are less frequent in science fiction, and for this reason the rarity of the Jew as a character in the magazine stories may be regarded as a blessing.

Perhaps, as the alien interplanetary explorers in Wilson Tucker's story "The Planet King" (*Galaxy Science Fiction*, October 1959) find, the last man on earth will be the Wandering Jew, 3,000 years old. Still misunderstood. Still taunted. Still waiting.

CIVIL RIGHTS:

ROCKETS TO GREEN PASTURES

The Negroes were moving out. By the tens of thousands they clogged the roads of the South, carrying with them their prized possessions. They left behind homes, jobs, white friends, and an ancestral history of slavery which blighted their attempts to be recognized as first-class citizens.

" 'Did you hear about it?' one Southerner asks another.

" 'About what?'

" 'The niggers, the niggers!'

" 'What about 'em?'

" 'Them leaving, pulling out, going away; did you hear?' "

That was the opening of Ray Bradbury's short story "Way in the Middle of the Air," as it appeared in the July 1950 issue of Ray Palmer's *Other Worlds Science Stories.* It was the most direct use of the color situation to appear in a science fiction magazine since David H. Keller wrote *The Menace,* a connected series of four short stories for *Amazing Stories Quarterly,* Summer 1928.

The Negroes were going to Mars. They had saved their money, built rockets, and now all in the South, at least, were leaving Earth forever. The entire story line focuses on the attempt of Samuel W. Teece, hardware proprietor, to prevent several Negroes, who either are under work contract or owe him money, from leaving.

It was surprising to see a new story by Bradbury in *Other Worlds Science Stories* at all. By 1950 Bradbury had already outgrown the pulps and was appearing in *The Saturday Evening Post, Collier's, The New Yorker, Mademoiselle,* and other mass-circulation publications. In forecasting the story, editor and publisher Raymond Palmer had bragged: "Ray Bradbury wrote this story for *Harper's!*" This seemed quite likely, and quite as obviously *Harper's* had rejected it. Then why hadn't it found a home in some other major publication or, at the worst, a leading science fiction magazine? The answer was that the story was to be included in *The Martian Chronicles,* scheduled to be published by Doubleday on May 4, 1950, and Ray Palmer was the only editor whose schedule permitted him to get the story into print even a few days before book appearance.

"Way in the Middle of the Air" was intended to be an allegory, and allegories are permitted a great deal of poetic license. *Road of Ages* by Robert Nathan (Knopf, 1935), wherein the remaining Jews of the world travel in a polyglot caravan across Europe and the wastes of Asia to Mongolia, has, in light of recent events, become *more* believable than the day it was written. That the rural Negroes of the South could assemble the technology and save the money to secretly build enough spaceships to take them all to Mars was unbelievable in 1950, and the years between have made it a screeching absurdity. The subject of racial intolerance had been a common one in science fiction. The previous issue of *Other Worlds Science Stories* (May 1950) had carried a touching novelette by Eric Frank Russell, *Dear Devil,* which told how Earthmen overcame their repugnance to a blue, tentacled, bug-eyed Martian who gradually guided a shattered world back to the path of progress. A few issues later, John Beyon, in a 20,000-word novelette, *The Living Lies* (November 1950), told of the fearful racial tension between the green, red, white, and black on the planet Venus and of a machine which can turn the colored races white.

Though weaknesses in the planning detracted greatly, Bradbury was not afraid to be blunt. The story involved Negroes, not blue men from Mars or green men from Venus. He also had the dubious distinction of reintroducing the word "nigger" into the text and attempted to add realism to his narrative through the use of the vulgarism "son of a bitch."

Just how forthright had science fiction been in its stand for or against the Negro? What were the expressions of its writers on the subject of the Negro in general and the American Negro in particular? What can be found in the literature that does not suffer from obliqueness?

One of the least known, yet most learned, fascinating, and important interplanetary novels of the nineteenth century was *A Voyage to the Moon,* written by Crysostom Trueman, a British clergyman (Lockwood & Co., 1864). The full title is *The*

History of a Voyage to the Moon, with an Account of the Adventurers' Subsequent Discoveries. An Exhumed Narrative, Supposed to Have Been Ejected from a Lunar Volcano. The details of the documentary are the finest day-by-day description of a space journey up to its time, similar in its specificity to "Hans Phaall—A Tale" by Edgar Allan Poe, from which it may have drawn inspiration. The antigravity metal for space propulsion is reminiscent of that utilized in *A Voyage to the Moon* by Joseph Atterley (Professor George Tucker), published by Elam Bliss, New York, in 1827. The use of shutters to accentuate or cut down the ship's antigravity potential in Trueman's novel appears to have been later picked up by H. G. Wells for *The First Men in the Moon* (1901).

The early part of this story, in which the mountains at the headwaters of the Colorado River are searched for the antigravity mineral, involves one Negro in particular, a free slave named Rodolph, who nurses Carl Geister, one of the two lead characters, through a severe case of illness in San Pablo, California. When Geister is joined by Stephen Howard, the "narrator" of the adventure, they listen in on a "nigger conversazione" which establishes Rodolph as an uneducated but wise black philosopher: " 'Lords o' creation and fellow-niggers,—de next head ob my discoorse are de stars. Gaze into de ferment on a cl'ar night—what do yer see? Hundreds o' lights, twinkin and blinkin wid radiance, scattered permiscus. 'Stronomers say dose are worlds. Gollies! what a notion! Next dey'll say dey got people in 'em, jis like dis world! Hu! git out! Don't stuff dis child, I tell ye.' "

Before this discourse proceeds much further Rodolph is wounded in the ear by an Indian arrow and there is a battle with mounted red men in which three Negroes are killed and scalped. This pattern of setting scientific adventure in the Wild West should be kept in mind, for within a very few years it would become the basic formula of the "invention" stories of the American dime-novel writers.

Though the speech patterns for Rodolph quoted above out of context may give the impression of the author gazing down from lofty white superiority upon the black man, this is not the feeling conveyed by the story. Rodolph is very clearly etched as an extremely intelligent and able man with high moral and ethical standards, capable of admirable resourcefulness, and possessed of distinct managerial skills. Simply stated, the Negro in this story was a literary device, utilized with considerable skill.

Certain points of similarity in the use of a Negro as a character exist in a later novel, *The Auroraphone* by Cyrus Cole (Charles H. Kerr & Co., 1890). Like *A Voyage to the Moon,* early Western adventures take place in and around Colorado. The inventor of an interplanetary telegraph, Gaston Lesage, is attended by a Negro who saved his life and whom he rewarded by buying him out of slavery and putting him in his employ. The Negro, Peter King, despite an inability to read, has gained a facility for transmitting and receiving messages by telegraph.

When Lesage begins getting information from humans on Saturn on his Auroraphone, the Negro is certain he has gotten into direct contact with Satan.

The Negro plays more than a comic role in the novel. Convinced that his employer is heading for perdition, he conquers his superstitious fear and telegraphs Saturn to terminate communication. The men of that planet destroy the Auroraphone by a tremendous solar flash of energy. Transmission is not resumed for ten years.

As early as its second novel, the greatest of all "invention" series, those of Frank Reade and later his son, Frank Reade, Jr., introduced a Negro character, Pomp, who was to remain integral to the entire life of the stories. Harry Enton, who eventually quit dime-novel writing to become a doctor, created Pomp in *Frank Reade and His Steam Horse,* published in the weekly *Boys of New York* from July 21, 1870, to October 20, 1879.

Frank Reade, genius teen-age inventor and prototype of Tom Swift, had as companions Barney Shea, a daredevil Irishman with a thick brogue, and Charley Gorse, a cousin from Missouri, in the first novel in the series, *Frank Reade and His Steam Man of the Plains, or, The Terror of the West (Boys of New York,* January 13 to March 31, 1879). Pomp enters the series in the second story as the servant of sixteen-year-old Charley Gorse. In appearance, Pomp is a grotesque figure: "He was no higher than four feet, his chest and shoulders were large and swelling, and from his enormously long body descended bandy legs of a little more than one foot in length, while his feet were the finest specimen in the heavy corn-crusher line that could have been met with . . . His head was very large, rounded off as smoothly as a cocoanut, and covered with hair that curled so tightly that he could not shut his mouth."

Although Pomp with his absurd proportions, odd appearance, and peculiarities of speech seemed to be intended for comic relief, out West, Pomp is shown to be one of the greatest horsemen who ever lived: outracing a pack of Indians, and outlaws, accomplishing a feat of picking them off one by one with a pistol while riding backward.

Pomp also strums away on an old banjo, keeping discordant time with the Irishman, who plays a fiddle. During the era when the Frank Reade series was written (1870–1898) the Irish were much maligned and discriminated against.

In making the two subsidiary characters broad caricatures to provide humor, the Frank Reade series can be considered to be perpetuating prevalent stereotyped notions of the two ethnic groups. The very real ability and heroism attributed to them must be considered a step forward. Though Frank Reade was clearly the superior of all, through natural genius, his attitudes towards his companions were completely democratic, and they were treated as equals.

When the publisher of *Boys of New York*, Frank Tousey, dropped Harry Enton after the fourth novel in the Frank Reade series and selected fourteen-year-old Luis P. Senarens (who he had never met and imagined to be a scientist) to continue the series under the pen name of "Noname," Pomp was retained as a major figure in the stories. The fifth story in the series, and the first by Luis P. Senarens, titled *Frank Reade, Jr., and His Steam Wonder* (*Boys of New York*, February 4 to April 29, 1882), informs us that the original Frank Reade has married, has made a fortune farming with steam-powered equipment, and one of his two sons, seventeen-year-old Frank Reade, Jr., has inherited his genius and carries on the inventive tradition.

Pomp is now twenty years older, but this in no way minimizes his usefulness. Whatever physical decline he may have suffered (not very apparent) is more than compensated for by the years of accumulated experience.

"The Steam Wonder" is a trackless, oil-fueled locomotive which proves to be particularly effective in stopping Indians in the West. Pomp is just as remarkably powerful and heroic as ever.

A pattern that was used in the Frank Reade, Jr., series up until its very end was a consistent good-natured squabbling between Pomp and the Irishman Barney Shea. It can be said that while the epithets, whether expressed for fun or realism, may make all those who desire progressive race relations squirm uncomfortably, they were the common expressions in use in their day. The Negro, Pomp, as well as the Irishman, Barney Shea, spoke like millions of others of their ethnic groups at the time. They were instantly recognizable by the readers.

The sharp line of demarcation occurs when the reader is shown by action that those very Negroes and Irishmen whom he may have regarded with condescension, the same ones he was likely to meet during his daily business, could perform deeds that were marked by considerable fortitude and great physical prowess, and that these deeds could be inspired by the highest concepts of fair play and patriotism. Furthermore, the Negroes and Irishmen he read about are not merely saddled with menial tasks, but operate at the pioneering end of scientific advancement in feats of adventure involving submarines, aircraft, space travel, and tanks.

Contrast Pomp with the characterization of Frycollin, Negro valet in *Robur the Conqueror, or The Clipper of the Clouds,* by Jules Verne, published in 1886. Verne had taken the entire concept of helicopter-driven aircraft from the Frank Reade series, as he had taken, and would continue to take, many more of its author's ideas in the future. It seems almost a certainty that Frycollin was inspired by Pomp, in order to lend "humor" to the story. Frycollin's *only* redeeming feature was that he did not "talk Negro," which, as Verne said, "was a consideration for nothing is more unpleasant than that odious jargon in which the use of the possessive pronoun and the infinitive is pushed beyond all bounds." In this manner, Verne dispensed with the necessity of attempting to simulate the Negro vernacular; otherwise Frycollin was depicted as follows:

> He was a pure-bred Negro from Carolina, with a stupid head on a weakling's body. Being only one-and-twenty, he had never been a slave, not even by birth, but he might as well have been one. Grimacing and greedy and idle, and a poltroon of the first order, he had been in Uncle Prudent's service for about three years. His master had been a hundred times on the point of kicking him out, but had kept him on for fear of getting something worse. With a master ever ready to venture on the most

audacious enterprises, Frycollin's cowardice had brought him many arduous trials. But there had been compensations. Very little had been said about his gluttony and still less about his laziness.

When Robur the Conqueror kidnaps Frycollin along with his master, Uncle Prudent, and a friend, Phil Evans, and carries them aloft on his gigantic, multi-vaned helicopter, the Negro's terror and sheer cowardice prove disgusting. Faint with fear, Frycollin crawls around the deck of the great ship on all fours, whimpering.

What a fantastic difference in *Frank Reade, Jr. in the Clouds* (*Boys of New York,* September 6 to December 20, 1884), when a flying craft of Frank Reade, Jr.'s is attacked by eagles, and Pomp, grabbing the legs of one giant bird, is pulled from the vessel to what seems certain death. His weight gradually draws the bird to the ground. When the novel was reprinted in *Frank Reade Library,* April 22, 1893, Pomp was given feature billing on the cover for this feat.

As to Frycollin, he spent most of the rest of *Robur the Conqueror* "shut up in the galley, he saw nothing of what was happening outside and might consider himself out of reach of danger. Wasn't he very like the ostrich, not only physically in his stomach, but morally in his stupidity?"

Fortunately, the Frank Reade and Frank Reade, Jr., stories, the largest circulated of all the "invention" novels, had started a precedent which held. When Edward Stratemeyer, outstanding dime-novel writer, editor, and author of the Rover Boys teen-age book series, launched *The Great Marvel Series* with *Through the Air to the North Pole* in 1906, a major character was an aide to inventor Professor Amos Henderson, a powerful, good-natured Negro who called himself Washington Jackson Alexander White. The Negro never used a small word where he thought a big one might do and a typical communication from him might be: "Heah's de stupendousness conglomeration dat eber transcribed dis terresterial hermisphere!"

While the Negro cooked meals and took care of the old professor, he also single-handedly overpowered culprits spying on inventions in progress, and was the engineer of a semirigid dirigible which sails to the North Pole, and later of the submarine in *Under the Ocean to the South Pole* (1907). The impression of him the reader got aside from the constant barrage of misused and mispronounced big words is of high intelligence, great strength, a fine sense of humor, pronounced mechanical skill, and pride in achievement.

The most popular series of boys' books ever published was the Tom Swift series, and Edward Stratemeyer was the father of them, the very first, *Tom Swift and His Motor Cycle,* appearing in 1910. Tom Swift, son of an inventor, riding down a country road on a motorcycle, accidentally knocks down an elderly Negro, Eradicate Andrew Jackson Abraham Lincoln Sampson. In attempting to make amends, Tom contrives a new brake for the old Negro's mule-drawn wagon and offers him work.

The same semiderogatory references are used in Tom Swift as in Frank Reade. When Eradicate, who has been struck down by the motorcycle, is asked to look around, he replies: "Ye dean't catch dis yearh nigger lookin' around!"

When Tom Swift apologizes, Eradicate speaks not unlike Washington White of *The Great Marvel Series* when he graciously replies: "It was mah fault fer gittin in de road. But dat mule Boomerang am suttinly de most outrageous quadraped dat ever circumlocuted."

Eradicate is an older man, not capable of feats of strength and daring such as those which personify Pomp and Washington White. He has little education and therefore cannot perform any highly technical tasks; yet while he provides humor, he is not made a buffoon. On his entry into the story he is an independent businessman who sells his services and gives a good day's work for a day's pay. In tight spots, he rallies his resources and with full regard for his limitations shows courage and common sense. He frequently helps Tom Swift out of difficult situations and is a loyal and good friend. In the early stories in the series he merely takes a fancy to Tom Swift, but later he goes to work for him.

The significant fact is, that teen-age science fiction, from 1879, when the Frank Reade series was begun, through to 1940, when the first Tom Swift series petered out, millions upon millions of white youngsters who read these boys' books were given a very friendly and positive view of the Negro.

The Frank Reade attitude toward the Negro was carried by dime-novel writers like Robert Ames Benet into adventure fiction for adults. With the ascendency of the pulp magazines,

Benet upgraded his writing standards so that he became a popular contributor to *The Argosy, All-Story Magazine,* and *New Story Magazine.* Today he is paradoxically best-known for his rare science fiction novel *Thyra, a Romance of the Polar Pit,* published by Henry Holt and Company in 1901. An exploratory expedition, searching for the North Pole, is carried by a balloon into an unknown area where prehistoric life, apemen, and giant descendants of the Icelanders still survive. One of the characters is Sergeant Black, a Negro formerly in the U.S. Army, but now the cook of the expedition. Though at one point Black almost loses his reason imagining the unknown horrors he may have to face, and though his position as the cook of the group is calculated to inject a small note of humor into the story, through most of its pages he is a fighting demon at the forefront of the dangers that face the party.

Negroes were cast in a villainous role in *When the Sleeper Awakes* by H. G. Wells, first serialized in seventeen weekly installments in *The Graphic* (January 7, 1899, to May 6, 1899) with illustrations by H. Lanos, one of the leading science fiction illustrators of the period and then published in hardcover by Harper and Brothers, 1899. An Englishman in suspended animation for 200 years awakes to find that bequests left him by wealthy businessmen during his sleep and cleverly managed by special investors have made him owner of half the world. At least one-third of the population of that future day lives in virtual slavery and, as they seek to revolt, blacks are brought in from Africa to subdue them cruelly. A Paris uprising is smashed by the Negro armies and now The Sleeper learns that a fleet of 100 airplanes is carrying a Negro army to London.

In a single plane, The Sleeper sets out to meet the oncoming fleet, to give London thirty minutes to set up antiaircraft which will win the day for them.

"No man of all that black multitude saw the coming of his fate . . . Those who were not limp in the agonies of airsickness, were craning their black necks and staring to see the filmy city that was rising out of the haze, the rich and splendid city to which 'Massa Boss' had brought their obedient muscles . . . They had heard of Paris. They knew they were to have lordly times among the 'poor white' trash."

An experienced pilot, The Sleeper wreaks havoc in their midst and antiaircraft does the rest, saving London.

M. P. Shiel, born in Montserrat, the West Indies, in 1865, was thoroughly familiar with the Negroes of that area. His fiction tended to show considerable contempt for the Negro, yet his short story "The Place of Pain" displays a certain amount of ambiguity. "The Place of Pain" was published in *The Red Magazine* before World War I, though it was not collected into book form until *The Invisible Voices* (Richards, London, 1935).

The central character in the story is a deposed Negro pastor, Rev. Thomas Podd of Small Forks, British Columbia, Canada. Reduced to starvation, he begs the white narrator to give him $3 a week in exchange for a tremendous secret involving life on the moon. "The payments wouldn't be for long, for I've developed consumption, I see—the curse of us colored folks . . . I'm mostly hungry—my own fault; but I couldn't keep on gassing to those big-lipped niggers, after seeing what I've seen."

Granted a dollar a week, he is rescued from hanging by the white narrator when the townsfolk quite accurately surmise that he has deliberately set three fires to prevent an electrical power plant being built on a nearby waterfall. With only hours of life left, Rev. Podd takes the white man to the base of the falls, where he has accidentally learned how to form a double-convex lens from the action of the water and has seen fantastic sights of life on the moon. The building of a power plant would destroy the natural lens, and he dies unsuccessfully trying to give the white man a glimpse of what he has seen.

The Reverend Podd is obviously an educated well-spoken man, capable of gratitude and unquestionably telling the truth of what he has seen. As though these positive points were too much for him to bear, Shiel, in describing Rev. Podd's downfall, says, "Anyway, the thin veneer of respectability came off him like wet paint, and he slipped happily back into savagery."

The highly controversial Ignatius Donnelly had published a novel, *Doctor Huguet* (F. J. Schulte & Co., Chicago, 1891), available in both hardcover and paper, which told of a landed southern gentleman, Dr. Anthony Huguet, who wakes to find himself a Negro. He recognizes the body he is in as that of a drinking no-good black, Ben Johnsing, and in turn his former body is now the habitat of the Negro.

Despite his knowledge of Latin and Greek, no school will hire him as a teacher. His fine speech and intelligence do not qualify him as a salesman in a white store and there are no Negro-owned stores. His fiancée is lost to him. When, in anguish, he protests his plight, he is arrested and later hunted by dogs.

Finally, he comes to terms with himself and begins a school for the ignorant blacks, but even this activity is resented by the whites.

On the other hand, the Negro in his body spends his time drinking, fishing, frequenting bawdyhouses, and recklessly spending his estate. He also "hates" Negroes, particularly the males, and leads white youths and Ku Klux Klanners against them.

Like the politician he is, Donnelly says the right things at times, but his own prejudices are shockingly revealed. Simply stated, a white man in a Negro's body ennobles the race, but a Negro in a white man's body defiles it.

Albert Bigelow Paine, the famed American biographer of Mark Twain, did not fall into the same trap in his short story "The Black Hands" in the American edition of *Pearson's Magazine* for August 1903 (the British edition ran it December 1903), mainly because he did not effect the body switch. A newspaper reporter awakes in a hospital after involvement in a train accident and finds the shock and the opiate have turned him black. A smashed nose makes him look all the more like a Negro. The colored elevator boy at first attempts to stop him from entering his own apartment. He encounters problems eating in restaurants, even where known. The landlord politely gives him an eviction notice, and his newspaper asks him to resign since it has been their editorial policy to claim that Negroes are genetically inferior, and to have one writing on their staff would hold them up to ridicule.

His fiancée had once told him: "It is for yourself, your soul that I care." He goes to her and she is horrified; as he reaches pleadingly towards her she exclaims, *"Oh, please don't touch me!"*

His mother and sister were in Rome at the time of the accident. Learning of his condition, his mother writes that for the sake of his sister they will stay abroad until everything is corrected. He goes to live among the Negroes, but they shun him as not one of their own.

He finally submits to the experiment of a doctor who tells him he may be able to restore his natural color, but there is a possibility that the process will kill him.

The story ends with the lines: "Will these hands be white if I return to the world of men?

"If not, then let me never awaken!"

Second only to the Civil War in its impact upon Negro life in America was World War I. With millions of men recruited for the service, and fantastic new production goals set for industry, the nation was faced with an acute labor shortage. Major industrial firms literally imported Negroes by the hundreds of thousands from the rural South and gave them a chance at well-paying jobs previously denied them. The beginning of a Negro middle class began to come into existence in the cities.

White reaction to this improvement was sharp and the severest practices against the Negroes were instituted in the South after World War I, and it was in the twenties that lynchings became a matter of world scandal.

Negroes of ability found their way blocked by color alone.

This frustration was used as material for a story by Eli Colter, "The Last Horror," in the January 1927 issue of *Weird Tales.* Richard Ballymair, a Negro, is born with white hands. In saving the life of an army captain from a lion in the Congo, he is clawed, and has a piece of white skin grafted to his body to replace his own. To his astonishment, he learns that it will remain white. With the aid of monies obtained from oil on land given him by the army captain, he sets about replacing his entire body with skin from whites he has kidnapped, so that he can comfortably take his place in the commerce and society of America.

A related theme was taken up by David H. Keller in four stories: "The Menace," "The Gold Ship," "The Tainted Flood," and "The Insane Avalanche," all published in the Summer 1928 *Amazing Stories Quarterly.* In "The Menace," a plot is uncovered by private detective Taine of San Francisco, in which Negroes have discovered how to make gold and are systematically buying up Harlem and other areas of New York City. They have also discovered a chemical which can turn their skin white. In the course of the narrative, Dr. Keller is brutally frank in his treatment of the race question. The other three stories deal with a series of other efforts by Negro scientists and leaders to destroy the United States for its behavior towards the Negro, almost succeeding before being foiled by Taine of San Francisco.

Both Colter and Keller agree that the Negro is capable of intellectual attainment, but in doing so have made the Negro appear far more sinister than anything the race riots have shown.

At the time "The Menace" was published, there was virtually no criticism of its theme. Twenty years later, when Keller began a comeback in the hardcover science fiction press, a whispering campaign criticizing the handling of the Negro in those early stories became audible among the science fiction fans.

Sometime in 1948, Walter Dunkelberger, a fan magazine publisher, issued *Fanews Magazine*, Number 340 devoted entirely to an article titled "In Defense of Dr. David H. Keller." It seems likely that this defense was written by Dr. Keller's wife, Celia, under the pen name of Cynthia Carey, though there is no direct verification of this. However, the defense pivoted on remarks that Keller's stories were "un-American." In so many words what Carey said was that though it was entirely conceivable that the stories were anti-Negro, they certainly were *not* anti-American, because being anti-Negro was the true American way of life!

The whispering campaign ended.

The gains of the Negro in society were not applauded, but were treated as a subject for alarm. Australian author Erle Cox had a book published by Edward A. Vidler, Melbourne, in 1925, entitled *Out of the Silence*. The book was acclaimed as one of the truly outstanding novels by an Australian writer. In this novel, a woman who has survived in suspended animation for possibly hundreds of thousands of years is found in a metal underground chamber. She is a specially bred superwoman preserved alive by a civilization that has long since perished.

In her own time all the colored races (hundreds of millions in number) had been exterminated in order to keep them from "dragging down" the whites. She has the secret of the weapon which will destroy all colored people, leaving the whites alive. So powerful is her will that no one can resist her. Describing the colored races of her era, she says, "Mentally and in everything but physical endurance they were beneath us. They could imitate, but not create. They multiplied far more rapidly than we did, and, led by ambitious men, they threatened to exterminate the white races by sheer force of numbers. In some places, where the two races lived side by side, the position became acute, and everywhere they demanded as a right an equality they were unfitted for." When an American protests her plan, she replies: "Dick, has your world not yet recognized that there are weeds of humanity as well as of vegetation?" The superwoman is finally killed by a jealous girl, whose man she has taken, and the entire plan aborted, but the reader is left with the uncomfortable feeling that her views were those of the author's.

A Negro scientific genius, Suun Yaar, whose laboratories are at the mouth of the Niger River in Africa, decimates the United States in "Man Created for Death" by Henry J. Kostkos (*Amazing Stories,* December 1934). The black scientist, who has unified Africa under Negro rule, intends to conquer the world and then the planets. The death toll among Americans is so great that artificial humans are created in the laboratory to maintain the strength of the working and fighting forces. The accelerated methods of bringing the artificial humans to maturity cuts their life span to a few years. A "test tube" genius, who foils the plans of Suun Yaar, develops to be a naturally born child who has been artificially stimulated to maturity. As he waits to receive his honors, the nation is sobered by the knowledge that this young, vibrant hero who has saved them all will die of old age in two years.

This story was in advance of its time in suggesting that a modern civilization could be constructed by the blacks in Africa. Despite its Negro villain, it is not a racist story and its ending has a memorable poignancy.

The anti-Negro intent of *Sown in the Darkness* by William Richard Twiford (Orlin Tremaine Company, New York, 1941), was never in doubt. It is quite probable that his novel was financed by the author. The owner of the publishing company was F. Orlin Tremaine, former editor of *Astounding Stories* and then the editor of the short-lived *Comet.* He had attempted to establish a publishing company and had issued several volumes of peripheral science fiction interest, including *Scare Me!* a collection of inexplicable supernatural and supernormal phenomena by the literary agent Ed Bodin, and *Who Do You Think You Are?*, an attempt to set up a theory and system for graphing an individual's tendencies through heredity, by the sometime science fiction writer Arthur J. Burks (based on some ideas of F. Orlin Tremaine).

Twiford, then a resident of Tennessee, presents the thesis that the mixing of the races through social equality has, by the year 2000 A.D., significantly lowered the intelligence of the average American. He quite accurately forecasts the growth of a separatist movement with Negro leadership in the United States. When those favoring separation of the races win at the polls and legislation is to be enacted to enforce it, all the black and yellow peoples of the world declare war against the United States.

The superiority of white intelligence triumphs over great odds. The Negroes who want their own nation are given one in Mexico under the protection of the United States. The whites deport all other Negroes to Africa and certain American island possessions.

That some whites were fully aware during the Depression of how uncomfortable it was to be a Negro in American society was evidenced in a short story "Pigments Is Pigments" (*Wonder Stories,* March 1935) by the youthful Mort Weisinger, later to become editor of the Superman comic magazine complex. A ruthless business executive is turned black through the injection of a chemical, by a scientist he has cheated. When the executive's wife sees his new color, she runs shrieking from the house and doesn't return. Finally, when he asks the scientist's price to restore his white color, he is told: "You look to me like a worried nigger. I think I can help you. Write out a check for two million dollars!"

That is the amount the executive eventually pays for the restoration of his white color and it happens to be his total net worth. So self-evident is the disaster of suddenly becoming a black man in American society that the author doesn't feel it necessary to offer supporting evidence to prove its undesirability.

It is easy to conclude that a rising tide of anti-Negro sentiment by indirection if not by direct intent was being reflected in the science fiction that appeared. This would be an incomplete truth, for major works were also published during this period in which the Negro fared well.

Electropolis, translated from the German of Otfrid von Hanstein (*Wonder Stories Quarterly,* Summer 1930), tells of the purchase by German interests of an area of desert in Australia the size of Kansas and the creation there of a superscientific community. This extremely readable novel contains one of the most memorable scenes concerning a Negro ever to appear in science fiction.

A white man has crashed his plane in the Australian wilderness. A bone fragment pressing on his brain will soon kill him. The Germans appeal to a cannibal tribe for medical help. An elderly naked savage comes forth, and with primitive instruments performs a brilliant brain operation, saving the white man's life. The description of the methods used by the native and the attitudes and impressions of the watchers must certainly rank among the strongest and most dignified sequences involving a primitive Negro written by a white man.

The same magazine published two novels, *The Moon Conquerors* by R. H. Romans (Winter 1930) and its sequel, *War of the Planets* (Summer 1931), presenting the Negro as descendant of a superior race which originated on the lost planet which broke up to form our asteroids. The blacks had built a mighty, scientific civilization and the whites were their slaves.

A Martian invasion of the Earth is defeated by the blacks, and the Martians mutate into the tiny ants which we see today. Decadence and constant forays by former white slaves, who have escaped, gradually crumble the Negro civilization.

A Negro plays a sympathetic if tragic role in Manley Wade Wellman's surprisingly well-plotted pulp short novel *Island in the Sky* in *Thrilling Wonder Stories* (October 1941). After one war too many the world is ruled by the airmen, in floating cities twelve to fifteen miles above the surface of the Earth. Blackie Peyton, who has done twenty years for involvement in a murder resulting from attempted robbery, is released from attending the atomic energy machines (slightly radioactive) as a reward for saving the life of a guard. He becomes a gladiator in the circuses which are part of the new civilization and gains as a friend and trainer a giant Negro named Willie Burgoyne. The Negro, powerful and athletic, has killed rhinoceroses in the arena with nothing more than a bow and arrow and a sword. He is potentially a master gladiator, but is psychologically incapable of taking the lives of men who have done him no harm.

Would the world perhaps be a better place if there were no white race? French author Yves Gandon doesn't think so.

His novel *The Last White Man*, first published in English translation by Cassell and Co., London, 1948, has the white men

65

wipe themselves out by introducing into warfare a disease that kills only those with Caucasian blood. The yellow and black men rule the world between them, and the one surviving white man is kept in a museum and displayed to the public two hours every day.

Ten years after the ascendancy of the dark races, he is permitted to revisit Paris accompanied by a young female Negro reporter, who will record his reactions. What he finds makes mockery of his most tender personal memories, but in the midst of his disillusionment the radio carried by the girl broadcasts a report of a severance in relationship between the dark races, a prelude to hostilities.

She asks him if he thinks there will be war.

He replies, "If wars were avoidable, how is it they have never yet been avoided?"

A similar situation is presented in *When the Whites Went,* written by British author Robert Bateman (Dobson, 1963). A strange virus kills every white man, and civilization begins to crumble as the highly technical facilities and services predominantly controlled by the whites collapse. In England, bands of Negroes with individual leaders form marauding armies while others attempt to establish workable communes.

Two white men who have been underground in a deep mine for two weeks have survived. They are not aware of what has happened and make contact with a Negro community. The pent-up hatred of the blacks bursts forth and an emotional tug-of-war takes place as to whether to kill what may be the last white men on the face of the Earth.

Ray Bradbury, who had brought the Negro theme boldly into the pages of the science fiction magazines with "Way in the Middle of the Air," now projected an all-Negro world in his sequel to that story, "The Other Foot," which appeared in the first, March 1951, issue of a literary magazine, *New-Story.*

The Negroes have for some time been settled on Mars. The news spreads that a spaceship is about to land with a white man in it. There is a bustle of activity. Guns come out of attics, ropes are prepared for lynchings, the streetcar is painted with the sign "For whites: rear section," the last two rows in the theater are roped off for whites, laws are projected against intermarriage, restaurants reserve the right to serve whom they wish. Then the rocket lands.

66

They learn that only a half-million people are left alive on the face of the Earth. The Negroes are begged the use of their rockets to rescue this remnant from an unlivable hell-world. The survivors will shine shoes, wash clothes, cook meals, and clean houses in exchange for refuge.

Isaac Asimov, in his novel *The Currents of Space* (*Astounding Science-Fiction,* October–December 1952), placed his story on the planet Florina, where the rulers are Negroes and the segregated workers whites, but it was done with such subtlety that the majority of readers missed the point entirely.

The literary device of having a superior Negro the final observer and narrator was used in *Childhood's End* by Arthur C. Clarke (Ballantine Books, 1953), wherein the entire aggregate of the races of man evolve to a higher level of intellectual and spiritual existence. Clarke's book was different in another way, inasmuch as his logic for the Negro as a hero figure derived directly from the growth of the United Nations, and the increasing publicity accorded statesmen from nonwhite nations.

Granting a Negro a superior status in a work of science fiction was now no longer an act of liberalism. Such Negroes visibly existed. It was reasonable to speculate upon their future.

In the future world of Philip José Farmer's *Moth and Rust* (*Startling Stories,* June 1953), there are African Negro nations living by the precept of nonviolence, reverting to a religion of primitivism including elaborate sexual orgies. These Negroes utilize depigmentation processes for creating "white" agents and dream of overthrowing France and taking control of the country. One of the agents of the Negro group is named Jim Crew, and members of various Negro sects have developed the "witch-doctor majic" into a valid form of extrasensory perception and projection. An impressive sequence in which Jim Crew's dying thoughts are tapped shows the observers visualizing through him a "dark and bearded man, stepping through the light, holding out his hand to Jim."

The massive problem of building a modern and viable structure for the newly freed nations of Africa was the subject of a series of stories by Mack Reynolds, a science fiction author who has spent a great deal of time on that continent. In "Black Man's Burden" (*Analog,* December 1961-January 1962), a team of well-educated Negroes from the United States, backed by well-financed organizations and advanced technology, commences a

67

long-range program to lure the thousands of diverse African groups away from their tribal customs and into the mainstream of modern life. The ingenuity they display in breaking the hold of tradition on the lives of Arab and Negro alike makes for good entertainment, and the description of existing customs has an air of authenticity to it.

A sequel, "Border, Breed, nor Birth" (*Analog,* July-August 1962), has one of the American leaders deliberately "become" a mythical hero to help unite Africa against the complex play of international politics. The mission, which had begun as somewhat of a lark, evolves into deadly grim battles in which most of the Negro leader's friends are killed or captured, though the prospect of an African union begins to take shape. It is now a mission which has lost all joy. Friends dead, interminable encounters ahead, the Negro turns to Isobel, a girl involved in the unification movement: "'You know, Isobel,' he said softly, slowly, 'in history there is no happy ending at all. It goes from one crisis to another, but there is no ending.'"

That, in an unrelated way, was also the message of John Jakes in his novel *Black in Time* published by Paperback Library in 1970. Jakes had the advantage of knowing the developments of the sixties in the civil rights movement. He also had the advantage of a new liberalism in the arts which permitted frankness in situations, words, and motives seen predominantly in underground works previously.

Three factions utilize a newly developed time-travel device, the Nexus, for different motives. A black, Jomo, intends to alter history so the Negroes will be dominant. A white minister, Whisk, is committed to changing it so the Negroes will stay in their place. Another Negro, Harold, realizes that he must set back to normal all their disruptions or none of them will be born!

The one thought that forcibly strikes home to the tamperers with time is that no matter how they change history, there will not be a better world. They decide to live and improve what exists, rather than to create a milieu in which they will not participate.

At no point in the past was science fiction in advance of the times in depicting the Negro. As whites stiffened their attitudes in the twenties, material appeared in science fiction magazines and books that reached the extreme of preaching genocide. It was fortunate that early writers of teen-age science fiction exercised personal responsibility or they could have infected white youths with an even greater virus of color hate.

With the onset of the United Nations and the "freedom" movements, science fiction reflected a more enlightened mood, but, except for the briefest flurry by Ray Bradbury, it had little to say about civil rights for Negroes. The accomplishments of super Negroes in uniting Africa, as written by Mack Reynolds, either did not anticipate the passions which exploded in the streets of the United States, or assumed they had long since been resolved. Science fiction which scarcely championed Negro rights, gloriously depicts a future in which the elevated, educated, superior Negroes shoulder their load in building the world of tomorrow. Today's novels which utilize the Negro revolt as a kickoff point for a plot situation are only exercising hindsight. Other stories reviewed, whose authors seem hopelessly bigoted by today's lights, were in cruel truth far more precise and even prophetic than the most gloriously relevant moderns. It would not be fair or accurate to accuse authors of a fiction form, whose primary purpose is entertainment, of hypocrisy; but it would be no more than honest to state that attributing social consciousness to them would certainly be a hollow gesture.

WOMEN'S LIBERATION:

WHEN WOMEN RULE

Readers of science fiction are predominantly male. It has been that way virtually ever since science fiction has been written.

Therefore, while love interest is a standard ingredient in most fiction, the same editors who give lip service to the need for more natural dialogue and clear-cut characterization fail to even note the omission of romance when equating the acceptability of science fiction. Stories in which female characters *appear at all* are in the minority in the magazines of prophetic literature.

Despite this, there is one theme spotlighting the female sex which, since the beginning, has been regarded as legitimately in the province of science fiction—that is the extrapolation of Woman Dominant: the female of the species completely independent of, or ruling over, the male.

The word "Amazon" is from the Greek and means "deprived of pap" or sans breast. Pliny the Elder wrote of a tribe of women warriors in Asia Minor who burned off their right breasts so as to make it easier to draw a bow.

Herodotus purports to tell of the origin of the Sauromatae nation from an incident involving North African Amazons. It is never completely clear whether the Amazons are white or Negro, though we get the impression they are the former. He tells of a battle between the Greeks and the Amazons (called *Oiorpata*, or "man-slayers"), which ends in victory for the Greeks. The Amazonian prisoners being carried back to Greece rise up and slaughter every man aboard the ship.

Unfamiliar with the art of navigation, they drift helplessly until cast up on the shores of Scythia.

The Scythians fight a pitched battle with them. When bodies

of the dead reveal their sex, the Scythians decide on a new tactic.

An army of young unmarried men is ordered to encamp near the Amazons at all times, but to refuse to engage in battle. After weeks of this, the women, feeling there is no danger, begin to make contact. Eventually the two groups begin living together. The Amazonian army, with their Scythian mates, takes up residence in a nearby land. The children of the union of Amazons and Scythians become the people of Sauromatae, who speak a corrupted Scythian, and whose women, though domesticated, still accompany their husbands on the hunt as accomplished horsewomen.

The Spanish explorer Francisco Pizarro, with Francisco de Orellana, a one-eyed knight, crossed the South American Andes in 1541 and sailed down a giant river. They survived many perils and claimed that toward the end of their journey they were attacked by powerfully built women warriors, from all-female tribes in the area. The story of these skirmishes led to the naming of the river they had navagated as the Amazon. These "Amazons" are actually believed to be the women of an Indian tribe on the banks of the Naranom, who assisted their men in battling the Spanish.

The Spanish were obsessed with the concept of the Amazon, for in 1510 Garcia Ordoñez de Montalvo wrote *Sergas of Esplandian*, which was popular enough to warrant other known editions in 1519, 1521, 1525, and 1526 (two). The novel told of a race of black women who lived on an island "on the right side of the Indies" called California. They were Amazons in every sense of the word, with their armor and weapons formed from gold, and sailed large ships with which they plundered nearby coasts.

Their island was the breeding ground of griffins, creatures with head, wings, and legs of an eagle and bodies of a lion. They caught baby griffins, training them as aerial mounts for combat, and fed them on killed and captured men, with a supplemental diet of male children.

Hearing of the campaigns against the Christians carried out by the Turks, the Amazon Queen, Calafia, convinces her nation that they should enter the foray for glory and gain. Her forces are greeted in jubilation by the Turks, who had been unable to force a fortified Spanish city. Mounting her women warriors on griffins, Queen Calafia swoops down on the beleaguered Spanish, who find that their swords and arrows cannot pierce the tight-packed feathers of the sky beasts. One by one, they are hauled aloft and either chewed up or dropped to their deaths.

The Turks mount ladders against the walls of the city to take it, but griffins indiscriminately repeat their deadly performance on their allies. The Amazons dismount and scale the heights of the city on ladders, swords in hand, but the attack is repulsed with heavy losses.

The queen and the Turkish leader challenge the Spanish king and his son to hand-to-hand combat to settle the issue, which cannot be resolved by clash of armies.

In this combat, the queen and the Turk are vanquished.

The captured Queen Calafia falls in love with Esplandian, son of the emperor, but when he marries Leonaria, daughter of the Greek king, Calafia bargains with the queen of the Spaniards, offering to convert to Christianity if she is given a husband of suitable rank. Further, she will change the ways of her island of California so that there will henceforth be a normal family relationship. The terms are met, Queen Calafia returns to California, and the story ends.

However, Edward Everett Hale, famed American theologian and author of *The Man Without a Country* and *The Brick Moon*, was to write still another chapter in the history of this colorful romance. At the meeting of the American Antiquarian Society for April 1872, he submitted a paper claiming a philological discovery to the effect that this story was the origin of the name of the state of California; that his researches indicated no appearance of the name "California" before first publication of *Sergas of Esplandian.*

He translated sections of the novel, which he titled *Queen of California,* for publication in *Atlantic Monthly,* and included it in his collection, *His Level Best* (Robert Brothers, Boston, 1873). Chronology appeared to favor Hale's hypothesis that Hernando Cortez, who christened California in 1535, secured the name from this book because, quite appropriately, it was "the right side of the Indies."

The Amazons described by Timothy Savage in *The Amazonian Republic, Recently Discovered in the Interior of Peru* (S. Colman, New York, 1842) were not as bloodthirsty as

72

the girls from California. A sailor, lost in the Peruvian jungles, is captured by cannibals. By chance, he is rescued by a party of Amazons. They have men who lack many masculine attributes, but are treated with utmost kindness. Their city is well-designed and run by an advanced form of government, which is very skillfully administered.

During the nineteenth century, the movements for the emancipation of women began to gain strength, and this was reflected in Utopian literature of that time. The most widely read novel championing the superiority of women was Sir Edward Bulwer Lytton's *The Coming Race* (Routledge, London, 1874), which presented an underground civilization inhabited by a highly scientific people able to control weather, manipulate plant biology, and fly with detachable wings. They also have an explosive so powerful it could destroy the world.

The women of the nation are physically and mentally superior to the men, fully capable of exterminating the opposite sex. Up until the day of their marriage, they aggressively do the courting and make the proposal. After marriage, they are extremely tactful in displaying their superiority, for their vows are renewable every three years.

A eugenically scientific, highly advanced form of the Amazonian society is found in *Mizora* by Princess Vera Zaravitch (pen name of Mary E. Lane), published in the *Cincinnati Commercial* in 1880 and 1881. Their land is in the polar regions and they have no need of the male at all. They reproduce by parthenogenesis, which is only one of the great marvels of their culture. Long before airships or radio existed in the outside world—they had them. They have also attained weather control and have invented a flexible glass with the versatility of plastics.

It is the eventuality presented in this novel that bothers males the most: that women might find a way to dispense with males, even for purposes of reproduction.

Undoubtedly the reluctance with which men conceded woman the right to vote and the slowness with which they permitted her to find independence outside of marriage was reflected by fears of something happening along the lines of Robert Barr's *The Revolt of the—*, "a page from the domestic history of the Twentieth Century" (*The Idler,* May 1894). Women have indeed "progressed." The wife of John Maddox is a business tycoon, with close-clipped hair, stand-up collar, bright bow tie, and jacket tailored like a tuxedo. There are high pockets in her tailor-made skirt. Mrs. Maddox smokes fine Havana cigars, but Mr. Maddox confines himself to Egyptian cigarettes.

While Mrs. Maddox is out in the commercial world, Mr. Maddox stays home and takes care of the children. She is not home very often, but he manages the children well, except that the girl cuffs the boy around a little more than necessary.

In an attempt to gain self-respect, he gambles on the stock market, taking a flyer at wheat. After a slight rise, the bottom drops out, and he and his friends lose a pooled sum of a million pounds to his wife, who has headed the group that cornered the wheat market. She comforts him with her personal check for 50,000 pounds and suggests he give up business and relax in Monte Carlo with the children. She'll be too busy to be home for a while.

Women need not become dominant because of natural superiority. The same result may be brought about by chance as in *A World of Women* by J. D. Beresford, published in America in 1913, but undoubtedly available in England a year earlier. Beresford had scored a critical success with *The Hampdenshire Wonder* (1911), and it was expected of him to come up with something equally imaginative, which he did in the form of a plague which killed only men and left the women alive. The novel focuses on one community of women, together with a single man, which reorganizes for survival. Jasper Thrale, one of the few men left alive, is marvelously adept with his hands and maintains the equipment needed to run a successful farm. However, his puritanical upbringing makes sex repulsive to him. When he finally forms a permanent relationship with one woman, he is regarded as somewhat more amoral under the changed circumstances than a man on a nearby farm, Sam Evans, who, acting almost like a stud, is doing much more to sustain the race.

The women prove unable to keep the mechanical civilization going and begin to take on strange beliefs and perversions. A gradual decline into savagery is forestalled when a ship arrives from America, where the plague struck with less virulence.

The publicity of the suffragette movement had begun to pervade the themes of fiction in the United States before World

War I. The most adroit purveyor of boy-meets-girl pap in the United States at the time was Robert W. Chambers, whose fantasies in the collection *The King in Yellow,* published in 1895, is one of the landmarks in American imagination. He began a series of stories in *Hampton's Magazine* for May 1911 which would eventually be collected as *The Gay Rebellion* and published in hardcover (Macaulay Company, 1913). Like a great many of Chambers's books, it sold exceedingly well, the subject matter concerning the Central National Female Franchise Federation, which formed clubs in every area to see that women advanced their rights. Women were out to set up new rules in the relationship between the sexes and among them was eugenic mating of the most perfect males with the most perfect females to create a better race.

Leading proponent of this philosophy was the New Race University, where young women captured men with nets, chloroformed them, and brought them in for physical and mental examinations.

The plan founders when the imperfect women—those who have vowed celibacy to improve the species—wonder why they can't have one of the tremendous reservoir of unfit men with such drawbacks as baldness, excessive thinness, potbellies, nearsightedness as a sort of consolation prize.

The popular all-fiction pulp *All-Story Cavalier Weekly* ran two stories in quick succession which satirized the situation. Two suffragettes and a professor are swept into the sea during a storm and cast up on a small island in J. Brant's "Equality Isle," in the issue of June 27, 1914. After several years on the island, the women prove superior to the man at providing food, and he becomes the cook. Eventually they both take to battling over him, and one kicks the other over a cliff. When the male tries to get away, he is knocked down by a stone hatchet and agrees to become the mate of the worthy victor.

An even more amusing situation occurs in "Votes for Men" by Percy Atkinson in *All-Story Cavalier Weekly* for July 25, 1914. A young man returning from abroad to the United States in the year 1923 is accosted by a woman on the streets who asks that he marry her. When he refuses, she has a policeman haul him off to jail. He learns that, since he has been away, a law has been passed making it illegal for an unmarried man to refuse a woman's proposal. He may either marry her, go to jail for two to ten years, or be auctioned off to the highest woman bidder for marriage. He selects the last method and arranges with his lawyer to have a young woman bid for him. She is outbid by an older woman, who stuffs him in a car to take him home, but they are attacked by male suffragettes and, in the ensuing melée, he gets away.

He meets the young woman who bid for him, and they are married by inserting five cents in a slot machine, which releases a phonographic record of the automated ceremony as their testimonial. Under the fugitive male law, he is safe if married. However, the lawyer never gave the young woman the money to bid for him, and she is so indignant at the idea that he thinks she would be party to such a scheme that she breaks the records and permits the older woman to repossess him.

Snide digs at women were safe in *All-Story Cavalier Weekly*, a pulp magazine with a higher percentage of male than female readers. A somewhat different approach had to be taken when women's liberation provided the plot focus in the "slick" and women's magazines, where advertising dollars were at stake. A most unusual example was found in *Collier's* for April 22, 1916, where the popular science fiction author George Allan England appeared with "June 6, 2016," a short story of America 100 years to come. In that future time, the women have the social right to pursue the male. A father gives his son both barrels at planning marriage to "that sort" of a woman: " 'The idea, Ellsworth! Letting a girl call on you, send you presents—Good God! In the good old days we men, and we alone, did the wooing, the proposing and all that. A woman who made so bold—' "

The twenty-first-century woman can "motor, swim, fly, dance, golf, discuss business, comment on current events and science, or banter small talk with equal facility."

In an attempt to keep his son from leaving his employ, the father confronts the girl and finds that, despite all her forwardness and accomplishments, she is utterly feminine and charming. He capitulates and the wedding will take place.

More remarkable than the women's liberation aspect was the incredible mass of invention and gadgetry which England incorporated as background to his story. We find vibratory electric toothbrushes, an ozonated sea shower, electric clippers, disposable paper pajamas and shirts, pushbutton breakfasts conveyed automatically to one's room, a rejuvenating bath that prevents hardening of the arteries and extends the life span, waste materials converted to gas to run engines which produce electricity and thereby cut down on pollution, air conditioning everywhere, complete elimination of dust, 210-story glass buildings, television, printing by electric inks on thin sheets of aluminum, dictation automatically typed onto paper, and numerous other scientific advances. Though dated, the story is fascinating on both social and technological levels.

The most literal renditions of the Spanish tales of the South American Amazons (with echoes of Greek lore) were two novels by Stephen Chalmers, both appearing in *Adventure* magazine. The first, *The Dance of the Golden Gods,* was published in four installments from the issue of February 3, 1919, to March 18, 1919. Sir Walter Raleigh has returned to England from South America with a supply of ore that proves to be fool's gold. Raleigh's friend, young Dickon Butshead, is mate on a ship with a mission to determine whether there is real gold to be found in a legendary city described by explorer Juan Martinez. In South America, the Indians take the crew of the British ship to view the Festival of the Love Moon, an annual ritual during which Amazon women of a certain island select their mates. The women pick the white men, ignoring the Indians. A fight breaks out, and the white men barely make it back to their river ships.

The sequel, *The Other Side of Beyond,* published complete in the issue for September 18, 1921, focuses entirely on the Amazons and purports to be "Extracts from the Narrative of Francis Sparrow, Scrivener to Sir Walter Raleigh, selected from the Original and Edited." Francis Sparrow and Hugh Godwin were left behind when Sir Walter Raleigh returned to England, and spent twenty-one years among the Indians. Their story begins in 1607.

After much adventure and searching, they reach the island of the Amazons, and the customs and mating procedures of the women are observed. The matriarchial society was established by native women who hid on an island after the destruction of their men by an enemy. The women became warriors and men born into the tribe were serfs. Mating was accomplished by invitation with men of selected outside tribes during a period of the year called Love Moon. Sexual relations with the lowly males of the Amazon tribe were not only forbidden, but a female suspected of such consort was subject to summary execution.

This short novel is easily one of the finest and most believable stories of the South American Amazons ever written. Historical names and incidents, legend and local color, are related with such an air of authenticity that it reads like dramatized history. Other myths are interwoven with those of the Amazons. The Greek legends tell of tribes in Atlantis with faces in their chests. Such a tribe is discovered on the Amazon, painting their bodies with eyes, nose, and mouth, lengthening their breechcloths to resemble beards, and draping straw covers over their heads so as to give the appearance of hair growing from the shoulder blades.

The possibility that women of the Amazon breed resided in the fabled lost Atlantis crops up again in Booth Tarkington's "The Veiled Feminists of Atlantis," a satire of the sexes he wrote especially for the Fortieth Anniversary issue of *Forum,* March 1926. Booth Tarkington was reputed to have been extremely fond of science fiction and was a member of The Fortean Society, which taunted scientists with a mélange of "unexplained" facts.

Written not too long after women had gained the vote, "The Veiled Feminists of Atlantis" tells of a land that was a virtual Utopia run by the men. As the women became educated, they cast aside the modesty of their veils, which also had granted them special privilege. They secure all the scientific wisdom of the men and then resume wearing the veil. The men protest, claiming that the women, having attained equality, now want superiority.

A war breaks out between the sexes with weapons far more potent than today's hydrogen bombs, weapons so powerful that they slow the rotation of the moon to its present rate. It ends with waves a thousand feet high deluging the land and sinking the continent.

With the onset of the all-fantasy magazines, the cropping up of the Amazon theme, with its delectable plot possibilities, was inevitable.

David H. Keller, who in dozens of stories showed small sympathy for women, wrote "The Little Husbands" (*Weird Tales,* July 1928), a short tale of tall women, rearing seventy feet high, who live upriver near the Amazon. They capture normal men whenever they can find them. The men are kept in a high stockade, pampered and well-treated as long as they amuse the women. They also must mate with them, and all male children are killed.

Should one of these giantesses' tiny consorts grow ill or begin to displease her, she either crushes him with her hands, buries him alive, or impales him on the giant cactus atop the fifty-foot walls as soon as a substitute is captured. As in most of Keller's stories, there probably was a strong note of allegory present, but the plot elements were handled so clumsily that it is ineffective.

Anything but ineffective is Dr. Keller's long novelette *The Feminine Metamorphosis* (*Science Wonder Stories,* August 1929), at once an accurate espousal of the position of women of that year and a savage attack on their loss of femininity and increasing masculinity.

Outraged by their inability to move into the higher echelons of the business world because of their sex, a group of brilliant women recruit and treat 5,000 superior females with male hormones that will give them all the characteristics of masculinity. The ultimate plan is a 100 percent female world with perfection of a means of parthenogenesis—female eggs which develop without being fertilized by a male sperm.

Their machinations are uncovered by Keller's laconic detective, Taine of San Francisco, posing as a dainty Chinese girl. The masculinized women are doomed to insanity by a latent disease present in the male hormones they have been treated with.

What if the women had succeeded in their ambitious plans? Wallace West, in his popular short story "The Last Man" (*Amazing Stories,* February 1929), painted a vivid picture of the future, when women have gradually usurped man's position and then finally exterminated him as a useless encumbrance, reproducing chemically in laboratory vats and incubators under controlled conditions. A male is born by accident, and they decide to let him live as an exhibit for their museum.

Most sex desires and feminine characteristics have been bred out of the women, who toil like bees in a hive in a civilization that has ceased to advance. A woman throwback, an Eve in the new Garden of Eden, entices the last male and runs off with him to the mountains to start a new natural cycle.

The late Dr. Thomas S. Gardner, father of the psycho-energizer drugs, deliberately wrote a counter to "The Last Man," appropriately titled "The Last Woman" (*Wonder Stories*, April 1932), in which he demonstrates what would have happened had the women lost their bid to overthrow the male. The men invent a chemical which channels their sex drive into a pursuit of knowledge. The scientists exterminate all females, children, and inferior men. They reproduce through the use of synthesized artificial ova. A single woman, born accidentally, has been kept as an exhibit in a museum to be shown not only to the men, but to visitors from other worlds as well.

An explorer, returning from a long space voyage, runs out of the drug which redirects his sex drive. He becomes susceptible to the woman, and she is drawn to him. He plots their escape, but his ship is intercepted and shot down. They are both tried and executed. Once again the world is completely male.

One of the relatively rare woman science fiction writers to take a crack at the theme in the magazines was M. F. Rupert, with "Via the Hewitt Ray" (*Wonder Stories Quarterly*, Spring 1930). Lucille Hewitt, in search of her father who is lost in the fourth dimension, enters a world where highly evolved women first obtained equality and then gained superiority. "The Sex War Epoch" ensued, and "eventually the women won, and we destroyed millions of the despised masculine sex. For untold centuries they had kept women subjugated and we finally got our revenge." Artificial laboratory births were tried, but the results were monstrous.

A pool of men of high intelligence was kept for reproductive purposes, and handsome men of low intelligence were sterilized and used to gratify the sexual desires of the women. Lucille receives permission to take one of the males used for reproductive purposes, who has shown criminal defiance, back to the third dimension with her. They are eventually properly married.

Following World War I, England had been plunged into an economic depression from which she never fully recovered. During the twenties the country was in so much trouble that it was thought that possibly women might do a more efficient job of running the government and at the same time put the damper on the killing. *When Woman Rules!*, a novel, appeared from John Long, London, in 1923, purported to have been written by "A Well-Known Member of Parliament." It projected the election of a woman prime minister, and female dominance in the decision-making offices of the nation. The book is more an exposé of the civil service in England than an exposition of women's rights.

One of the most abysmal pictures of the utter subjugation of men by women appears in *Woman Dominant* by E. Charles Vivian, published in 1930 by Ward, Lock & Co. Ltd., London. In a tropical land that would have to be in Africa or Indochina, but is neither because the Smoky River, along whose shore the action takes place, does not exist, three men discover a matriarchal tribe of natives. For three generations, the men have been fed a powder by an old black woman which renders them dull-witted and obedient even to commands that would cost them their own lives.

The intrusion of the white men results in the overthrow of the matriarchal system, and the knowledge that in a generation the men may regain their dominance.

Probably the best single novel of women as a ruling class, particularly from the standpoint of superbly sound science and philosophical argument, was written by Owen M. Johnson, best remembered for *Stover at Yale* (1911) and other light, rollicking novels of campus life. *The Coming of the Amazons* (Longmans, Green, 1931) would have delighted literary integrationists with its excellent blend of science and sex.

John Bogardus is quick-frozen in 1929, and is revived by seven-foot-tall, blonde, blue-eyed women in the year 2075. They, too, have the Frigidrome for suspended animation. Scores of small planes take off and land on the air-decks of gigantic dirigibles, anticollision devices are built into their vehicles, servants are hypnotically instructed, specialties of great chefs are frozen and withdrawn to be eaten fifty or one hundred years later as though they were vintage wines.

A woman genius had invented a ray which virtually exterminated most of the races of the earth. The men are regarded as second-class citizens, degenerating into swivel-hipped fops. Marriage is for six months. The women continue to grow in strength and intelligence. There has been a movement to restore the vote to men, but it has been resisted.

John Bogardus leads men in revolt by reversing the ancient "weapon" of Lysistrata in refusal to grant sexual relationship to a female. The book brilliantly retains interest, despite lack of action, by the device of examining the Amazon civilization, and in the process, mirroring our own. A dream ending almost spoils the story, but the author rescues the work artistically with a clever last-page trick.

The women of an up-to-now undiscovered planet between Neptune and Pluto unwillingly take over when their men have virtually destroyed themselves, in "The Woman from Space" (*Wonder Stories Quarterly,* Spring 1932) by Richard Vaughan. They develop an extraordinary science and successfully clear the asteroid belt, then move their planet into that orbit to be closer to the sun. The earth, almost rendered uninhabitable by a star that has brushed too close to our solar system, has lost a majority of its women. The two worlds, one almost devoid of men, the other short of women, agree to a happy accommodation.

So logical an attitude was not long to prevail in science fiction. Within little more than a year, Edmond Hamilton, in "War of the Sexes" (*Weird Tales,* November 1933), had both factions at each others' jugulars again. Allan Rand of the twentieth century, by an apparent miracle of science, finds his brain in the body of a man 20,000 years in the future, who is Thur, ruler of the Males. For 8,000 years, the males and females have been in separate camps warring upon one another. Both sexes have discovered the secret of laboratory production of humans. The ruler of the Females is shot down while air-blasting a male city. Thur offers to let her go, after demonstrating the ancient art of kissing, if she will convince her women to call off the war. She pretends to agree, but knocks him out and flies him to her headquarters. At the last minute, she finds she does not have the heart to execute him, but other females depose her and both are "killed." Allan Rand comes to in the laboratory in his own time, to learn he has been unconscious and has apparently never gone to the future at all.

Bossed around by a mother and three sisters, Edmond Hamilton expressed his resentment at this domination by returning to the theme again, in "World Without Sex" (*Marvel Tales,* May 1940). *Marvel Tales* had switched to a briefly held policy of featuring sex (two issues), so Hamilton assumed the *nom de plume* Richard Wentworth. In this world, sex is abhorrent to both men and women, children are produced in the laboratory, and by design, a steadily decreasing quota of males are created, stirring a revolt. The women destroy most of the remaining men and condemn a few survivors to death. The males escape, overpowering four women, and take them along to the hills. A mutually painful period of overcoming inhibitions and disgust about sexual relations is followed by the birth of a child and a normal rapport among mother, father, and offspring. When a political change in the women's world makes it possible for them to return to civilization, they refuse and find that more females seek to join them. At this point, Edmond Hamilton makes perhaps the most valid and psychologically probable observation on the theory that the elimination of men would end war, as he concludes his story with the females factionalized and destroying each other.

The type of thing that *Marvel Tales* considered to be sex-tainted was so mild, *even for the standards of that day,* that to imply that element almost seemed fraudulent. In England, Victoria Cross was producing a series of suggestive novels which at least told the reader that some hanky-panky was involved, including *The Eternal Fires, The Night of Temptation,* and *Electric Love,* and among them was a monument to women's liberation titled *Martha Brown, M.P., a Girl of Tomorrow* (F. Werner Laurie, 1936).

In England of the future, political power has gradually passed into the hands of the women, who begin to assume men's roles. They run the country, while the men are gradually relegated to raising the children and taking care of the home.

Sexual freedom begins for the woman at the age of sixteen, when she may bed down with any man who takes her fancy. If she becomes pregnant, nothing is thought of it. Living with a man or getting married is all the same, and the more well-to-do women, such as the heroine, Martha Brown, may have four husbands and a string of lovers.

Most of the men take to wearing dresses, making up, and spraying themselves with perfume. The women on the average begin to get bigger and stronger and are the aggressors in all things.

Under the beneficent influence of the women, the family structure has been virtually destroyed, but they have also almost eliminated prisons, prostitution, greatly cut down on crime, and found more effective ways of getting rid of garbage.

The women only have children to please and occupy their

husbands and have little or nothing to do with them.

Just when, at the age of thirty-five, Martha Brown is next in line to become prime minister, a powerfully built twentieth-century-type American man from the Northwest comes into her life. He has read her books and thinks very highly of her. He is completely unlike British men, larger and stronger than she, with a note of authority in his voice and a degree of masculinity she has rarely seen.

She falls in love with him and hopes to add him to her list of lovers or husbands, but he is not interested. He will not even have an affair with her unless she gives up her career and her husbands and returns to America with him. After an agonizing decision, which almost costs her life when one of the jealous jilted husbands tries to kill her, she throws over her fame, fortune, and families for the old-fashioned kind of love.

It seems a little farfetched, but, in a way, this might be termed a moralistic novel!

Some measure of sophistication and style came to the theme of woman dominant as seen in the pulps, when "The Priestess Who Rebelled" by Nelson S. Bond appeared (*Amazing Stories,* October 1939). In a devastated world of matriarchal tribes, where three basic strata exist: warriors, breeders, and workers, with a few men as studs, Meg, who aspires to be ruler of the tribe, makes a required pilgrimage to the Place of the Gods. Her meeting with a superior man from an unknown distant land, her realization that the gods had been *men,* and that her tribe's present way of life is doomed, is adroitly and pleasingly told. The internal evidence makes it obvious that Nelson Bond received his inspiration from "The Place of the Gods" by Stephen Vincent Benét (*The Saturday Evening Post,* July 31, 1937), which has a similar situation, mood, and locale.

A sequel, "The Judging of the Priestess" (*Fantastic Adventures,* April 1940), saw a reuniting of the sexes under threat of invasion of the Japcans, who still possess deadly weapons. However, this story is marred by weak humor and pulp treatment, though it possesses entertainment value. There is a final novelette in the series, *Magic City* (*Astounding Science-Fiction,* March 1941), where the matriarchy still nominally lingers, but is now set on bringing the Wild Ones, outcast men, into the fold. In the process, the ruins of New York are revisited, and certain old truths rediscovered.

Though there seemed to be infinite opportunity for originality and divergence in the notion of a world run by women, the plain truth was that writers displayed almost a religious devotion to a worn formula. "Amazons of a Weird Creation," an ineptly constructed story by Jep Powell (*Fantastic Adventures*, June 1941), finds a scientist and a reporter in the year 2450, when ancient crones rule a world without men, where reproduction is carried on by parthenogenesis, and where an atavistic female helps the men escape in their time machine. In "Drummers of Daugavo" by Dwight V. Swain (*Fantastic Adventures*, March 1943), American and Nazi agents during World War II vie to steal from an Amazon tribe in the jungles of South America a formula, whereby the women reduce the men to a foot or two in height, and the secret of a force ray which these women possess. "World Without Men" by Robert Moore Williams (*Amazing Stories*, June 1950) has two men carried into the future by the queen of an Amazon city, with wild males roaming the perimeter searching for mates, as in "The Priestess Who Rebelled." A sympathetic girl assists the men in their efforts to escape, which finally ends in a wild orgy as the hordes of wild ones force their way into the city.

Australia's first science fiction magazine to consistently publish new stories, *Thrills Incorporated*, devoted the cover of its seventeenth issue (published about December 1952) to "Amazons of the Asteroids" by N. K. Hemming, wherein women warriors ride flying horses between three tiny worlds supporting a communal air bubble. They are decadent descendants of the inhabitants of the original planet whose destruction created the asteroids.

Fifteen-foot-tall females rule the world of Krinn, with husbands half their size. The women carry on all the work and business, while the men take care of the home. In "Woman's World" by Ted Taine (*Fantastic Adventures*, March 1953), an earthman is assigned the task of getting the women to join the Federation, a well-knit confederation of worlds that started on earth. In order to do so, he organizes a revolt of the "undersized" men.

The same issue contained "Land of the Matriarchs" by E. Bruce Yaches, a trivial tale of an all-female order on Venus, of one of their haughty, independent adherents who is rescued from a monster by a man, and of her warm appreciation after she has cleaned up at his hut.

Some attempt to apply logic to the literary device of over-sized Amazonian women was earlier supplied by Clark Ashton Smith in "The Root of Ampoi" (*Arkham Sampler,* Winter 1949). A Cockney sailor hears of a tribe of giantesses who live on a plateau in Malaya and who will trade rubies for beads and trinkets. He locates this tribe and confirms the fact that, while the women average eight feet in height, the men are of normal size. They are a quite civilized and friendly people. The queen becomes attracted to him and they marry. He learns that the women attain their great size by eating a special root that is forbidden to men. When a female child is born to the Cockney and the queen, a supply of this root is brought into the home. He secretly eats quantities of it, grows eight feet tall, and has every intention of asserting himself, but he is overpowered and excommunicated from the village. Back in civilization, he spends the rest of his life as a circus freak. The story is moralistic in tone, implying that to seek superiority for its own sake is to risk destruction of happiness, security, and general respect. The story ranks high in literary craftsmanship.

Science fiction has had its share of superwomen. There was The Black Margot, beautiful warrior ruler of Urbs, Stanley G. Weinbaum's creation in "Dawn of Flame" (*Dawn of Flame and Other Stories,* 1936); Violet Ray was John Russell Fearn's entry in "The Goldon Amazon" (*Fantastic Adventures,* July 1939), a character who gained remarkable popularity as the extraordinary heroine of a long series of newspaper novels; and Erani, specially bred female mental genius of a race that lived before recorded history, revived in present-day Australia with the mission and means of destroying all the colored races of the world in Erle Cox's novel, *Out of the Silence* (1927).

They were all one of a kind. Typical of an entire culture was Dyann the Amazon in Poul Anderson's "Captive of the Centaurianess" (*Planet Stories,* March 1952), a beautiful, good-natured, formidable fighting machine from Alpha C3, a planet where all women were like her and men were the weaker sex and homemakers. As a bunkmate on the space ship *Jovian Queen* with Earthman Ray Ballentyne and a tentacled Martian genius who has evolved a logical theory for faster-than-light travel, she is involved in a bloody but joyous struggle to forestall the aggressive inhabitants of Jupiter's moons from kidnapping the Martian. Though the tale is a deliberate romp, the aggressive sexuality of the Amazon women and female warriors strike a more believable note than many Amazon stories written "straight."

Poul Anderson was to have still another go at the Amazon concept in "Virgin Planet," which led off the first issue of *Venture Science Fiction,* January 1957, a companion to *The Magazine of Fantasy and Science Fiction,* which had as its policy stories that were a bit stronger meat than those commonly found in other science fiction magazines. The titillating part of this story, of a man who lands on a planet where Earthwomen abandoned there centuries earlier have continued to reproduce a one-sexed race, consists of inquiries as to the use of the "special" organ he possesses as well as several near-seduction sequences. Unlike the Amazons of most previous stories, the women in "Virgin Planet" actually worship the legend of men and believe that someday a suitable delegation will arrive to join them.

One of the truly outstanding literary efforts involving a dominant female society to be published during the fifties was L. Sprague de Camp's *Rogue Queen* (Doubleday, 1951). The locale is a planet of a distant sun, peopled by a mammalian humanoid race which procreates through an egg-laying queen fertilized by a male. The warriors and workers of the society are all female but virtually neuters as far as sexual desire is concerned. Males exist solely for their reproductive function and occupy a status scarcely more elevated than that of a drone bee.

The landing of an Earth ship, and the impact of a monogamous society in which males occupy a position of superiority, results in a traumatic change in the philosophical outlook of the aliens. The story ends with the overthrow of the old system and the creation of a heterosexual society, but not before the author outlines one of the most elaborately fascinating civilizations yet depicted in science fiction.

Reading like some bachelor's daydream are the Lalitha of Philip José Farmer's *The Lovers* (*Startling Stories,* August 1952). The *Lalitha* are not human at all, but an insect parasite which has evolved in the shape of a woman, because their only method of reproducing is with a human male. This group of "females" exists as a separate society. Ages past, they had

87

helped bring the downfall of the humans by becoming mates or concubines and thereby influencing their decisions. When pregnant, their bodies slowly form a hard outer shell, and they die, then the "grubs" eat their way out of the body to be cared for by the other "women." Pregnancy is prevented indefinitely by the *Lalitha* drinking alcoholic bug juice. The Earthman, who has been secretly carrying on an affair with one of these creatures, substitutes another beverage for the alcohol, causing her pregnancy and death. Unaware of her true nature, the revelation fails to alleviate the sorrow and remorse he feels, for he truly loved her.

Another masterpiece in this genre is John Wyndham's long novelette *Consider Her Ways,* written as an original for Ballantine Books' paperback anthology *Sometimes, Never* (1956). Jane Summers, M.D., through drugs, regains consciousness in the body of an obese woman of tomorrow, a breeder of that civilization. The society of the future is divided into three castes, all women: workers, breeders, and "warriors," as found in "The Priestess Who Rebelled," except that technology is well advanced. As in "A World of Women," the men died off in a single year, from circumstances attributable to a single scientist.

A woman psychologist of that distant day listens to every argument given her by Dr. Summers about the positive values of a world with men and counters them with matchless logic. A superb dialogue between the two points of view is capped with a clever ending, when Jane Summers revives in the present in her own body and kills the scientist who she believes will set off the chain of events that will result in a manless world. Unfortunately, she has not been observant enough to note that his son, who is also a scientist, bears the same name!

Younger writers began to accept the Amazonian theme as a basic. Early in his career, Harlan Ellison wrote of a special agent sent to Arka III by Galactic Center in the guise of a female in "World of Women" (*Fantastic Science Fiction,* February 1957) to investigate reports that one of a five-woman matriarchy had gone insane and wiped out the entire male population. In Robert Silverberg's "Woman's World" (*Imagination Science Fiction,* June 1957), a man awakes from 500 years of seeming suspended animation to find the earth ruled by women, and himself involved in a male bid to regain power. Like Allan Rand of Edmond Hamilton's "War of the Sexes," he awakes to find that he has imagined the experience while undergoing a laboratory test.

Telling the all-female civilization story from the viewpoint of one of the women was the major contribution of Charles Eric Maine in *World Without Men* (Ace Books, 1958). Charles Eric Maine is the pen name for British author David McIlwain, which he first used for an amateur story in the fan magazine *The Satellite,* October 1938, titled "The Mirror." In *World Without Men,* a birth-control drug ends female capacity to bear males. Women in this manless society are not sexless; to the contrary, they are all required to accept a lesbian relationship. The discovery of a perfectly preserved male body frozen in the polar wilderness sets off an emotional reaction, because the cadaver may be the source of chromosomes which will make possible the artificial creation of a male fetus, a project laboratories have been working on for 5,000 years.

When success is achieved and a male infant incubated, the computer which runs the world orders its destruction. The assistant to the cytologist who has brought the child into being disregards the order and flees with the baby. Word of its existence spreads, and violence against the existing order flares. As the story closes, it is evident that the male will be permitted to live and a bisexual society restored.

Despite a heaviness of style, due in part to the elaborateness of detail, *World Without Men* is one of the outstanding stories of its type. It sustains interest throughout, and at times achieves dramatic intensity, pointing the way to a more artistic approach to a subject frequently treated flippantly.

There is little question that the theme of the Amazon, the matriarch, the woman superior, will remain a permanent plot staple in science fiction, and without major changes in format. To underscore this conclusion, one but has to read the three-part novel *Amazon Planet* by Mack Reynolds (*Analog,* December 1966 to February 1967). Of several thousand civilized worlds of United Planets, only one, Amazonia, is a matriarchy. Originally settled by women, it is believed that no rights are accorded to any male born into the society, and female warriors are permitted a male harem numbering up to three. Women have appeared at United Planets conferences, but no man has ever been permitted to enter or leave that world.

A man, who is an agent from United Planets, is allowed a visa for purposes of arranging an exchange for a metal badly needed by the women. The story line utilizes a physical action format, ending with the revelation that the women have actually given a substantial amount of equality to the men, and that the impressive display of armed women warriors in a setting of Greek pageantry was a façade calculated to frighten off those who might visit for the purpose of subversion and to cover the fact that the planet actually had no armed forces and could not repel an armed invasion.

The fictional creation of an Amazon world, as has been documented, is one of the oldest themes in science fiction. It has appeared with regularity ever since the Greek empire flourished. If anything, the battle for equal rights started by women more than 150 years ago has probably contributed to the frequent use of the plot.

Men, in every case, seem uneasy about this "equality," claiming that it will end in domination for the reasons given by Booth Tarkington in *The Veiled Feminists of Atlantis:* that women will also insist upon retaining their special privilege which will give them superiority. The intensity with which these feelings are held is underscored by the very high percentage of stories in which women literally exterminate the males upon achieving domination. Disquietingly, the same "inevitability" is expressed by the several women who have written stories of their sex gaining the upper hand.

The implication is almost that a male and a female are two completely different species instead of two indispensable sexes of the same animal. It requires only a few moments of rational thought to conclude that either an all-male or an all-female society makes no sense from the standpoint of nature and is a sterile blind alley for civilization. The theory that if women ran the world there would be no war reminds one of the same view held by the Marxists if only the entire world were communistic.

Though women have technically gained legal equality with men today, they not only seem no closer to ruling the world, but show small interest in desiring to do so. The "overbearing, domineering" men continue to drive themselves, most with no more sinister motive than providing a better life for their wives and children.

Philip Wylie summed up the matter succinctly in *The Disappearance* (Rinehart & Co., 1951), describing what would happen to each of the sexes separately, if the other, without warning, completely disappeared. In terms of a single family, as well as for the entire world community, he vividly dramatizes the meaninglessness of life in a single-sexed world and describes the almost religious ecstacy of thanksgiving when, after four years apart, the sexes are abruptly united. They have learned many things by their bizarre experience, but most important appeared to be that, though the sexes possess obvious differences, there are overwhelmingly more points of similarity.

BIRTH CONTROL:

Better the World Below Than the World Above

The name of Sidney Fowler Wright is enshrined in the hall of fame of great science fiction writers primarily for his epic *The World Below*, a work of storytelling magic, imaginative power, and poetic evocation that frequently transcends its influences and imitates with honor.

Distrustful of scientific advance and the men who made it possible, he was nevertheless hypnotized by it and displayed a consistently erudite, even brilliant, base of scientific credibility in describing the technological progress he excoriated.

His diatribes against science were made not so much because he feared its misuse would bring destruction of civilization (he welcomed that since it would mean that Man would revert to a simpler state), but because he knew it might achieve Man's dream of elimination of strife, want, and insecurity and he felt that goal would inevitably deprive life of all meaning.

Only a superb literary technique and superior imagination gained him respect despite his "message" and rescued him from the label of "crank" which he deserved.

The controversial author of the acclaimed *The World Below* was born in Birmingham, England, January 1874, attending King Edward's High School in that city. Upon graduation in 1895 he secured a position as an accountant and, thus established, married Nellie Ashbury the same year. She bore him three sons and three daughters and died in 1918. He "retired" from accounting in 1920 and married a second time to Truda Hancock, who was to present him with one son and three daughters. From the foregoing, it can be established that his lifelong, never-ceasing battle against birth control, as expressed repeatedly in his science fiction, was a sincere and not a frivolous notion.

The economic circumstances which made it possible for him to dispense with accounting as a means of making a living after twenty-five years are not clear. At the age of forty-six he emerged as the editor of a magazine titled *Poetry* (later to be retitled *Poetry and the Play*). This post he held continuously through 1932. His interest in poetry was, without question, a deeply felt one. *Scenes from Morte d'Arthur,* his first book published in 1920, was verse, as was his second, *Some Songs of Bilitis,* in 1922. There would be three other volumes of poems as well as the editorship of numerous anthologies. Some of them had the air of vanity publishing to them, specifically the series of which a typical title was *Contemporary Poetry of Shropshire, Worcestershire, Herefordshire and Monmouthshire* (1929).

The World Below was actually his first serious work of fiction and was intended as a trilogy, the third portion of which was never written. *The Amphibians, a romance of 500,000 Years Hence,* the first novel in the contemplated series, was set up and relatively poorly printed by the Merton Press, London, in 1924. The plates were transferred to the Swan Press, Leeds, in 1925 and 1,000 buckram-bound hardcover and 5,000 softcover copies published. As acknowledged in the first chapter, the novel was a critical success and deserved to be.

The initial premise was a twist on H. G. Wells's *The Time Machine.* A British subject is propelled 500,000 years into the future. Instead of encountering degenerate descendants of mankind, he is placed in contact with several mutated human species whose intelligence is transcendentally beyond ours. One is a furry race of amphibians, entirely feminine in characteristics (though sexless), and the other a towering group of giants known as "The Dwellers." So far beyond the abilities of today's *homo sapiens* are these civilizations that their motives and actions are virtually incomprehensible to the hero. The most gallant and heroic feats of valor scarcely minimize the contempt with which these races regard the sojourner into the future; not only his thought processes and his actions, but his very touch, is repulsive to them.

Circumstance throws the hero into alliance with the amphibians in a series of adventures through lands, and with creatures, spawned from a nightmare. Though a degree of spiritual comradeship develops, romance is no more possible than between a human and an ape.

Wright's first book in the United States was not *The Amphibians*, but a nonfiction tract, *Sermon on the Mount for Today*, published by Scribners in 1927, which is an obscure and virtually unknown presentation of his outlook. However, his second publication, a novel titled *Deluge: A Romance*, took the country by storm and became a best seller when published early in 1928 by Cosmopolitan Book Corporation (an affiliate of *Hearst's International Cosmopolitan Magazine*). There had been fine stories of another inundation before, the most notable of them *The Second Deluge* by Garrett P. Serviss (*The Cavalier*, July 1911 to January 1912), but it, as others, dealt primarily with the broad spectrum of the *physical side* of the disaster. Wright placed his entire stress on the human aspect, stressing the efforts by the few survivors to form a primitive social arrangement.

A passionate disciple of Jean Jacques Rousseau, Wright took his cue from *Discours sur les Sciences et les Arts*, which purported to show that science and art were perverting mankind. "They had used their boasted intelligence to evade the natural laws of their beings, and they were to reap the fruits of their folly," Wright wrote in *Deluge*. It was not only that they were physically ill-adapted for life on the earth's surface, but the minds of most of them were empty of the most elementary knowledge of their physical environment.

It went for nothing that Rousseau's book was originally written in 1750 when man's scientific knowledge was infinitesimal even compared to what it had become in Wright's day, and that natural disasters and wars had been survived with a hardihood and genius by the "decadent" civilized humans, whereas primitives in tune with nature either adopted the methods of the advanced races or disappeared from the face of the globe.

Wright's philosophy was again underscored in a lost-race novel, *The Island of Captain Sparrow*, which had appeared in England and was rushed into print by Cosmopolitan in 1928. Riding on the popularity of *Deluge*, it enjoyed wide readership. A castaway on an unknown Pacific island witnesses the end of an ancient white race in conflict with descendants of pirates who had settled there centuries earlier. The island is also inhabited by satyrs, hunted by the pirates for food. After a superbly related series of adventures, the castaway and a stranded

French girl, the last adult humans on the island, disdain return
to civilization, prefering their elemental "Paradise."

Wright was in his glory now. Not only could he preach his
"Sermon on the Mount for Today," but he was being well paid
and acclaimed for doing so. With alacrity he pushed to completion a sequel for *Deluge* titled *Dawn.* This novel dealt with the
struggle for power (and women) after the waters had receded.
An exercise in grim realism against a highly imaginative setting,
it was well done, with moments of poetry. In its pages Wright
is revealed as a proreligionist if antiscientist. Indoctrinated by
one and drawn by the other, he seems unable to reconcile his
disparate desires, so he castigates science unrequitedly so that
he may always have it near him.

The publishers seemed themselves convinced of the market-
ability of primitivism, for they had translated from the Russian
Sons of the Mammoth, by Waldemar Bogoras (1929), a novel of
prehistoric times wherein the protagonist, driven from his tribe
because of heresy, tames nature for himself and his women with
nothing but his hands and a few crude tools.

The most important short-range influence of *Deluge* upon
the literary world was its affect on John Collier, a fellow British
author. Collier had already made his mark with the publication
of *His Monkey Wife* in 1930, a satire built around a man's
choice of a female chimpanzee as a wife in preference to a
woman. Like Wright, he had preoccupied himself with verse
from 1920 to 1930, a few selections of which had been collected
in *Gemini,* published in a limited edition of 185 copies (Ulysses
Press, London, 1931). As a short-story writer, Collier was obsessed by fantasy and was inclined to follow works of that character. "Full Circle," published in 1933, and clearly patterned
after *Deluge,* was laid in 1995, when after a prolonged war the
remaining survivors try to start all over again. The story was
kept in narrow focus, Collier concentrating on the problems of
a few individuals and a single small band involved with the
catastrophe. This technique was to become a standard in science fiction to be adopted in recent times by such authors as
John Wyndham and John Christopher.

The philosophy of *Deluge* was to be extended further when
it was released under the same title as a motion picture by RKO
in 1933, starring Sidney Blackmer and Peggy Shannon.

Whatever the reason, its sequel, *Dawn,* did not share the

success of *Deluge*. Perhaps, despite its smoothness, it was regarded as an appendage to a tale already told. More likely,
issued in the year of the Depression, it was forgotten in the flood
of economic woes. The Depression was also to terminate Cosmopolitan's book publishing activities and Wright was obliged
to find himself a new publisher.

With his reputation, this was no problem. He had written the
second in the contemplated trilogy of which *The Amphibians*
was the first, titled *The World Below*. Under the latter title, the
two were combined and issued by Longmans, Green and Co. in
1930.

While Wright had still been one of their prize possessions,
Cosmopolitan had been prone to honor him. They had published several small volumes of his verse from which they could
scarcely have made money, but more important, they had issued his translation of Dante's *Inferno* in 1928. Actually, the
translation was begun by Sir Walter Scott, the famed novelist
and poet, and never completed. Wright finished it. He would
later write *The Life of Sir Walter Scott* (1932) and go on to
complete Sir Walter Scott's partly done novel *The Siege of
Malta* (1942). The researches and effort Wright put into *Inferno*
are reflected in fair measure in *The World Below*.

The second portion of what was published as *The World Below* parallels in future tense the situations in Dante's *Inferno*.
As Everett F. Bleiler put it in his introduction to Shasta Publishers' reissue in 1949 of *The World Below*, "The hero's descent,
the Amphibian psychopomp, the various hells, the legalistic
Vulturemen, the satires on the brilliant but wicked lizards, and
the Killers, all recall the *Inferno*."

This was not obvious to the purchasers of 1930, predominantly science fiction readers and authors. Writing in the June
1930 issue of *Amazing Stories*, literary editor C. A. Brandt sum-
marized the early adventures of the novel's hero succinctly
when he wrote, "He arrives in a strange world where trees
scream while they attack, where the hot soil projects rubberlike
roots to trip up the intruder, where voiceless froglike monsters
are peeled and eaten *à la banana* by gigantic human beings
called the 'Dwellers,' a world where the seas are peopled and
controlled by furry human-like, yet sexless females, who telepathically communicate their thoughts to one another regardless of distance."

Advertised for two years in *Wonder Stories, The World Below* became part of the library of the dyed-in-the-wool collectors. Yet, though some eventually related the second portion to Dante, the debt of *The Amphibians* to A. Merritt's *Moon Pool*, even the adoption of the title of "The Dweller" for an underground alien, was overlooked. More understandably, no one linked the book to *The Night Land*, a strange novel initially issued in 1912. *The Night Land*, deliberately written in eighteenth-century English, was the work of the near-genius William Hope Hodgson, whose short stories had seen limited circulation in America up to that time, but whose novels were read only in England. Reprinted in an abridged form in 1921, it contains many elements that appear in *The World Below.* Hodgson's work, in common with Wright, shared certain elements traceable to Dante.

The World Below, though its concepts would echo in the works of American science fiction writers for years to come, and though it received serious reviews—*The Saturday Review of Literature* for July 5, 1930, saying, "The strength of the book lies in the adventures, related with a combination of extravagant imagination and sober verisimilitude which makes Mr. Wright unique. 'The World Below' is an almost painfully absorbing story"—it was not a financial success. It lowered the curtain on the United States as a sphere of influence for Wright. It would be six years before another of his books would appear in this country.

Dream (Harrap, London, 1931), a fantasy which appeared only in England, tells of a woman who is projected a million years back in time to an age in which humanlike creatures are completely exterminated by an evolving ratlike mammal. When she returns to the present, she finds that the victor as well as the vanquished disappeared into the evolutionary maw of time.

The loss of the American market was more ego-deflating than financially damaging to Wright. In 1929 he had scored with a mystery, *The Bell Street Murders.* This was to be followed by *The King Against Anne Blickerton, By Saturday, Arresting Delia,* and a parade of others under the pen name of Sidney Fowler. Sold predominantly in England, these were to prove his bread and butter, while science fiction would henceforth become an avocation.

97

"The author of 'The Deluge' has written for this magazine, . . ." the editor of *Weird Tales* stated with pride in a pre-issue announcement of the appearance of "The Rat" (*Weird Tales,* March 1929). It was apparently the first short story by S. Fowler Wright to appear in the United States. A scientist who makes a rat immortal kills a distasteful child who has been bitten by it for fear the bite will grant eternal life to an undesirable. This story possibly inspired the acknowledged masterpiece *The Eternal Man,* by D. D. Sharp (*Science Wonder Stories,* August 1929), which dealt with an interminable hatred between an ageless man and an immortal rat.

Possibly the best short-story sale that S. Fowler Wright made was when the June 1929 issue of *The Red Book Magazine,* then one of the leaders among women's magazines in the United States, carried on its cover the announcement: "An astonishing Love Story of the Future by S. Fowler Wright who wrote 'Deluge.' " The story was entitled "Love in the Year 93 E. E." (Eugenic Era) and captioned "Love laughs at eugenic locksmiths." The blurb raved: " 'Deluge' sensationally proved Mr. Wright's skill at thinking in terms of the future. His interesting speculation about civilization's end made it instantly a best seller. Here he shows what love and elopement may be, when we are all eugenic." A photo and biographical note was published in the "Tune with Our Times" section which reported on people that were making news. Wright was characterized as "being endowed with one of the most audacious and interesting minds of our day. He became world famous upon the appearance of his novel 'Deluge' . . . his book became a best-seller both abroad and in this country."

Aside from the sales value of the name of a best-selling author, even women's magazines were reluctant to publish Simon-pure science fiction—which "Love in the Year 93 E. E." certainly was. The difference rested in the editor of *The Red Book Magazine,* Edwin Balmer, who later collaborated with Philip Wylie on two of the landmark science fiction novels of this century, *When Worlds Collide* and *After Worlds Collide.* Every now and then he sneaked science fiction into *The Red Book Magazine,* and he made sure that its men's adventure companion, *The Blue Book Magazine,* never was without it!

"Love in the Year 93 E.E." reaffirms the theory of the *Del-*

uge, that the superior man should have more than one wife. As in the *Deluge,* the women should make the selection. In 93 E. E. (2029 A.D. in today's reckoning) machines scientifically select mates, and in order to avoid its decision, two lovers escape from the society in a plane. They head for a forest area of Brazil where they presumably can continue life in a more primitive state. "The Rat" and "Love in the Year 93 E. E." were the first two of a series of short science fiction stories, collected in 1932 by Jarrolds, London, under the title *The New Gods Lead.* Taken individually, some of the stories in *The New Gods Lead* were of consummate artistry. Considered collectively, they were the assembled testament of Wright's philosophy. Here are the points of the plots of the other stories in that book (in which the title of "Love in the Year 93 E. E." was changed to "P.N.4 D."):

"Justice" tells of the aged and infirm becoming such an oppressive burden upon the fewer young (due to birth control) "because the advances of preventive medicine and operative surgery have extended life," that declining penalties are given for killing old people through automobile accidents, and past the age of sixty-eight the driver can sue for his loss of time and inconvenience.

"This Night" relates an incident in a world where scientists rule and brides-to-be are pressured to report to the apartment of one of the ruling group prenuptially, so that the first child will be of superior caste.

"Brain" would have the future legislative scientists take their pick of babies for experimental and vivisectional purposes.

In "Automata," the practice of birth control brings robot children into popularity. Eventually, the last worker fails to meet his quota and a machine quietly leads him to euthanasia.

"Rule" has insurance companies taken over by a power play and rates forced down to one-third. Banks are compelled to lower interest, and all income taxes are abolished. No workers are permitted to be laid off because of automation.

All stories are warnings of the pitfalls of progress and happiness. Some contain Wright's "solutions" to our immediate "problems." The repetition of references to some of the "horrors" of a scientific state makes it apparent that he is *endorsing* rather than deploring them.

Critics have compared Wright to M. P. Shiel because both

had highly unusual literary styles, but the comparison is faulty. Shiel was vituperatively opposed to religion and blinded by his faith in science. The Jews, to Shiel, were behind most of the world's problems. There were remedies. Besides the elimination of religion and Jews, deep breathing, exercise, and a diet of honey and nuts would set everything right.

Wright, his fanatical opposite, was for religion, and a dedicated foe of scientific progress. Science would bring about birth control, selective mating, child experimentation, licentiousness, too many old people, robot children, and eventually machines would either exterminate Man or the human breed would seek death because of the absence of spiritual values in a too-comfortable state.

Solution?

He gave the formula in *Power* (Jarrolds, London, 1933), where a young man becomes dictator of England and sweeps aside most existing laws and forbids the passage of new ones. The *elimination* of scientific progress is specifically called for. "Science gives richly; but are they not a devil's gifts at the best? Religion taught standards of conduct, and science offers standards of comfort."

In *Vengeance of Gwa* (Thornton, London), published under the pen name A. Wingrave in 1935, his obsession against birth control and the compulsion that women bear more and more children becomes almost paranoid as Bwene, king of a land in a forgotten era of prehistory, is consumed by hatred for his mate because she cannot give him a son. The queen has saved the life of the daughter and only child she did bear, when by custom she should have been put to death. Wright's predilection for more than one wife for his lead character is again displayed, as is his contempt for all who seek to establish a stable and trouble-free community.

Wright's protestations and philosophy were not confined merely to his fiction; he wrote books on purely political subjects, with titles like *Police and Public* and *Should We Surrender Colonies?* Interest in politics found him in Germany in 1936 when Hitler was readying for conquest. The result was a perceptive work of "fiction" published that year in England as *Prelude in Prague* and in the United States as *The War of 1938.* It simulated a behind-the-scenes postulation of the circumstances and actual military strategy by which Hitler would overrun Czechoslovakia. It predicted that "Germany might have lit a fire which she would not quench."

This early warning of disaster was translated into "a dozen" European languages arousing the ire of the Nazis, who made determined efforts to prevent its sale and distribution. This was S. Fowler Wright's shining moment.

He muffed it in a sequel, *Meggida's Ridge* (R. Hale, London, 1937), in which the Germans join hands with the Russians to war against England.

The most persuasive advocate of political views which in fervor, if not in fact, remind one of Wright was Ayn Rand, destined to establish a cult centered around the philosophy promoted in her books *The Fountainhead* and *Atlas Shrugged*. In 1938 she had published a short novel titled *Anthem*. In that work a man and a woman flee a controlled society to return to primitivism and individualism. This was one of the earliest expressions of Rand's philosophy, that the individual should work for himself and not for the group.

Both Wright and Rand feared socialism or collective action of any sort and championed a system of near-anarchy. Both called for a return to primitivism as the means of making a new start. Both feared that technological progress might lead to socialism and serfdom. Rand would applaud scientific invention if employed for capitalistic individualism, while Wright felt the use of science for public good was the beginning of decadence and corruption.

Appearing in the same year as *Anthem*, Wright's *The Adventure of Wyndham Smith* showed fundamental similarities in spirit. He displays again his remarkable facility for getting the reader immediately into the situation, his logical inventiveness, and a poetic style. The hero finds that he has been snatched into the future to offer arguments as to why the five million humans of that day (the figure is kept constant by birth control), who are enjoying unparalleled harmony and good living, should not commit mass euthanasia. His remonstrations prove unavailing, humanity incinerates itself, except for a handy contrary-minded female. The last portion of the story builds with considerable power as the last two remaining humans find themselves a cave, are joined by some friendly dogs, and survive a grim chase by automata which have been built not only to farm, but to hunt animals by scent.

The voices of Wright and Rand, preaching a complete reversal of either scientific or sociological development, were indeed eloquent ones, but their science fiction audience had an even more charismatic spokesman for the other side. He was Olaf Stapledon, author of *Last and First Men* (1931), whose thundering prose and towering imagination were at the peak of their powers when *The Star Maker* appeared in 1937, on sale contemporaneously with the books of reaction. Stapledon preached the community of man, the most daring evolution of body and spirit, and the ultimate of the cosmic mind. Stapledon, an admitted socialist, personified everything that Wright hated and feared, so their philosophies were antipodal. Neither author would have more than a minute effect upon the course of *world* events, but in the science fiction microcosm, Stapledon would triumph through the acceptance of his positive conviction that Man was destined to colonize the galaxy. This principle was adopted as an implicit order of faith by the bulk of the emerging science fiction writers of that period.

Whether it was special circumstances related to the onset of World War II or sensitivity over the lack of reader enthusiasm for his philosophical precepts, Wright ceased his private fight until peace prevailed. Immediately following the war in 1946, a group of his short stories was collected by Books of Today and titled *The Witchfinder*. It contained what was by all odds one of the most skillful of his short stories, "Original Sin."

A utopia is attained where "there is no disease. There is no dirt. There is no hunger or thirst. There is no pain. There is enough for all of all things that a man can need, so that there is no cause either to envy or hate, either to strive or long." "Naturally," under such a set up, Man wants out; the entire human race agrees to end it all. Two people, a man and a woman, conspire to live on. All humans but them and one girl are dead. The man is about to inject the girl with the fatal needle. He hesitates, and suggests she need not die. His woman companion reaches over and drives the needle home.

"Should we survive, and found a new race," the man records, "we ought to make a better world than it was before. But it seemed to me that it was a bad start." The story was later included in his Arkham House collection, *The Throne of Saturn.*

This was the beginning of a mild revival for Wright. The anthologists Raymond J. Healy and J. Francis McComas se-

lected his short story "Brain" for an anthology that would prove
to be a best seller, *Adventures in Time and Space.* This was its
first American appearance. In England, 1947 opened with
Books of Today reprinting *Vengeance of Gwa* under his own
name. The big year was 1949; Arkham House published *The
Throne of Saturn.* Though its sale was limited, the quality of
Wright's short stories was recognized by people who counted,
and many of the titles were selected for anthology appearances.
The same year Shasta Publishers, Chicago, reissued *The World
Below* in a handsome autographed edition. This led *Galaxy
Novels* in 1951 to release the work as two separate paperbacks.

When the two novels that made up *The World Below* were
first combined, the British edition (1929) preceded the American (1930) by some months, and critics in England had come to
grips with Wright's theories. The result was a special preface to
the American edition stating, "My aim in writing was to offer
an imagination only. I was not concerned with an argument."

Twenty years later, his work was accepted on that basis (with
the sole exception of L. Sprague de Camp's incisive observa-
tions of Wright's philosophy in *The Science Fiction Handbook,*
1953). Was that the way Wright really wanted it? Had time
mellowed if not erased his antiscientific militancy?

The answer was swiftly forthcoming in *Spiders' War* (Abelard
Press, 1954), a sequel to *Dream* (1931). Marguerite Cranleigh,
the same girl who had been magically shunted into the past,
now arranges with her friendly magician to be sent into the
future. Wright's purpose in sending her on this trip was to
provide a vehicle for a commentary on our civilization, as evalu-
ated by the people of tomorrow. Upon the arrival of the new
girl in the future, she is captured by a leading figure in a semiru-
ral, near-primitive society. He decides (at her suggestion) to
take her as his wife. *Since he is already married, he facilitates
things by driving a dagger into his wife's stomach, cuts her into
roasts, and the couple dine sumptuously on the carcass for the
next few weeks.* This procedure is approved by the culture.
Wright now sets out to establish that this man and this civilization are morally and spiritually *superior* to our own.

Why?

We have birth control.

We have taxes.

We kill people with automobiles.

We permit the working poor to outvote the minority rich.

We promote scientific progress.

The added years brought no softening. When Groff Conklin, who had used "Automata" (dividing its three episodes into three segments) in his anthology *Science-Fiction Thinking Machines* (1954), asked Wright if he had a story involving mutants, he got a surprising result. Instead of suggesting an old story, Wright penned an original, "The Better Choice," which appeared in *Science Fiction Adventures in Mutation* (1955).

The theme?

A woman is changed into a cat for "kicks."

How did she find it?

"She had the time of her life. She had teased dogs. She had stolen food without fear of criminal law. She had had adventures upon the tiles."

When the time comes to change back, she approaches the window where her husband is watching.

"There was so little to return to: so very much to resign. He saw her turn and leap back into the night."

Wright died February 25, 1965, aged ninety-one, of complications of aging but he had passed on some of the techniques he borrowed and sharpened. The evidence is very strong that John Collier owes to Wright not only the inspiration for *Full Circle*, but the format of sophisticated presentation of the shocking which has built for his short stories a deserved reputation. Among the magazine science fiction writers, Jack Williamson, particularly in the story "The Moon Era" (*Wonder Stories*, February 1933), is considerably in Wright's debt. The idea of an invisible bridge across a chasm which appears in *The Amphibian* is the focus of the title for A. Hyatt Verrill's adventure tale of the discovery of a Mayan city with advanced scientific discoveries, "The Bridge of Light" (*Amazing Stories Quarterly*, Fall 1929). Verrill would have had to have picked up and read the British book earlier, for *The World Below* would not appear in the United States until the following year. Whether Ayn Rand was influenced to use the science fiction media for her theories because of its effectiveness in Wright's related concepts can only be conjectured.

As for Wright's philosophy, kindness is not in order. He was far, far from the first to put such ideas on paper. "Citizen 504" by C. H. Palmer, which appeared in the December 1896 issue of *The Argosy,* needs only the transposition of the by-line to be a perfect S. Fowler Wright "beware of progress" story. "Easy as ABC" by Rudyard Kipling (*The London Magazine,* March and April 1912), included in *Diversity of Creatures,* 1912, is of the same breed. Much closer to Wright's own active prose period was the publication of *We* by Eugene Zamyatin (Dutton, 1924), which transposed the Russian system to the United States so effectively that George Orwell is said to have taken his cue from it for *1984.*

Ever since the turn of the century the antiutopia and the antiscientific story have become so prevalent that Chad Walsh, even though writing an entire book on the theme, *From Utopia to Nightmare* (1962), barely skimmed the surface of the subject. The world did not need Wright to tell it that overstressing science could prove disastrous.

Therein lies the crux of the matter. Most antiutopian writers were warning against the *misuse* of science, not for an end to progress; they were afraid that if technology outstripped morality Man might not only enslave, but destroy, himself.

Wright was not afraid of war. He expresses his feeling in the line: "The worst wars have their heroic side." In fact, war, to him, was a desirable thing if severe enough to return the survivors to a primitive state.

He was afraid that Man might make it.

In succeeding, there would probably have to be planned parenthood for controlled population increase. Rather than agree to that, Wright would forego Heaven, and that is precisely what he advocated.

What do we call a man who asks a couple in Paradise with eternal life ahead ("The Choice," included in *Throne of Saturn*) to drop all that and insist on reincarnation? To resume contributing to the population explosion, and in compensation for their sacrifice promises only: "You will know remorse and shame. You will desire things which you cannot reach, or you will find your gains to be worthless. You will know pain that is more dreadful than sorrow, and sorrow that is more dreadful than pain. You will do evil to others, and you will suffer evil continually. At the last, you will die

105

miserably, facing the curtain of death without assurance of immortality."

What do we call a man who derives his greatest inspiration from endless recasting of Dante's Inferno, and who even titles one of his books *The World Below?*

The Devil's disciple?

PSYCHIATRY:

The Invasion of the Incredible Headshrinkers

The world at large always suspected that readers of science fiction were candidates for the couch, but that the subject matter could infect the psychiatrist as well as the patient must have come as a bit of a shock to them when they read a 20,000-word account of just such a circumstance in the popular book *The Fifty-Minute Hour* by Dr. Robert Lindner (Rinehart, 1955) titled "The Jet-Propelled Couch." When the chapter was reprinted in *The Magazine of Fantasy and Science Fiction* (January 1956), editor Anthony Boucher termed it "an article," underscoring the author's claim that this piece, like others in the book, was based on actual case histories.

With the skill of a master storyteller, Dr. Robert Lindner tells of the referral of a young physicist to him by a physician in a southwestern government project. The patient, whom he calls Kirk Allen, has read a series of books in which his name appears as the protagonist, and he fancies that the novels are an actual account of his adventures in the future. From hints given by the author it becomes apparent that Kirk Allen's real name is John Carter, and his "imaginary" land the Mars of Edgar Rice Burroughs.

Confronted with a difficult case, Dr. Lindner takes the desperate expedient of attempting to enter the dreamworld with his patient in hopes of finding errors and discrepancies.

His qualifications are impeccable, for as he points out: "I can only say that I have been, since learning to read, an *aficionado* . . . introduced to *Amazing Stories* by a schoolmate. . . . my passage from BEMs through Burroughs to Wells, Heard, and Stapledon was swift. At forty I remain a rather reluctant addict, fighting the temptations of van Vogt, Bradbury, and Co., but succumbing blissfully to the appeal of a new Orwell (alas, there will be no more from him), a Wylie, or a Huxley."

Eventually he notices an increasing lack of interest on the part of his patient in carrying the game any further. *Kirk Allen has been cured for some time but is now carrying on a pretense so as not to spoil the psychiatrist's quite evident involvement and enjoyment.*

"The Jet-Propelled Couch" was in an unwitting sense a rebuttal to psychiatrist Robert Plank, LL.D., M.S.W., who had asserted in a long article in the July 1954 *International Record of Medicine and General Practice Clinics,* titled *The Reproduction of Psychosis in Science Fiction,* that the plot outlines of science fiction stories are "to a higher degree than other literature, morphologically similar to schizophrenic manifestations, especially of the paranoid type."

When asked by George Dusheck, a reporter from the *San Francisco News,* for a comment on Dr. Plank's statement, John W. Campbell, editor of *Astounding Science-Fiction,* who was attending the Twelfth World Science Fiction Convention in San Francisco at the time, replied for the September 4, 1954, edition: "I would be more impressed with Plank's view . . . if psychiatry had any good notion of what it is talking about when it uses the word 'schizophrenia.'"

Yet, in its own way, Dr. Plank's article was more friendly than hostile. He was a regular reader of science fiction, and the president of MD Publications, which issued *International Record of Medicine and General Practice Clinics,* was the late Felix Marti-Ibanez, M.D., a writer of fantasy who had three stories in *The Magazine of Fantasy and Science Fiction* and whose cultural medical publication *MD* ran frequent features on various phases of science fiction.

True or otherwise, "The Jet-Propelled Couch" epitomized a phase that science fiction was passing through at the time, spearheaded by Horace L. Gold and *Galaxy Science Fiction,* that was so pronounced that for a period the science fiction fans referred to the publication as "the magazine of psychiatric fiction."

While *Galaxy Science Fiction* printed the largest share of such stories, they were also to be found quite frequently in *The Magazine of Fantasy and Science Fiction* and *Astounding*

Science-Fiction. Because *Galaxy Science Fiction,* between the years 1950 and 1955, paid just about the top rates in the field (three cents to five cents a word), writers trying to sell Gold wrote what they thought he would buy and those stories he did not buy which possessed merit appeared elsewhere.

When writing of the psychiatric in science fiction, it should also be made clear that the great body of "mad scientist" stories that was part-and-parcel of the early years of magazine science fiction is excluded. The "mad scientist" was a literary device, not a mental aberration.

The greatest and perhaps the very first of all science fiction based on a psychiatric theme was *The Strange Case of Dr. Jekyll and Mr. Hyde* by Robert Louis Stevenson, telling of Dr. Henry Jekyll, who discovered chemicals that could alter his personality, releasing the dark side of it, and then finds himself helpless to restore permanently his true state.

The rise of LSD has converted *The Strange Case of Dr. Jekyll and Mr. Hyde* from an allegorical horror fantasy into science fiction, for the "mind-expanding" drugs are capable of mentally bringing about changes similar to those attributed to chemicals in Stevenson's work.

The publication of *The Strange Case of Dr. Jekyll and Mr. Hyde* was historic on more than its science fiction count. Released in January 1886 by Longmans, Green and Co., London, the publisher decided on a daring experiment. He would bring out a cheap edition *first.* This cheap edition would be paperbound, printed by the tens of thousands, and sell for only a shilling (about twenty-five cents).

Sales proved phenomenal. The publisher had a best seller on his hands. As a result, Stevenson, at a single thrust, gained a reputation as a major writer which had eluded him for thirteen years. The story, interestingly, had been inspired by a nightmare, and had taken only six days to write (three if he had not burned the first version and rewritten it).

No major figure followed Stevenson's lead in science fiction based on mental disorder for thirty-eight years.

That man, like Dr. Robert Lindner, was also a psychiatrist, David H. Keller, M.D. When he appeared on the scene with "The Revolt of the Pedestrians" (*Amazing Stories,* February 1928), specialized science fiction periodicals were not quite two years old. New writers of importance were being attracted to the medium, among them A. Hyatt Verrill, Miles J. Breuer, M.D., Bob Olsen, and Francis Flagg. None of these men were youngsters, and most were professional men. Their subjects were considerably more adult than might have been expected from a fledgling literature, and Keller was by all odds the most thoughtful of them all.

"The Revolt of the Pedestrians" was Keller's first sale, and it was made at the age of forty-seven. It was a savage satire based on the popularity of the automobile and the gradual loss of the use of legs by humans as they succumb to the lure of this form of transportation. Humanity is divided into two groups: the Automobilists, with legs shrunken from nonuse, but with advanced technical knowledge, and the Pedestrians, people with normal legs, who are regarded as less than human because of it and hunted down in a policy of extermination. When a daughter of a powerful leader of the Automobilists proves a throwback and makes active use of her legs, "thousands of suggestions" are made "from psycho-analysis to brutal splinting and bandaging of the girl's lower extremities," to correct this social defect.

She is one of the few survivors when the Pedestrians invent a device that stops all power, and the legless Automobilists, helpless, die by the millions.

Overnight, Keller was a big name in science fiction.

The first story had only once mentioned the word "psycho-analysis" in hyphenated form, but the tales that followed moved even more strongly in that direction. "Unlocking the Past" (*Amazing Stories,* September 1928) was a moving story of an invention that would make it possible for a child to tap ancestral memory, which stopped just short of becoming a valid piece of psychiatric science fiction. Keller hit the target full on with "The Insane Avalanche" (*Amazing Stories Quarterly,* Summer 1928), the fourth in a related series of stories published in the one issue under the unifying title of *The Menace.* In the first three stories, the Negroes had failed in three major attempts to destroy the white power structure and gain superior status. Their leaders retreat to an equatorial island where they are joined by Dr. Abraham Flandings, a mulatto, who has been prevented from advancing himself as a psychiatrist because of his race: "I have always been interested in the mind and preferably in the abnormal, the unusual, the diseased mind," he explains. "My color made it hard for me. The study of medicine was difficult and the endeavor to become a psychiatrist almost insurmountable . . . In the United States there was practically no opening for anyone of my race." Dr. Flandings submits that he has an idea which he feels, if implemented, could topple the white race.

Back in the United States, techniques for construction with the use of glass advance tremendously. Soon, not only one-family homes but apartments and commercial buildings are poured from glass, dropping prices far below anything previously believed possible. Even elevated highways are successfully constructed from glass. Then, in a nation prosperous and happy, there comes a frightening rise in mental disorders.

It is eventually discovered that the effect of the rays of the sun, filtered through the glass, is the basic cause of mental disorders, but by that time 120 million people have been put into suspended animation to cut down on care costs. The glass trust turns out to have been a device of the Negro power group, who are tracked to their island lair by Taine of San Francisco.

Keller followed this tale immediately with "Stenographer's Hands" (*Amazing Stories Quarterly*, Fall 1928), where big business breeds men and women for their ability to type and transcribe material. The "mechanization" ceases when the specially bred workers develop nocturnal epilepsy from strains of in-breeding and after 200 years the entire plan collapses.

Still more directly in accord with the psychiatric (though with considerably more tongue-in-cheek) was his tale "The Moon Rays" (*Wonder Stories Quarterly*, Summer 1930). As an experiment, a small nation is selected and valuable prizes offered to those people who can "see" the most imaginative objects in the face of the moon. People by the millions spend hours every night staring at the lunar orb, trying to conceive of ever more original images. Quickly the crime rate increases, people tend to lose their inhibitions, there is a record number of marriages, and a sharp increase in all types of mental disorders.

In the late twenties, psychiatrists were rare, and knowledge of the science limited. Keller had virtually no competition in this area of science fiction. One other popular science fiction writer, Miles J. Breuer, an internist with a laboratory in Lincoln, Nebraska, had touched on the subject with passing references in a few of his stories. A considerable knowledge of psychoanalysis was displayed by him in "The Inferiority Complex" (*Amazing Stories,* September 1930). To lend realism, this highly unusual story was illustrated with photographs, with superimpositions, supplied by the author showing gigantic bacteria threatening a man in locations near a lake and in a laboratory. "The Inferiority Complex" dealt with a scientist who claimed to have bred in his laboratory huge bacteria, bigger than a man. He was found to be suffering from "micromania," a condition said to be quite common, in which the patient believes himself to be very small in size. Inferiority complexes are actually a *mild* form of micromania, which explains the title of the story.

Breuer might have made a mark for himself in science fiction based on psychiatric themes, but he did not try that vein again, whereas Keller persisted not only in the science fiction magazines but in *Weird Tales,* bastion of the supernatural. There he had published "Creation Unforgiveable" (April 1930), concerning a writer (obviously Keller himself) who builds a small writing shack (which he had himself done) and becomes immersed in the writing of a prehistoric tale in which a brave caveman and an Amazon girl are captured by half-humans-half-apes and tied to a stake to be eaten by a scaled monster. Then, away from his typewriter on a social call at this crucial moment in his plot development, he is convinced his characters will perish if he does not write them out of the situation in time. Rushing back to help them, he falls and knocks himself unconscious. When he comes to, the shack and the typewriter are smashed, there are evidences of blood and large distinct tracks that sink a foot into the ground and lead to the entrance of a cave on the grounds.

This was a prelude to what is perhaps Keller's greatest tale of horror, "The Thing in the Cellar" (*Weird Tales,* March 1932), which could technically qualify as science fiction. The story concerns a child born in an old English house, who is irrationally afraid of the cellar. He is even uneasy in the kitchen, from which a stairway leads to the cellar. The cellar is ordinary in most respects and has served generations of families. To cure the child's obsession, a doctor advises he be locked in the kitchen with the cellar door open to prove his fears are unfounded. When they open the door to release him, he is found clawed to death.

The bereaved father shakes the doctor and demands to know

what killed his son. The answer is indecisive but stunning in its psychological implications:

"How do I know, Tucker?" he replied. "How do I know? Didn't you tell me that there was nothing there? Nothing down there? In the cellar?"

Almost as fine a story, but never truly appreciated because of its subtlety, was Keller's "No More Tomorrows" (*Amazing Stories*, December 1932). A psychologist pinpoints the portion of the brain wherein man plans for the future. He devises a test batch of a serum which will destroy that ability, making one incapable of comprehending or believing in a tomorrow, living only for today. He makes a deal to sell that secret to the Russians so they can use it to immobilize the world and seize control. His girl feeds him the chemical in a drink and he loses not only the ability to plan ahead, but faces death from the Russians, who will think he has double-crossed them. The Russians inform him that they plan to kill him the next day. Instead of pleading for life he laughs: "Oh this is too much . . . Why, if you are going to wait till tomorrow, you will never be able to kill me . . . *You cannot kill me tomorrow for I have no tomorrow.*" There the story ends on a note of sublime irony.

Keller's own background and life was almost as bizarre as his fiction, and from it he drew a great deal of the substantive horror reflected in his works. He was born in Philadelphia, December 23, 1880, and traced his family in America back to before 1645. A sister, eighteen months older than he, was the focus of his mother's attention, and he was ignored. At the age of six, when sent to school, he could speak so few words of English that he was sent home as language-retarded. The only person in the world who could divine his needs and in any manner interpret his meaning was his older sister. When she died at the age of seven, he was cut off from the world, unable to communicate coherently with anyone.

The loss of her daughter, and the thought that her son's deficiency might reflect on her, motivated his mother to start a personal program of education at home to supplement private schooling. In three years the boy had achieved norm, with the exception that, having been taught English as though it were a second language, simplicity became the keynote of his expression.

He put this phase of his life into the story "The Lost Language" (*Amazing Stories*, January 1934), concerning a little boy who appears normal in every respect but will not talk. He begins to write a strange language which no one can understand. Eventually it is determined that the language is an ancient form of Welsh, which only one old woman in the world might conceivably be able to interpret. She dies before they can reach her. The story ends when an older sister vows to devote herself to learning the boy's language and to keep him with her so that she may be his link with the world.

A great struggle against the powerful will of his mother for control of his own destiny caused Keller to strike out for independence after his graduation from medical school in 1903. He married and finally set up as a country doctor in Russell, Pennsylvania, a town of only three hundred people. Living almost by the barter system, he eventually gave up and tried again, spending a "bitter" year at Pleasantville, New Jersey. Faced with complete professional and economic failure, he finally accepted a post as a junior physician in the Anna State Hospital of Illinois, a mental institution, in 1915.

American entry into World War I found him a first lieutenant in the medical corps. While in the service, he wrote a primer and first reader for use in his school for illiterates at Camp Lee, Virginia. He then was assigned the job of trying to help shell-shocked soldiers at Camp Cody, New Mexico. He did outstanding work in restoring men to normalcy in a field that was little understood at the time.

At the close of the war he took a post as Assistant Superintendent of the state hospital for the mentally ill at Pineville, Louisiana. He spent ten years there and drew heavily upon his experiences for stories he later wrote. He resigned when Huey Long became governor of the state.

He was early among psychiatrists in an American mental institution to attempt to employ Freudian theories in an effort to cure his patients. "This revolutionary work deeply interested me and I read everything obtainable pertaining to it," he wrote in *Through the Back Door (Life with the Abnormals)*, a 125,000-word inside story on the workings of a mental institution completed in 1941 and circulated only in manuscript.

It was while actually working in institutions for the mentally ill that Dr. Keller wrote his science fiction and fantasies on psychiatric themes. He was actually involved in the environ-ment of the abnormal most of his working hours, and a Freudian at a time when the theories were still not widely accepted. As a result he had virtually no competition in the science fiction world and ironically exerted only a limited amount of influence, because there was literally no one capable of duplicating his themes or approach.

An excellent case in point is "The Tree of Evil" (*Wonder Stories*, September 1934). After leaving Louisiana, Keller had taken a post in Bolivar, Tennessee, and used that community as the background for his story (involving Taine of San Francisco) of a town that gradually loses its sense of morality as a result of eating leaves from a very special tree.

"The Tree of Evil" was but a prelude for a short novel which Keller was to write which may very well be the most remark-able single story based on psychiatry in the science fiction for-mat. Before World War II, Keller had written half of a novel titled *The Abyss*, and put it aside. It finally was completed and appeared in hardcover from New Era Publishers, Philadelphia, 1948, under the title *The Solitary Hunters and the Abyss*. That was the only book ever turned out by that firm, organized by two Philadelphia science fiction enthusiasts, Robert A. Madle and Jack Agnew, during a period when specialty book publish-ing houses for science fiction and fantasy were common. In this novel a chemical is discovered in the bodies of the insane which appears to be a major cause of abnormality. Synthesized, this chemical will temporarily produce the same symptoms in "nor-mal" human beings. The drug is included in chewing gum, and through absorbing it, the individual throws off 2,000 years of superficial culture and philosophy and assumes behavior pat-terns similar to those of the days of Rome.

The population of New York City is subjected to this "mad-ness" for thirty days. The accounts of the rise of cultism in Harlem and the attitude toward the white race by the Negroes is little short of brilliant.

The preciseness with which Keller drives home his argument that there is a *physical* as well as *mental* cause of abnormal behavior reveals that, despite his admiration of psychoanalysis, he now realized that Freud had only part of the answer. The parallel between Keller's chemical and LSD is too obvious to elaborate upon.

David H. Keller died on July 13, 1966, deeply involved with his writing and frustrated that it had not brought him more attention. He was unique in that so great a portion of his work involved psychological and psychiatric subjects set to fiction, usually science fiction, fantasy or horror fiction, and that he was by education, training, and experience singularly well qualified for that specialty.

As early as 1939, one writer plunged into a psychiatric theme with such power that it clearly foreshadowed the success that was later to be his. That author was Robert Bloch, with his masterpiece "The Strange Plight of Richard Clayton" (*Amazing Stories*, March 1939). The first man alone on a flight to Mars loses his time-sense. He experiences a series of adventurous and horror-packed dreams, until, even waking, he has increasing difficulty telling fantasy from reality. He has no idea of how much time is passing, but knows it must be great since his hair is whitening. Finally, the ship lands and he staggers forth to die of old age, though he has been in the ship only one week and, due to a malfunction, it never left the ground!

The magazine that began to point the way to psychiatry as a source of plot ideas for science fiction was not a science fiction magazine in any true sense. It was a magazine called *Unknown*, edited by John W. Campbell, editor of *Astounding Science-Fiction*, and devoted to the proposition of fairy tales for grown-ups. Plots were drawn from legend, myth, superstition, religion, witchcraft, spiritualism, and Forteanism, and there were few stories that a trained psychiatrist could not have related to a true human aberration. Robert A. Heinlein contributed an outstanding short story, "They" (*Unknown*, April 1941), about a man held under observation because he believes everything taking place in the world about him is a gigantic plot. It turns out to be just that, his entire world a series of props and façades for no reason that he can determine. This bent achieved its epitome in a psychological fantasy by L. Ron Hubbard titled *Fear* (*Unknown*, July 1940). This short novel carries its lead character through a surrealistic nightmare as he attempts to recapture four lost hours from his memory, culminating in the discovery that he had murdered his wife during that period.

Hubbard was himself imbued with an interest in psychiatry that reflected itself in the movement of Dianetics which he sponsored in 1950. His best-selling book *Dianetics: The Modern Science of Mental Health* (Hermitage House, 1950) presented a number of racy couch case histories. A follow-up book on the subject, *Science of Survival,* by L. Ron Hubbard (The Wichita Publishing Company, 1951), outlined techniques for "auditing" a Dianetics patient which differed scarcely at all with the popular view of psychoanalysis. Considering that a long article, *Dianetics: The Modern Science of Mental Healing,* by L. Ron Hubbard preceded the book in the May 1950 issue of *Astounding Science-Fiction,* plots involving mental problems might quite reasonably be expected to receive more space in science fiction periodicals.

There were frequently such implications in Henry Kuttner's stories previously, particularly in "Shock" (*Astounding Science-Fiction,* March 1943), where a man from the future is found to be an insane genius who has been taking shock treatments.

Kuttner's effort was effective but bluntly direct, without nuance. By contrast, Clifford D. Simak's "Huddling Place" (*Astounding Science-Fiction,* July 1944), the second in his famed "City" series, was a sophisticated and delicately subtle telling of a surgeon from Earth, asked to go to Mars to save the life of a close friend on the verge of completing a philosophy that will set mankind ahead a hundred thousand years. For generations Earth has decentralized and there has been little need to go anywhere. In the end the man's agoraphobia prevents him from leaving.

A British author, writing under the name of Peter Phillips, gained a reputation with his first science fiction sale "Dreams Are Sacred" (*Astounding Science-Fiction,* September 1948), by mechanically permitting his consciousness to be directed into the dream-world of an insane science fiction writer. He introduces so many extraneous factors into the dream that he destroys the pattern and forces a return to sanity. This story preceded "The Jet-Propelled Couch" with a fundamentally similar idea.

The willingness of *Astounding Science-Fiction* to include material in a psychiatric vein whenever the use enhanced the story was underscored in "The Strange Case of John Kingman" by Murray Leinster (May 1948), where it is discovered that a man has been held in a mental institution for 162 years and modern tests determine that he is an alien from outer space, but nevertheless actually paranoid. An attempt to cure him results in a reversion to infantilism.

Despite Leinster, stories with a deliberate psychiatric approach were not that common. There were frequently outstanding stories in which a psychiatrist played a major role. Foremost among them was "In Hiding" by Wilmar H. Shiras (*Astounding Science-Fiction,* November 1948), concerning a psychiatrist who gradually wheedles the disclosure from a boy about whom his teacher has a "feeling," that he is a true intellectual mutation resulting from a radiation accident when he was a child.

The author who made the most effective use of the psychiatric between the dominance of David H. Keller and the emergence of *Galaxy Science Fiction* was Ray Bradbury, who made a major but largely ignored use of hallucination on the part of an Earthman landed on Mars in "Defense Mech" (*Planet Stories,* Spring 1946), who imagines that he is viewing a variety of Earth tableaux on that planet. When Bradbury altered the idea slightly to have an entire crew of a spaceship in "Mars Is Heaven" (*Planet Stories,* Fall 1948) experience similar but more elaborate hallucinations, he wrote a story which became one of the true pillars of his success.

Is Bradbury conscious of the frequency of psychological themes in his work? Most probably!

The science fiction editor who was most fascinated by psychiatric themes in science fiction and most actively encouraged the writing of and promoted the popularity of such stories upon the introduction of his *Galaxy Science Fiction* (October 1950) was Horace L. Gold. Gold had written science fiction for *Astounding Stories* as far back as 1934 under the pen name of Clyde Crane Campbell. He had for a period before his entry into the armed services in World War II worked as an editor for Standard Magazines, publisher of *Thrilling Wonder Stories* and *Startling Stories,* and had sold fiction to *Unknown* magazine. A two-year stint in the Pacific during World War II resulted in personal problems that required psychiatric help. His involvement with psychiatrists and his familiarity with their methods made him lean toward stories which explored mental abnormality in a future tense.

Certain authors displayed a definite aptitude for this type of fiction. Richard Matheson, with "The Waker Dreams" (*Galaxy Science Fiction,* December 1950), tells a successful story of how future man, though believing he has been relieved of all work through automation, is mentally confused into performing scores of essential, minor tasks to keep his world functioning. Matheson repeated again with singular effectiveness in "Lover, When You're Near Me" (*Galaxy Science Fiction,* May 1952), where a station keeper on a distant planet battles agonizingly, but unsuccessfully, to prevent what appears to be either telepathic seduction or a special form of psychosis induced by the presence of an abhorrent humanoid female of that world.

Theodore Sturgeon, too, found himself proficient at the story of psychiatry in science fiction terms. His *Baby Is Three* (*Galaxy Science Fiction,* October 1952), the novelette which formed the basis of his great classic, *More Than Human,* literally starts and ends in the psychiatrist's office. The psychiatrist draws out the incredible revelation that the patient is part of a gestalt organism, acting as the central teen-age control of a number of humans functioning in telepathic concert. *Baby Is Three,* through Sturgeon's ingenuity, lifted itself off the psychiatrist's couch to achieve the distinction of being the best story on gestalt psychology to appear in science fiction up to that time.

Sturgeon appeared to enjoy playing with abnormal psychology as much as did Gold, and it was to become a powerful element in a number of his stories. Certainly, his most intensive use of the psychiatric was in "Who?" (*Galaxy Science Fiction,* March 1955), where a lone space traveler imagines he is talking to someone behind the bulkhead of his spaceship on a long space journey, only to learn that a device has been planted in his brain to keep him in communication with the child within himself.

As intensively psychiatric was Sturgeon's "The Other Man" (*Galaxy Science Fiction,* September 1956), where a man's alter ego and ego, which have been battling for ascendency and causing erratic patterns of behavior, are modulated electronically so that both personalities blend into a harmonious whole.

It can be seen that, despite the spaceships and gadgetry like the psychostat in "The Other Man" for taking a man's personality apart and putting it back together again, the basic premise of *all* three of Sturgeon's stories is the theme of "possession." This theme is almost as old as mankind; it is the basis of the first and greatest psychiatric science fiction story, *The Strange Case of Dr. Jekyll and Mr. Hyde*, and it has been most fundamentally exemplified in *The Dybbuk* by S. Ankski, generally considered to be the finest of all plays written originally in Yiddish.

A substantial portion of the tales of the psychiatric in science fiction published since the onset of *Galaxy Science Fiction* boil down to little more than variations on the theme of possession. "Silent Brother" by Algis Budrys, writing as Paul Janvier (*Astounding Science-Fiction,* February 1956), utilizes symbiotic intelligences from Alpha Centauri to offer Man guidance; Philip José Farmer in *Strange Compulsion* (*Science Fiction Plus,* December 1953) tells a story of *physical* possession by a parasite, resulting in actions on the part of its host which are seemingly irrational and antisocial; indirect possession is found in "The Dreaming Wall" by Gerald Pearce *(Galaxy Science Fiction),* which surrounds a city on Fallon's planet, where the night is punctuated by people screaming in nightmare as strange dreams and stranger thoughts encroach upon their slumber. The problem is solved when an ancient wall which "protects" the city is determined to be interpenetrated with a mindless life-form, which receives, stores, and transmits telepathetically all thoughts emanating in its area.

It is worthy of noting that when an actual psychiatrist such as Keller writes a broad spectrum of science fiction based on his specialty, possession as a theme is rare. With the dilettante it is common, for his knowledge of psychiatry is usually too limited to make him aware of the recurrent plot trap.

Since 1950, the quantity of science fiction on psychiatric themes has grown so vast as to provide a fertile field for a scholarly volume. Such a volume might be of particular interest if it were written by, or in collaboration with, a psychiatrist.

Psychiatric stories have been published of the intensity of "Hallucination Orbit" by J. T. MacIntosh (*Galaxy Science Fiction,* January 1952) or "The Yellow Pill" by Rog Phillips (*Astounding Science-Fiction,* October 1958), wherein every word is devoted to the subject's problem and a guessing game ensues between the reader and the lead character as to what elements are real and which are psychiatric syndromes. Inevitably, there have also been stories where the psychiatric element was tongue-in-cheek.

"Something Green" by Frederic Brown (*Space on My Hands,*

Shasta, 1951) was a master spoof, where a spaceman, stranded for thirty years, has seen the color green only when he discharges his seemingly inexhaustible ray gun at a wild beast. When a rescue ship lands, he learns Earth has been blasted and the color green is to be found on no other world. Rather than face up to that fact, he destroys his rescuer and retreats again into his green-blasting hunt fantasy.

Henry Kuttner, in teaming up with his wife C. L. Moore in "A Wild Surmise" (*Star Science Fiction Stories,* edited by Fred Pohl, Ballantine Books, 1953), again utilizing "possession," had a human and a Martian psychiatrist exchange bodies through a subject who imagines he lives on both worlds. It was really Robert Bloch who wrapped up the psychiatric spoof in "Dead-End Doctor" (*Galaxy Science Fiction,* February 1956), where the last psychiatrist on Earth fights a losing battle to hold his business against gland serums which compensate for almost all mental ills. He finally sells his couch and starts a new career in the treatment of mental problems of robots, performing the first successful "prefrontal robotomy."

It is an easy and natural thing to laugh at a substantial part of the stories involving psychiatric problems which appear so frequently in science fiction, particularly since so many of them are written by authors who are playing their psychiatry by ear. Yet the record clearly shows that the benefits to science fiction have been more on the plus than on the minus side. Psychoanalysis plays an increasing role not only in our lives but in our literature. Adding this element to science fiction has brought the field in line with the general trend, and incontestably contributed some superior stories to the roster.

CRIME:

From Sherlock to Spaceships

There has always been a great affinity between the more involved followers of the detective story and the lovers of science fiction, possibly because a single writer, Edgar Allan Poe, is literary father to both. Science fiction was the older child, sired as "Hans Phaall—A Tale" in the May 1835 issue of *Southern Literary Messenger.* A virtual documentary, this story kept in extraordinarily tight focus the hour-by-hour scientific problems of getting a space vessel to the moon. It was this single story that proved the "divine" inspiration of Jules Verne and turned him into a science fiction writer. Six years later, "The Murders in the Rue Morgue," appearing in *Graham's Lady's and Gentleman's Magazine* for April 1841, popularized the use of deduction and analysis by a crime expert to solve a "murder," in this instance committed by an orangutan. Not only the literary method, but the brilliant deductive talents of C. August Dupin as chronicled by his anonymous narrator were acknowledged by A. Conan Doyle as providing the pattern that was to result in the much-cherished stories of Sherlock Holmes and Dr. Watson.

Both science fiction and the detective story became distinct literary forms, each with its coterie of devotees. It was far from uncommon to find authors who wrote both, as well as readers who enjoyed them equally, yet certain elements in the two types of stories made a successful amalgamation rare. Science fiction required only a single basic connection with reality, and the rest of the story could expand into outright fantasy, providing the progression maintained a consistent logic. The detective story required that the reader be supplied with all the facts necessary to determine the perpetrator of the crime, and those not provided had to be implicit in the familiar world. The problem of a writer supplying adequate background of the world of the future, a planet light-years off, or a technology that was capable of traveling in time, and still giving the reader a fair shake at guessing the ending, was monumental.

There was little point in attempting to combine the two disparate categories of fiction, until the unprecedented world acclaim given Doyle's stories of Sherlock Holmes made the hero detective not only popular but increasingly learned and scientific. M. P. Shiel had early produced Prince Zaleski, a sort of Holmes Gothic with immense erudition; Jacques Futrelle's Augustus S. F. X. Van Dusen was so cerebral that he was called the Thinking Machine; Joyce Emmerson Muddock's Dick Donovan was frequently involved in cases where crimes were complicated by hypnotic and drug syndromes; and Dr. R. Austin Freeman's Dr. John Thorndyke was a master of the laboratory and appeared to have an encyclopedic knowledge of theft that put Sherlock Holmes to shame. Particularly with the Dr. Thorndyke stories it was no longer possible for the reader to anticipate the author, so a hard rule was broken.

It was only logical progression to hypothesize an improvement of an existing device or the invention of a new one to mechanically assist the detective or criminologist in his solution of the crime. This technically spilled the detective story over into the realm of science fiction. The authors who took that small but irrevocable step forward, and in doing so set into motion a chain of events that would elevate the detective story to unprecedented popularity in America, have scarcely been given adequate acknowledgement in books on the history of the detective story. It is not that the critics intend to be unfair, but that their works are for the most part obscure, and where they are known a peculiarity of copyright dating has influenced readers to believe they rode with a trend rather than originated it. Ironically, one of those authors is highly regarded in the science fiction world—for he is the man who plotted and then co-authored with Philip Wylie those interplanetary classics *When Worlds Collide* and *After Worlds Collide*—Edwin Balmer! His collaborator was William B. MacHarg.

The editor of *Hampton's Magazine*, upon introducing the first Luther Trant "psychological detective" story, "The Man in the Room" by Edwin Balmer and William B. MacHarg (May 1909), could scarcely be faulted on perspicacity:

> This initial story, one of a series of six [there proved to eventually be at least twelve] deserves special mention because it tells of a new sort of a detective—the psychological detective. To make a bold statement, this new detective theory is as important as Poe's deductive theory of "ratiocination" and may be pursued even further than that brilliant method in the actual practical business of thief-catching. It must be borne out in reading these tales that they are not mere dreams of the imagination. Such devices as Luther Trant employs to run down criminals are in use every day in the psychology laboratories of our universities, and could as readily be applied to the world of crime as they now are to the world of scientific experimentation.

In that first story, Luther Trant, a dissatisfied assistant in a psychological laboratory, uses a chronoscope to measure the time-lapse in an association word-test given to suspects to solve a suspicious death. The focus of suspicion is kept on the woman in the case, but the true fascination of the story centers on the mechanical device which is so convincingly described as "standard in psychological testing laboratories." The technique and the mechanism are characterized as "merely the methods of the German doctors—Freud's methods—used by Jung in Zurich to diagnose the causes of adolescent insanity."

Edwin Balmer's father, Thomas Balmer, was then regarded as one of the nation's most outstanding advertising men, and the son's interest in psychology in part derived from the older Balmer's publication of a book on the psychology of advertising. Edwin Balmer was a newspaperman, a consulting editor of *Hampton's Magazine,* and his first book, *Waylaid by Wireless* (1909), had a scientific plot device. His collaboration resulted from William Briggs MacHarg's marriage to Balmer's sister, Katherine, on June 10, 1909. MacHarg was a graduate engineer who for a time wrote short fiction and verse for Chicago newspapers, then entered the employ of a company contracting for architectural ironwork. In January 1909 he left contracting work and teamed up with Balmer on the Luther Trant stories. The literary collaboration between the two men would encompass many successful books into the early twenties. Balmer was to become editor of *Red Book Magazine* in 1927, a position he held until 1949. MacHarg's work would continue to appear into the 1950s.

The Luther Trant stories ran monthly throughout the remainder of the year in *Hampton's Magazine,* copiously illustrated, sometimes in two colors. The second story, "The Fast Watch" (June 1909), solved a crime through the use of the galvanometer, which measures the moisture on a man's palms under questioning to determine his truthfulness; "The Red Dress" (July 1909) employed an automograph registering involuntary motions of interrogated suspects; "The Man Higher Up" (October 1909) sees a big corporate crime solved with the aid of a plethysmograph, a device which revealed the increase and decrease of blood in the hands under stress in concert with the pneumograph, which transmitted the reaction of the respiratory system under emotion; "The Eleventh Hour" (February 1910) brings into play the psychometer, which causes a light to move off center of a screen when a change in blood pressure or perspiration flow indicates someone is lying; and "The Hammering Man" (May 1910) utilizes a sphygmograph, an automatically penciled record of the human pulse, to solve a mystery. This story was later reprinted in *Top-Notch Magazine* for May 1, 1915, under the title of "Decidedly Odd."

The first nine Luther Trant stories were issued in hardcover by Small, Maynard and Company, Boston, in early 1910, under the title of *The Achievements of Luther Trant. The New York Times,* in a review of the book in its edition of April 23, 1910, said of the stories: "All are to be envied into whose hands these fall for its readers may be sure of some hours of surcease from whatever 'damnition grind' is their lot in life. For its literary quality also [the book] is to be recommended."

Beyond that, the stories appeared to have made no general stir in the literary world, except with the editors of *Cosmopolitan,* who took them very seriously. At that time *Hampton's Magazine* was making a circulation drive that would carry it from a low of 13,000 readers in 1907 to a high of 444,000 in 1911. In achieving this, it patterned its policy and format almost identically after the affluent *Cosmopolitan.* Both magazines featured muckraking articles against the "villainous" giant corporations (in fact, the villain in "The Man Higher Up" is an unscrupulous big company executive); both magazines were printed in what has come to be known as "pulp" size, on fine-coated stock, featuring fiction and nonfiction; both ran the works of Jack London, Rex Beach, George Randolph Chester, Gouvernor Morris, O. Henry, and Elbert Hubbard; both were lavishly illustrated throughout in two colors; *Hampton's* ran fantasy (including new fairy tales!) as well as science fiction, and *Cosmopolitan* had first serialized in America H. G. Wells's *War of the Worlds, The First Men in the Moon, Food of the Gods,* and *In the Days of the Comet.*

When "The Case of Helen Bond," the very first adventure of Craig Kennedy, a professor of chemistry who became "The Scientific Detective," appeared in the December 1910 *Cosmopolitan,* it had been rejected by Robert H. Davis, fiction editor of Munsey's magazines. It was seized upon by the editor of *Cosmopolitan* as its answer to Luther Trant, whose latest adventure, "Matter of Mind Reading," had appeared in the October 1910 *Hampton's Magazine* only two months earlier.

What was eyebrow-lifting, however, was that the plot and device of the first Luther Trant story, "The Man in the Room," were repeated in "The Case of Helen Bond." The device was a machine for registering the reaction time of a woman to a word-association test. Since Arthur B. Reeve was also a contributor to *Hampton's Magazine,* having seen published an article titled "Men and Monkeys—Primates" in its January 1909 issue only four months before the appearance of the first Luther Trant story, coincidence appeared unlikely. It also explains why Robert H. Davis, one of the greatest fiction editors of all time, let it go.

When the first volume of Craig Kennedy stories, titled *The Silent Bullet,* was published by Dodd, Mead, in 1912, "The Case of Helen Bond" was included second, after the title story (except for several hundred words of introductory prologue on "Craig Kennedy's theories"), and the name changed to "The Scientific Cracksmen." The twelve stories were otherwise published in the precise chronology in which they appeared in *Cosmopolitan.* Most of the other instruments used in the Luther Trant stories eventually showed up in the Craig Kennedy stories, but few of them quite so blatant a copy as in the first.

A Craig Kennedy story now appeared in every issue of *Cosmopolitan* and would continue to do so through 1918.

"The Silent Bullet" (January 1911), the title story of Reeve's initial book, his second Craig Kennedy story (announced as "The Mystery of the Silent Bullet"), referred to a murder through the use of a silencer, which is solved by recording the physical pressure on the arms of their chairs by prime suspects under questioning. "The Bacteriological Detective" (February 1911) advanced the theory that certain illnesses are reflected in a person's handwriting, and thereby criminals are caught by the use of a sphygmograph, an instrument that records the "force and frequency of the pulsation," as a person writes; "The Deadly Tube" (March 1911) has Craig Kennedy bug a room with a sensitive microphone, with a stenographer taking down the statements of two men participating in a fraudulent lawsuit; "The Seismograph Adventure" (April 1911) finds the movements of a medium at a seance exposed through the use of an earthquake detector, a seismograph. The quantity and variety of the detectors in his stories comprise probably the most comprehensive review ever made of the subject.

Kennedy was no stylist, but he was direct, lucid, and his science was convincing enough to attain "willing suspension of disbelief." Scientific methods were frequently involved in the *crimes* as well as their solutions. Readers were uncritical; the papers were daily recording scientific miracles—why not in crime detection, too?

Within two years, as his stories appeared unflaggingly, month after month in *Cosmopolitan,* Arthur B. Reeve's popularity quickly outdistanced that of any detective-story writer in the United States. His stories were collected and issued in book form and his books proved best sellers of their type. Craig Kennedy was frequently called "the American Sherlock Holmes."

The stories were syndicated in newspapers throughout the nation. A Philadelphia resident buying a copy of *The Evening Bulletin* on December 13, 1913, in addition to all the paper's other features, would find on page thirteen: "The newest adventure of Craig Kennedy—Scientific Detective, *The Invisible Ray*" and be treated to a description of a machine alleged to be able to convert baser elements into gold and read minds at the same time! Actually, the primary function of the mechanism was to blind people!

In England, *Nash's*, a popular all-fiction magazine which became almost entirely a reprint of America's *Cosmopolitan—*

covers, stories, most of the illustrations, and even some of the articles—published the Craig Kennedy stories monthly, and he instantly caught on. In *Nash's,* Craig Kennedy became a British detective and the locale of his stories was England, just as Bruno Lessing's stories of New York's East Side Jews were changed to London's East End.

One of the leading British monthlies, *The London Magazine,* started a similar detective series almost immediately in its March 1911 issue, written by Max Rittenberg. Titled "The Strange Cases of Dr. Wycherly," the series concerned a psychological detective who, through self-hypnosis, can pick up thought waves from residual vibrations in a room. He could read minds, even in a crowded theatre, by injecting himself with pyridye-novocaine which rendered him temporarily deaf, permitting him to concentrate on thought waves around him. He also utilized basic elements of psychoanalysis to help solve murders. In a real sense, when he dispensed with his psychic powers, he was more truly a psychological detective than were Luther Trant or Craig Kennedy, who employed mechanical gadgetry to obtain similar results.

Max Rittenberg was an Australian-born author, educated in England, who built a reputation for himself as an authority on mail-order sales. Some of the stories, particularly those where some elementary form of psychoanalysis is employed, are quite good. The series was picked up in the United States by *The Blue Book Magazine* under the title of "The Strange Cases of Dr. Xavier Wycherly," beginning with its June 1911 issue. This series and other similar detective works by Max Rittenberg were run almost monthly through to March 1915. *The Blue Book Magazine* had previously reprinted several of William Hope Hodgson's horror stories of the sea from *The London Magazine,* so there may have been some sort of arrangement between the two publications.

A more highly scientific series was that created by author Michael White for Street & Smith's *Top-Notch Magazine* in 1911. A chemical criminologist called Proteus Raymond, whose great ambition in life is to be able to drop crime detection and devote himself to scientific research, after solving ingenious crimes in his stories "Eternium X" and "Force Mercurial," attempts to disappear from sight by leaving for the West Coast. There he walks into his most fantastic case, described in "The

Viper of Portland" (*Top-Notch Magazine*, February 15, 1912), where highly radioactive Saturnium rays projected into a zinc-lined cabinet are used to reduce human bodies to vapor, eliminating all evidence. Michael White had a second scientific detective, Charles Dagett of Dagett's Chemical Institute, who in "With Rays of Violet" (*Top-Notch Magazine*, February 1, 1913) utilizes a Radiograph emitting ultraviolet rays, to prove a famous diamond is a fake.

Arthur B. Reeve inevitably followed the same road as imitator Michael White to more fantastic inventions in his novel *Exploits of Elaine* (Harper's, 1915), using a laserlike death ray, and having Craig Kennedy as an associate of U.S. Intelligence in *The War Terror* (Harper's, 1915) involved with an electromagnetic powderless gun which can fire a noiseless high-velocity shell with a very small barrel; invisible ultraviolet light rays for reading messages hundreds of feet away; a radiograph for reading documents in sealed envelopes; and most brilliantly in the chapter "The Artificial Kidney," describes in extensive scientific detail the device in actual use today. Reeve was most believable and effective when discussing medical aspects of his plots, but these stories were in the minority.

Another author involved in detective stories who rose to popularity about the same time as Arthur B. Reeve was Sax Rohmer (Arthur S. Ward) with *The Insidious Dr. Fu Manchu* (McBride, 1913). This novel was borderline science fiction by virtue of the fact that Fu Manchu's master strategy encompassed conquest and domination of the white world. The hapless Commissioner Nayland Smith and his trusted aide, Dr. Petrie, can do little more than fight a delaying action against their highly endowed adversary, with his cruel Oriental tortures and strange ethical codes. Fu Manchu remains more a series of atmospheric tableaux than a true fantasy, yet in this archfiend and the enigmatic mystery of his beautiful female slave, the Egyptian Karamaneh, Arthur B. Reeve discovered elements which he thought he could incorporate with profit into his Craig Kennedy works.

Long Sin as a Chinese villain compatriot of an archcriminal known as the Clutching Hand was a character type and the infrared death ray was an advanced weapon which both remind one of elements from Fu Manchu when blended into *The Exploits of Elaine* by Arthur B. Reeve. This is a Craig Kennedy novel with action-romance interest which reads like a silent movie script, because that was just what it was and it developed to be the rage of United States and England when made into a movie serial by Pathé in 1914. *Elaine* offered action thrills that competed with Pauline of *The Perils of Pauline.*

A sequel in 1916, *The Romance of Elaine,* was a "natural," and this time a super Chinese villain, appropriately named Wu Fang (Popular Publications would issue a magazine titled *Wu Fang* in 1935), easily as resourceful and wicked as Fu Manchu, links up with Long Sin. Craig Kennedy's wireless-controlled torpedo is stolen by Wu Fang, to be turned over to an enemy nation that will use it to conquer the United States. A third film in 1918, *The Triumph of Elaine* (the title of the last chapter in *The Romance of Elaine*), was also made. As World War I drew to an end, Arthur B. Reeve was at the zenith of his career. No other detective writer in the United States was even a close runner-up in popularity. In achieving his stature, Reeve had immensely broadened the market for the detective story in this country. There seems to be little question but that his phenomenal sales emboldened Street & Smith to issue *Detective Story Magazine,* the first specialized pulp in history, whose first issue was dated October 5, 1915. They had been publishing the dime novel character Nick Carter, but Craig Kennedy's popularity proved that the vogue for that type of hero was waning, so they incorporated that character into the new magazine. (He was also given the editor's title!)

Arthur B. Reeve was credited by many then, as now, with fathering the scientific detective in America, a claim that has not previously been challenged because of an inexplicable copyright notice in the Harper's editions of his first book, *The Silent Bullet,* given as 1910, and lack of specific reference as to in what publication and at what date the Luther Trant stories appeared. Actually, *The Cumulative Book Index* and *The Book Review Digest* conclusively list the first Reeve book as appearing in 1912 and it was also reviewed during that year by various publications.

Sanctification of his position seemed to come with the publication of a twelve-volume matched set issued by Harper's in 1918 and sold in tandem with a ten-volume set of the works of Edgar Allan Poe for twenty-six dollars, payable in thirteen two-dollar installments. A quote from Theodore Roosevelt was used to launch the sales promotion which stated: "I particularly enjoyed half a dozen rattling good detective stories by Arthur B. Reeve—some of them were corkers." Among other publications, a series of advertisements was run from February 1919 on in such popular adventure publications as *The Argosy, The Popular Magazine, People's Favorite Magazine, The Blue Book Magazine,* and various others. Considerable thought went into the promotion, and the advertisements were changed monthly with a different intriguing situation from one of the stories highlighting each advertisement with illustrations. Sales were extraordinarily good, and the set, titled on the binding "Craig Kennedy Stories" and on the title pages "The Craig Kennedy Series," is more common in used book stores than single copies of Arthur B. Reeve's books.

Arthur B. Reeve was born October 15, 1880, in Patchogue, Long Island, and died August 9, 1936, at the age of fifty-five in Trenton, New Jersey.

A graduate of New York Law School, Arthur B. Reeve never established a practice, but entered the editorial field as an assistant editor on *Public Opinion* from 1903 to 1906 and then moving on to the editorship of *Our Own Times* from 1907 to 1910. His first serious writing was nonfiction, initially on the potentials of the human mind, and then a series on crime detection contributed to *Survey,* a magazine of social reform on whose staff he briefly served during 1907, which was concerned with laboratory methods of solving crimes.

During 1908 he contributed several articles to Frank A. Munsey's *The Live Wire,* the first magazine in history printed entirely in two colors or more, including one with the marathon title of "Towering Buildings, that Grab Gales from the Skies, Snatch Electricity from the Earth, and in many Other Ways 'Butt In,'" in its March issue.

When *The Live Wire* was absorbed by *The Scrap Book,* he contributed more than a dozen articles in 1909, 1910, and 1911 on subjects as different as "'Why Not' Own Your Own Home" (March 1910) to "Cipher Secrets Revealed" (December 1910). In essence he was a journalist and the sale of fiction made up almost an invisible part of his income, if any, before the advent of the Craig Kennedy series.

Yet, he had both an interest in writing fiction and in the fantastic aspect of fiction even at college. While attending Princeton University, from which he was graduated in 1903 before going on to New York Law School, he was a contributor to that institution's *The Nassau Literary Magazine.* He wrote a very fine critique titled "Rudyard Kipling" for its October 1902 issue, in which he said of that author: "To him, the phantom 'rickshaw, and the pit of the cataleptics, where dwell 'the dead who died not, yet may not live,' and the ghostly billiard players of the dâk bungalow, are matters of familiar story. In depicting the weird, the mysterious and occult, none other save one has excelled him—on Kipling has fallen the mantle of Poe, which rested for so brief a while upon the shoulders of Guy de Maupassant."

The previous year he had written for the May 1901 issue of *The Nassau Literary Magazine* a fantasy titled "The Golf Dream," regarding a gridiron star and master golfer, who, while drowsing on a hammock, dreams he is approached by a stranger named Colonel Bogey with whom he takes to the links. After a close game he is defeated by one stroke, but as he turns to tender his congratulations, the stranger is nowhere in sight. Far more significant than the story is the name of the hero, which is Craig Kennedy!

In a later biographical sketch in *Dime Detective,* Arthur B. Reeve attempted to establish priority over Edwin Balmer and William B. MacHarg for the creation of a scientific detective by citing this early story, difficult to check outside of Princeton University's own library. *It is not the same Craig Kennedy and it is not by the remotest logic a detective story.*

After World War I, a more mature Reeve sensed that the trend was changing. Craig Kennedy stories, written in a style barely a notch above Tom Swift juveniles, were not going to catch the public's fancy forever.

Arthur B. Reeve dropped the old formula, and in his novel *The Soul Scar* (Harper's, 1919) used Freud's theories on the nature of dreams as the basis for a much more mature plot.

We find Craig Kennedy stating: "Anxiety may originate in psychosexual excitement—the repressed libido, or desire, as the Freudians call it. Neurotic fear has its origin in sexual life and corresponds to a libido, or desire, which has been turned away from its object and has not succeeded in being applied." The lie-detector tests remain, but are administered much more half-heartedly. Craig Kennedy became a philosopher, deeply immersed in psychoanalysis, moralizing on life, death, and sex in

Atavar, the Dream Dancer (Harper's, 1924). In that book, the outline juvenility of earlier volumes disappeared, even from the chapter headings.

On the basis of that novel and other stories, Arthur B. Reeve claimed that he wrote the "first story with the Freud theory before Freud was even translated." At first glance that seemed to be true, but on investigation it develops that Edwin Balmer and William MacHarg, in a never-reprinted and little-known Luther Trant story titled "The Daughter of a Dream," which appeared in *Hampton's Magazine* for June 1911, based a story on Freud's theory of dreams.

Edith Coburn has repeatedly had dreams in which she finds she cannot keep up with hosts of other people ascending a staircase. As she falls behind, another woman always takes her hand and leads her away.

Luther Trant, utilizing the techniques of Freud, reveals to Edith Coburn that she is the daughter of a Negress. The woman who comes in the dream is her mother, Linette. The meaning of the dream is that she cannot hope to enter into or keep up with the white world. The dreams are caused every time the odor of prussic acid is present, which triggers an associational response. Unable to accept the facts of life, Edith Coburn takes poison.

The Ellery Queen duo writing in their book *Queen's Quorum* (reissued by Biblio & Tannen, 1969) included *The Achievements of Luther Trant* as one of the 125 most important detective works ever written on the basis of historical importance as well as quality and also stated that it "has been the victim of indifference and neglect."

The exact circumstances whereby Arthur B. Reeve connected with his Craig Kennedy stories at *Cosmopolitan* are not clear. Probably it was a chance submission. He had the scientific education and knowledge of criminology to write the scientific detective story, but had been writing virtually no fiction. Having launched the character in that magazine, which for the next seven years rarely published an issue without Craig Kennedy, it is puzzling that he was permitted to sell stories with the same character elsewhere—but he was!

A short novel, *The Treasure Vault,* led off the July 1, 1912, issue of *The Popular Magazine* and solved a problem and crime with the use of a telautograph, an apparatus for transmission of writing by long distance over the telephone. This was followed by a two-part novel beginning in the April 1, 1913, issue of the same magazine, titled *The Death Thought,* dealing with a criminal's attempt to dispose of a body by freezing it with liquid air at a temperature of 320 degrees below zero so that it would crystallize and then shatter into tiny particles. Both stories were up to Reeve's standards of that period and did not read like rejects.

Adventure magazine also published Craig Kennedy in 1913.

Arthur B. Reeve ran another series of stories about a scientific detective named Guy Garrick in *Red Book Magazine.* A representative story was "In the Cave of Aladdin" in the June 1914 issue, where a Selenium cell is put inside a bank vault that is being systematically robbed even though it is apparently impenetrable; the cell rings a bell if a light goes on. Guy Garrick is a younger man than Craig Kennedy, but a scientific genius who puts his talent to work to defeat crime. These stories were collected under the title of *Guy Garrick* by Harper's in 1914.

The scientific detective after World War I had lost its popularity in big time magazines of the standing of *Cosmopolitan,* but the residual interest of several million purchasers of Arthur B. Reeve's books in the United States and another million in England was still worth tapping for lesser magazines.

Everybody's Magazine, which had been one of the world's leading general magazines during the first decade of the century, had gone into a general decline, and in 1921 it dropped from large flat size to the same size as the pulps, still with slick paper, but with untrimmed edges, and printed entirely fiction. It picked up the idea of scientific detective stories which *Cosmopolitan* had dropped, and introduced with its December 1921 issue Dr. Goodrich, *"the new* scientific detective . . . His stories give us the scientific truths of the future in the guise of fiction." The new character was the creation of Stoddard Goodhue.

There were five Dr. Goodrich stories published in *Everybody's Magazine,* the first, "The Phantom Auto," in the December 1921 issue and the last, "The Subconscious Witness," in the February 1925 issue. Dr. Goodrich, who worked for the city police in a scientific capacity, was not as good as his advance notices. The level of thrills may be calculated by the novelette

The Magic Wheel, in February 1925, where he discovers that a roulette wheel is being controlled by radio signals from another room and with a little ingenuity interrupts the gambler's system and superimposes his own.

Arthur B. Reeve quite obviously recognized Dr. Goodrich as an opportunity for selling *Everybody's* and began a new series for it in the September 1923 issue with "Thicker Than Water," in which he solves a case by taking pore prints from forehead smears; brings a drowned girl back to life with a series of adrenalin shots right into the heart in "Dead Men Tell Tales" (October 1923); and uses "wireless" in "The Radio Wraith" to simulate a voice from the dead in a séance and solve a crime (November 1923).

Arthur B. Reeve was still an attractive name when the Frank A. Munsey Company, publishers of *Argosy-All Story,* issued a weekly companion of detective fact and fiction in a pulp format called *Flynn's* beginning with the issue of September 20, 1924. The titular editor of the magazine was William J. Flynn, renowned detective who had spent twenty-five years with the U.S. Secret Service.

The man behind the throne was Robert H. Davis, the editor whose innumerable major literary discoveries on *All-Story Magazine* and *Argosy-All Story* had earned him an international reputation. Robert Davis had been one of the earliest editors to buy from Arthur B. Reeve, offering a market as early as 1907 when essays and articles were all that was available. He had published very little by Reeve since that author had scored his success as a fiction writer. When Arthur B. Reeve entered his office in February 1924, possibly by invitation, since Davis was recruiting authors for *Flynn's,* he photographed him coming through the door. If this seems unusual, it should be stated that Davis was rated as possibly the world's leading amateur photographer of his period.

Discussing the various plot gambits that Reeve had covered, Davis suggested as new areas: "North, east, south, west; air, earth, fire water; seeing, hearing, tasting, smelling, feeling."

To the thirteen, Reeve added one more, "The sixth sense—common sense." *Flynn's* third issue, October 4, 1924, presented an entire new series of Craig Kennedy stories, four in number, dealing with air, fire, earth, and water individually. A photograph in four colors of Arthur B. Reeve in a laboratory setting was featured on the cover for the opening story, "Craig Kennedy and the Elements—Air."

In that story a plane comes down to earth with a dead pilot. There have been thirty similar engine failures by French planes over Germany, so the latter country is suspected of perfecting a deadly new ray. This merely confuses the issue until Craig Kennedy discovers that the pilot's death was actually due to a heart attack from insufficient air when an attempt at an altitude record is made.

The second story in the October 11, 1924, issue which dealt with fire, finds Craig Kennedy suspicious when the body of a dead woman glows slightly in the dark and he correctly surmises she has been poisoned by Radium salts and Phosphorus. The final two stories about earth and water lacked any scientific ingenuity or originality whatsoever.

There were two other similar series, *Craig Kennedy and the Compass,* beginning in the December 13, 1924, issue, in which four consecutive stories involving North, East, South, and West were the motif; and another on the Six Senses, beginning with the January 31, 1925, issue. Both of these series featured four-color cover photographs of Craig Kennedy, but the stories were run-of-the-mill and the science in them was small and strained.

The three series were collected in a book titled *The Fourteen Points,* published in 1925 by Grosset and Dunlap with an introduction by Robert H. Davis telling of the origin of the stories and prefaced by the photograph he took of Arthur B. Reeve walking through his office door.

Robert H. Davis, whose past editorial record had shown an exceptional interest in publishing science fiction and fantasy, did not bar them from *Flynn's.* There were two in the November 12, 1924, issue, "Hate That Would Not Die" by Maurice Coons, where detective Hartley Learned solves the murder of a judge as actually committed by an ape into whose skull has been transplanted the brain of a criminal whom the judge had sentenced to death; "Murder Music," by Douglas Newton, a British author who wrote a great deal of science fiction, told of a series of deaths of men and women while listening to music by players who have developed notes that can kill certain people. A particularly interesting plot was that of a man who invents a hush machine, suggested by Hiram Maxim, that muffles all sound, so that a shot from a gun cannot be heard, as told by Robert Russell in his story "The Silent Menace" published in the June 6, 1925, number.

Though the scientific detective was becoming less common in the general magazines, interest stirred from a most unexpected source. Hugo Gernsback, then publisher of *Electrical Experimenter*, was in the process of changing that magazine into *Science & Invention* and had started a policy of featuring two pieces of fiction an issue. He was no particular detective-story fan, but he liked the idea of exploring the capacities of the utilization of science to commit crimes or to catch criminals. "Educated Harpoon" by Charles S. Wolfe in the last, April 1920, *Electrical Experimenter* was his first scientific crime story, and quite appropriately was illustrated by the late famed science fiction artist Frank R. Paul. An executive is stabbed to death in his office on the sixteenth floor of a skyscraper. Three secretaries vow no one got in or out of his office, and no clues present themselves, not even the murder weapon. Joe Fenner, a student, wireless telegrapher, and scientific dabbler, deduces that a tiny gasoline-engine-powered airplane, guided by radio from a skyscraper a quarter of a mile away, flew through an open window, struck the victim in the back, reversed its propellers, and took off with the needlelike dagger which extended from it.

Scientific detective Joe Fenner became almost a monthly feature and among his best ideas were those in "The Phantom Arm" (*Science & Invention*, June 1920), where a rifle is automatically fired at a moving target by a man playing pool miles away; "The Master Key" (*Science & Invention*, August 1920), in which an electromagnet is used to get a man out of a room bolted on both sides; and "The Devil's Understudy" (*Science & Invention*, March 1921), involving electrocution by a current conveyed on a beam of ultraviolet light.

Scientific detective stories were contributed by many other authors, including Harold F. Richard's "The Unknown Avenger" (September 1920), dealing with the use of Radium as an ingenious killing agent; Nellie E. Gardner's "A Subconscious Murderer" (October 1922), employing an actual patented invention of Hugo Gernsback's, the hypnobioscope, a device for learning while one is asleep, as the means of accomplishing a murder; and "Hunting Criminals in the Year 2,000 A.D.," translated from the German of Felix L. Goeckeritz (May 1923).

During the same period scientific detective stories appeared frequently in *Radio News*, a companion to *Science and Invention*, also published by Hugo Gernsback.

Until the first issue of *Amazing Stories* was published, dated April 1926, there was no way of judging whether the science fiction specialists regarded any portion of the scientific detective stories as within their domain. The affirmative answer came when Hugo Gernsback ran Edwin Balmer and William MacHarg's Luther Trant story "The Man Higher Up" in the December 1926 *Amazing Stories*. This was followed by "The Eleventh Hour" (February 1927), "The Hammering Man" (March 1927), and "The Man in the Room" (April 1927), the latter receiving the *cover* by Frank R. Paul, showing in detail the equipment required to measure a woman's reaction to the word-association test. Of particular interest was the reprinting of "The Hammering Man" (a sphygmograph records rise and fall of blood pressure to ascertain truth), for this story, which originally appeared in *Hampton's Magazine*, was never included in the book. This meant that Gernsback's reprint consultants had obtained the story from its original magazine source, a fact further made logical by their reprinting in June 1926 of "An Experiment in Gyro Hats" by Ellis Parker Butler (a stovepipe hat with a gyroscope to keep drunks from falling down on their way home), which appeared originally in *Hampton's Magazine*, June 1910.

From *Science & Invention*, *Amazing Stories* also reprinted Charles Wolfe's scientific detective stories "The Educated Harpoon" (December 1926) and "The Master Key" (April 1928). However, his most interesting tack was the introduction of five different criminologists, all patterned to a great extent after Luther Trant and Craig Kennedy: Robert Goodwin, scientist, inventor, and "head of the great Chicago laboratory and experimental plant which bore his name," utilizes a sphygmomanometer (blood pressure recorder), a dictaphone to bug conversations, a camera which automatically takes photos of burglars, as well as fingerprints, to trap men who try to sell him stolen platinum in "White Gold Pirate" by Merlin Moore Taylor (April 1927); Dr. Edmund Curtis Thorne, an anthropologist with a deep insight into criminal psychology is almost proved brilliantly wrong in solving a "murder" which develops to be an accident in "The Psychological Solution" by A. Hyatt Verrill (January 1928); Prof. Fiske Errell, world's greatest criminologist, foils Oriental Lakh-Dal, who has a machine for driving men insane in "Lakh-Dal—Destroyer of Souls" by W. F. Hammond (March 1928); while David S. Harris, investigator of crime, rated the cover of the July 1928 *Amazing Stories,* for blocking thefts conducted through transferring matter by radio (with a female genius the culprit) using a sphygmomanometer in the process in "Super Radio" by Charles Cloukey; and Dr. Milton Jarvis proves that atomic hydrogen welding has made it possible to cut open a bank vault and *seal* it up again in "The Atomic Doom" by Edward S. Sears in *Amazing Stories Quarterly,* Winter 1928.

By far the most remarkable detective Hugo Gernsback's authors ever produced, and the one who scored the biggest impact with the readers, was a little man named Taine of San Francisco, who made his debut in four short stories titled "The Menace," published together in the Summer 1928 *Amazing Stories Quarterly.* The stories may never be reprinted again because their theme deals with Negroes who have perfected a chemical for turning their skins white. They have secured a method of economically extracting gold from seawater and are systematically buying up blocks of New York and renting apartments only to Negroes. It is their intent to buy all of New York, turn Negroes' skins white, and usurp the white power structure. Many exchanges of conversation are brutal in their directness. For example, when Taine of San Francisco is caught in his investigations by a Negro woman, Ebony Kate, who runs a new religion to recruit adherents to the projects, and as he is to be fed to a thirty-foot boa constrictor, he tells her: "You are not really trying for justice but for revenge. You may turn the black man white but ultimately he will remain—just—a—nigger."

An attempt to turn all the whites in New York black by slipping a chemical in the water system is foiled by Taine, as was a previous effort to flood the United States with synthetic gold. An epidemic of insanity due to the prevalence of glass construction of buildings is laid to the white-Negro machinations. After thirty years Taine tracks the Negro leaders to their island lair, does them in, all except Ebony Kate, who comes back to San Francisco with him to work as a domestic. "In the years that followed Ebony Kate delighted in telling the little Taines how

their grandfather and she had fought those white-black boog-
ers."

What the plot outline cannot reveal was David H. Keller,
M.D.'s insight into sociological problems, not only of race but
those brought about by increasing mechanization. As to his
detective, Taine's one great talent was at disguise. In person he
was so undistinguished as to be difficult to remember. He often
carried a puppy around in his pocket. He made $200 a month
(supplementing it from special assignments), was completely
henpecked by his wife, suffered from dyspepsia, and when offered a cigarette would reply: "No thank you, I never smoke,
for nicotine injures the delicate enamel of the teeth and once
that is gone, decay soon follows." No one knew that he had a
false set of uppers and lowers!

While "The Menace" derived its theme from discrimination
against the Negro, *The Feminine Metamorphisis,* a short novel
in Hugo Gernsback's new August 1929 *Science Wonder Stories*
(started after losing *Amazing Stories* and *Amazing Stories
Quarterly*), employed prejudice against women as the reason
5,000 outstanding females decide to be operated upon and be
given male characteristics so they can dispense entirely with
the unfair sex. Taine cracks the case disguised as a woman.

The scientific detective story had not completely disappeared from *Flynn's Weekly* (changed to *Detective Fiction*
with June 18, 1927, and *Detective Fiction Weekly* with June 2,
1928). A series by Douglas Newton on the archvillain Odoric
Dyn, a Norwegian who set out to form a master race of Nordics
to rule the "serf races" (all dark-haired or dark-skinned people),
is hunted and finally destroyed by Raphel Phare and Martin
Sondes in six exciting bonafide science fiction stories starting
with "Gold and White Beauties" (*Flynn's Weekly*, March 26,
1927) and concluding with the destruction of a scientific island
community in "The City of Tomorrow" (*Flynn's Weekly*, April
30, 1927). The stories were collected under the title of *Dr. Odin*
and published by Cassell, London, in 1933. Arthur B. Reeve's
new Craig Kennedy stories appearing in *Detective Fiction
Weekly* in 1929 seemed rather unimaginative after Odoric
Dyn.

Despite this, Hugo Gernsback was now the leading proponent of the scientific detective story of the type originated by
Arthur B. Reeve, and he launched the first and only magazine

in history specializing in such stories, titled *Scientific Detective Monthly*, with the first issue dated January 1930. Arthur B. Reeve was made "editorial commissioner" (though he had no editorial power) and a Craig Kennedy story ran in *each* issue, all reprints from his first few years of writing. The magazine was large format, containing ninety-six pages, and in addition to the Craig Kennedy story "The Mystery of the Bulawayo Diamonds," solved by a bolometer which "can measure the heat of a woman's blush," the issue contained the Luther Trant story "The Fast Watch," a serialization of *The Bishop Murder Case* by S. S. Van Dine, featuring Philo Vance, and detective stories by science fiction writers R. F. Starzl, Captain S. P. Meek, U.S.A., and Ralph Wilkins.

In his editorial Hugo Gernsback stated: "And while *Scientific Detective Stories* may print detective stories whose scenes lie in the future, it should be noted that whatever is published in this magazine is based on real science; and whatever will be published will be good science." Actually *Scientific Detective Monthly* was a science fiction magazine with the emphasis on crime detection.

Hugo Gernsback defined the stories he ran in *Scientific Detective Monthly* in his article "How to Write 'Science' Stories," published in the February 1930 *Writer's Digest*. His definition was: "A Scientific Detective Story is one in which the method of crime is solved, or the criminal traced, by the aid of scientific apparatus or with the help of scientific knowledge possessed by the detective or his co-workers."

Most issues ran a Craig Kennedy and a Luther Trant story; Taine of San Francisco regularly chronicled his youthful experiences before he became a big time scientific detective, and a Dr. Thorndyke story by R. Austin Freeman was resurrected. A new scientific detective, the Electrical Man, Miller Rand, was created for the May 1930 issue by Neil R. Jones, author of the famed Professor Jameson series in science fiction. The Electrical Man wears bulletproof clothing, including his mask, gloves, and socks. His clothing is electrified, stunning any man who touches it, and his power is transmitted to him by radio.

After five issues the magazine found it wasn't making it, so with its June 1930 number the name was changed to *Amazing Detective Tales*. The content remained the same, but covers which were usually technical and had even included radio-powered robots were changed to scenes of horror. The editor, Hector G. Gray, was dropped with the July 1930 issue and David Lasser, who edited *Wonder Stories* and *Wonder Stories Quarterly*, assumed the duties. Science fiction writers Otis Adelbert Kline, Clark Ashton Smith, Ralph Milne Farley, Ed Earl Repp, and Eugene George Key were among those who contributed, but the publication received little support from either the science fiction or the detective fans. With the advantage of hindsight, it is possible to say that the magazine was extraordinarily good *for what it purported to be,* rounding up all the then-available talent and cultivating some of its own. With the tenth issue, October 1930, it announced it was going pulp size, but no further numbers appeared under Hugo Gernsback.

A story titled "Murder on the Moonship," by British author George B. Beattie, was announced as forthcoming and was published in the February 1931 *Wonder Stories* instead. It promulgated five mysterious deaths on a spaceship with the finger of suspicion pointing everywhere. The killer turns out to be a poisonous prehistoric flying reptile brought back to life by space radiations and the emanations from the atomic engines. Beattie's story was a harbinger, Craig Kennedy would continue to appear elsewhere, but the lie detector, a marvelous adjunct to a detective in the year 1909, was by 1929 a rather unexciting device. The scientific detective could no longer sustain an audience with a gadget alone. Arthur B. Reeve had early added Freudian sex to gadgetry, a formula which made Ian Fleming's James Bond the sensation of the sixties, but he took himself too seriously in his crusading and failed to arouse interest.

Hugo Gernsback sold his title *Amazing Detective Tales* to Wallace R. Bamber, an air-story writer who had raised some money and begun publication of *Far East Adventure Stories,* a magazine in certain respects similar to Farnsworth Wright's *Oriental Tales.* It was Bamber's opinion in 1930 that the pulp western was on the decline and that the adventure and the action gangster story was on the rise. He raised some capital and organized Fiction Publishers Inc., at 158 W. 10th St., New York. Having already launched an adventure magazine, *Amazing Detective Tales* was to provide the second hedge to his market appraisals of pulp categories on the rise. Writing in the December 1930 *Author & Journalist,* he stated: "We have reduced the size to the standard seven by ten and increased the number of pages from 96 to 128. No longer will detective stories with a particularly amazing or scientific slant be used, but in their stead the standard, orthodox detective yarn . . . No unusual stuff, just the same old hokum that has been shoved down the detective readers' throats for a decade or so, with a tendency, if there is any variance, to a little more action and blood-spilling than in the old deductive detective yarn."

Amazing Detective Tales was published under the new owner, arousing for many years a controversy, unresolved until now, as to whether or not it had any relationship to Gernsback's magazine, since the content of the revival was so antipodal. *Far East Adventure Stories* did well for at least a short while, offering in late 1931 rates up to four cents a word. It did not survive long, nor establish a pulp magazine genre.

One series which did survive *Amazing Detective Tales* was Taine of San Francisco.

Readers loved the droll and laconic Taine, who, when introducing himself to a prospective client in "Euthanasia Limited" (*Amazing Stories Quarterly,* Fall 1929), said: "Some weeks ago you asked the Chief of the New York Secret Service to send you a detective that was brilliant and at the same time looked like an imbecile. I am the man, Taine, from San Francisco." A master of disguise, Taine solved that case by posing as an Oriental servant, uncovering a device that drained all electrical current from the human body, producing death from no seeming cause.

When the head of Secret Service at Washington, D.C., sends to San Francisco for the best man they have to help them solve the baffling disappearance of 503 college students in "The Cerebral Library" (*Amazing Stories,* May 1931), Taine arrives.

"I never heard of you," is the complaint.

"That may be true," Taine replies. "But some of my best work has not been broadcast. I married the Chief's daughter. He likes me. Of course, she does too, but she is busy now, so the old man sent me. Want me?" Taine, now disguised as an Oriental surgeon, cracks the case in time to prevent the transplantation of the brains of the college students into an electronic complex that will form a great information bank.

Taine's last appearance in a science fiction magazine (exclusive of reprints) was in "The Tree of Evil" (*Wonder Stories,* September 1934), where he solved the mystery of an entire town that was slowly losing all notions of morality from a drug whose effects seem remarkably close to LSD. A nonscience fiction Taine story, "Hands of Doom," appeared in *10-Story Detective*, October 1947, where Taine proves that two great bronze praying hands, driven by a mechanism, did not crush the skulls of several victims, but were a decoy to distract attention from the real murderess.

Enough interest was created by his scientific detection to warrant the beginning of a "Scientific Detective Series" of booklets by ARRA Printers, Jamaica, New York, publishers of the early science fiction fan magazine, *Science Fiction Digest*. "Wolf Hollow Bubbles," a 6,000-word Taine of San Francisco story concerning cancer cells large enough to engulf a man, was published in May 1933, and autographed copies were advertised at ten cents. The action in the story takes place while Taine is still courting his wife. This was the only story issued in the Scientific Detective Series by this press.

The collected stories of Keller's popular little detective (including several never previously published) were announced for hard covers in 1948 by the Hadley Publishing Co., Providence, Rhode Island, under the title *Taine of San Francisco*, but never appeared.

The Taine stories were uneven in quality and loosely constructed. A number of them were not even science fiction. They were frequently imaginative, employed humor effectively, but their popularity rested in the creation of the character of Taine, who was a standout by any criteria.

A contributing reason for the popularity of the Taine of San Francisco stories was that when one was written for a *science fiction* magazine, it could qualify by the most stringent definition of the term as part of the genre. Though the publication of Hugo Gernsback's *Scientific Detective Monthly* and *Amazing Detective Tales* had done much to refine the art of the scientific detective story, progress was not continuous, nor was it uniform in all publications. The thinking of the science fiction editors of that day was that if a crime is committed or solved through the utilization of established scientific principles, it constituted a legitimate science fiction story, regardless of whether any element of fantasy was present.

Their logic was not shared by their readers for, other than Taine, scientific detective stories enjoyed small popularity, though editors continued to use them. An example in point was a 10,000-word novelette contributed by popular science fiction author A. Hyatt Verrill to the April 1930 *Amazing Stories* titled *The Feathered Detective*. In it, Big Ben, a former sailor, and his pet bird, a rare African tourace, are murdered. The tourace is a green bird, whose plumage runs red when wet. The murderer, who has come in out of the rain and wrung the bird's neck with wet hands, is caught by the red stain resulting from the bird's feathers. One otherwise unusual series that perpetuated this flow was written by A. L. Hodges; the first two stories, "The Pea Vine Mystery" and "The Dead Sailor," both appeared in *Amazing Stories* for May 1930, and were only 300 and 400 words long respectively. In the first, the man is strangled to death by fast-growing pea vines, and in the second, a sailor is killed by a chance bullet of water. The final story in the series, "The Mystery of Professor Brown" (*Amazing Stories*, August 1930), stretched to the interminable length of 600 words, solved the death of a lab instructor by showing that when he inserted his head momentarily into an electrical induction furnace, its action melted a piece of metal in his skull, causing it to drop through his brain.

Of the same order of interest, though much longer, was "The Radio Detective," by Lincoln S. Colby (*Amazing Stories*, May 1931), where interference of a radio set uncovers the fact that a former convict is slowly killing the judge who sentenced him by sending heavy dosages of X-rays through a wall into his bedroom.

Utilizing the same formula, Alfred John Olsen, Jr., a popular science fiction writer of fourth-dimensional stories, better known as Bob Olsen, inaugurated a new series built around the mental wizard Justin Pryor, head of the research department of the advertising firm of Wright and Underwood, with *The Master of Mystery* (*Amazing Stories*, October 1931). In that first story, a man found dead in bed with a crushed skull, in a locked, burglar-proofed room, is discovered to have been killed by the impact of a thirty-pound piece of dry ice placed to drop on his head. The evaporation of the ice eliminated the murder weapon. A second story, *Seven Sunstrokes* (*Amazing Stories*, April 1932), has seven prominent men dying of sunstroke induced by injections of a chemical that makes them overheat when subjected to ultraviolet rays. The third and final story in

145

the series, *The Pool of Death* (*Amazing Stories,* January 1933), may actually be classified as science fiction, when it is discovered that a man who has dived into a swimming pool and is never seen again has been digested by a massive amoeba. All of the stories were long novelettes.

Olsen also had published the first of what appeared to be a new scientific detective series, featuring "The Lone Monogoose," so named "because he's a whiz at hunting and killing snakes." The story, titled "The Crime Crusher" (*Amazing Stories,* June 1933), was based on a camera that could photograph events up to thirty days *past.*

The greater imagination which Olsen displayed as his stories continued to appear (and the diminution of other scientific detective stories without some note of fantasy) was to a degree forced by magazines and authors outside the science fiction field, among them Erle Stanley Gardner.

Today, the late Erle Stanley Gardner is renowned as one of the world's best-selling mystery authors, having hit the jackpot with Perry Mason. In 1928 he was a hard-working pulpster, no better known for his detectives than for his westerns. Stories of the western desert were his particular forte, and at times his western character, Bob Zane, became a desert detective, fortuitously combining two of his creator's strongest talents. Finding himself going stale on westerns, Gardner one day in 1928 outfitted a truck like a camp wagon and struck out across old prospectors' trails to recharge his plot banks. On the trail, a story he claims was told him by a prospector gave him the foundation for his first try at science fiction, "Rain Magic" (*Argosy,* October 20, 1928). That story, with its intriguing description of ants that build houses out of little sticks of wood, and malevolently bright monkey men, was a noteworthy effort. He didn't stop there, but went on to write a number of others, most of them short novels for *Argosy,* but none was to recapture the special charm of his first.

It was inevitable that he would attempt to incorporate the crime and detective theme into his science fiction, just as he had done in his desert yarns. "A Year in a Day" (*Argosy,* July 19, 1930) was based on a drug that could speed a person's movements up 100 times, enabling a murderer to enter a room filled with people, kill a selected victim before the eyes of all, and still remain unseen. In "The Human Zero" (*Argosy,* December 19,

1931), men vanish, leaving all their clothes on the floor, in the arrangement in which they were wearing them. It develops that electrical transmission of temperatures of absolute zero, through powder sprinkled on their hair, has shrunk their cells to the point where they disappeared.

Garrett Smith had written a prophetic harbinger of the use of closed-circuit television to guard against criminals in " 'You've Killed Privacy!' " (*Argosy,* July 7, 1928), which was a noteworthy effort, but undoubtedly the crime story in a science fiction setting that created the greatest impact during this period was Murray Leinster's "The Darkness on Fifth Avenue" (*Argosy,* November 30, 1929). In that story, a criminal discovers the means of plunging any given area into an abyss of impenetrable blackness. Armed with special lenses, his men can plunder at will. The efforts of the police force to offset the paralyzing effects of darkness and track down the culprit involve the use of blind men and hair-raising sequences where police cars run along the grooves of trolley tracks to keep them on the road. In referring to the supplementary crimes committed under the cloak of darkness by people in the darkened area, Leinster also provided graphic sociological comment. "Darkness on Fifth Avenue" was a true detective story, initially intended for *Detective Fiction Weekly,* but the three sequels, "The City of the Blind," "The Storm That Had to Be Stopped," and "The Man Who Put Out the Sun," involve so great an escalation of the scope and effectiveness of the scientific terrors that an evil genius is leveling against mankind that they become primarily tales of mass disaster and only incidentally detective stories.

Leinster would use the detective and scientific invention both in and out of the science fiction magazines. The title "The Sleep Gas" (*Argosy,* January 16, 1932) indicates a device employed by the criminal element to achieve their ends; "The Racketeer Ray" (*Amazing Stories,* February 1932) finds the bad guys with a gadget that can draw all metal to them as well as electrical current; and "The Mole Pirate" (*Astounding Stories,* November 1934), his banner achievement in this vein and one of his finest stories, concerning a scientific criminal, utilizes a machine that can move through the ground as a submarine moves through water.

The foregoing tales of Erle Stanley Gardner and Murray Leinster were actually popularizers and prototypes of a formula involving a criminal genius threatening a city, country, or planet with scientific horror and an official or specialized agent battling the menace. This formula would eventually form the entire basis of a magazine like *Operator 5* and become a plot bulwark for others such as *Doc Savage, The Spider, Secret Agent X,* and even to some degree *The Shadow.* To that extent their influence was even stronger on the pulp magazines as a body than it was on the science fiction magazines specifically.

Exposed to the obvious greater popularity of the more imaginative superscientific mysteries of the class of Erle Stanley Gardner and Murray Leinster, a less reserved plotting was inevitable in detective stories that appeared in the science fiction magazines. As early as 1930, Hugh B. Cave's "The Murder Machine" (*Astounding Stories of Super-Science,* September), told of the invention of a device by Michael Strange to hypnotize people at long distance and use them as murder tools. Edmond Hamilton's "Space Rocket Murders" (*Amazing Stories,* October 1932), added a somewhat more sophisticated dimension to science fiction when an investigation to solve a series of deaths of space rocket experimenters (including one named Braun) reveals that the disguised Venusians on Earth have been attempting to slow down Earth's progress in this direction until we become less combative.

Despite his outstanding attempts to popularize the detective story in science fiction with *Scientific Detective Monthly,* Hugo Gernsback had at times been as guilty as *Amazing Stories* of continuing to promote such stories without any true element of fantasy. Several such examples appeared in a group of neatly printed booklets he published titled "The Science Fiction Series," which sold through the mail for ten cents each or six for fifty cents. His June 1932 *Wonder Stories* announced six more titles in the series; No. Seventeen billed "two surprises for the lovers of scientific detective mysteries." The first, "The Spectre Bullet" by Thomas Mack, suggested live actors in conjunction with moving pictures, and had one of them murdered by a shot that ostensibly came from the screen; the second, "The Avenging Note" by Alfred Sprissler, contained nothing more scientific than a concealed poisoned needle, driven by a spring into a woman's finger when she attempted to tune a harp.

Yet it was Gernsback who would again make one more strong effort to give the scientific detective story a respected place in science fiction. Evidence that he would try again came in the blurb of "The Missing Hours" by Morton Brotman (*Wonder Stories*, April 1935), where he said: "An occasional scientific-detective story is well suited to this magazine, and the present one has much merit and everything that a good detective story should have." The story told of armored truck drivers who arrive at their destination hours late, with no memory of what happened in the lost time, except that their money is gone. Their undoing has been a hypnotic ray quite similar in action to the one in "The Murder Machine" by Hugh B. Cave.

What Gernsback was really up to was revealed in the same issue where it was announced: *"The Waltz of Death* by P. B. Maxon is our new serial starting next month, and we challenge you to show us a more satisfying scientific detective murder mystery."

In blurbing the first installment of the serial which appeared in the May 1935 *Wonder Stories*, Gernsback justified his experiment on the grounds "that *Liberty Magazine*, the well-known slick publication, which boasts of the largest magazine circulation, conducted a contest last year in which our present serial, 'The Waltz of Death,' was awarded honorable mention."

The Waltz of Death, judged by the mystery writing standards of its period, was a superior work. The author catches reader interest in the first few pages where the unexplained death of a young, healthy man sitting in an easychair in full view of a number of people is graphically described. This occurred with nothing more sinister than a piano recital of a Brahms waltz in progress. There was no mark on him, but a box of aspirins in his pocket had gone up in a puff of white powder as though the tablets had exploded.

Interest is sustained as an autopsy reveals that the dead man's insides are badly torn, as if from an internal explosion. The story concludes, after some 60,000 words of mystery, as a legitimate work of science fiction. The murderer turns out to be the pianist, who is also a scientist. He has been working on exploding the atom by the use of vibrations. He has succeeded in getting a limited explosion from the atoms in aspirin through repetition and buildup of certain sound dissonances. When he notes that a guest, who has inadvertently caused the death of the girl he loved, has taken three aspirins, he elaborately builds up the proper sound dissonances on the piano until the aspirins explode internally, accomplishing his purpose.

The Waltz of Death was a good story of its type, but an extremely bad story for Hugo Gernsback to have published in 1935. That was the year when his magazine *Wonder Stories* was fading under the competition of the "thought variant" story policies of the field-leading *Astounding Stories* edited by F. Orlin Tremaine. Readers were being fed an exciting diet of far-out themes, treatments, and handlings of science fiction. By contrast, British reader Sidney L. Birchby was right in complaining of *The Waltz of Death:* "It was the slowest waltz I've known. On and on for three months, taking up half the magazine. A marathon dance?"

The mystery of what happened to the author of *The Waltz of Death* was to prove more baffling than that posed in the story. P. B. Maxon's agent was the late Ed Bodin. A very close friend of F. Orlin Tremaine, Bodin had shown him the story first, but was correctly told that while a creditable mystery, it didn't fit in with the dynamic presentation of ideas that was building *Astounding Stories* at the time. Tremaine suggested *Wonder Stories* (inadvertently hurting his competition, which would sell out to Standard Magazines after its April 1936 number). *Wonder Stories* paid on publication, so many months passed between the time the story was first submitted and the check forwarded to the author. The letter containing the check was returned with the information: "no such party at this address." Notices in the writers' magazines produced no results.

When interest was expressed by Arcadia House, Inc., in putting the novel in hard covers under their Mystery House imprint, Ed Bodin managed to get a spot on Dave Elman's radio program "Contact," which specialized in appeals to people who had money coming to them. On October 12, 1940, 9:30 P.M., Ed Bodin described the details of his dilemma and asked anyone with information to get in touch with him. No reply was forthcoming.

F. Orlin Tremaine, in taking up the editorship of Bartholomew House, a paperback offshoot of McFadden Publications during World War II, remembered the novel, and placed it into soft covers under the imprint of "A Bart House Mystery" in 1944.

A trip to the last place of residence by Bodin finally disclosed that the author, P. B. Maxon, had dropped dead in a rented

150

room the very night he had mailed the manuscript.

The poor reaction to the publication of *The Waltz of Death* by the readership of *Wonder Stories* was not lost on the field. Scientific detective stories in science fiction magazines became infrequent, and publicity identifying them as such, rare. Outside the science fiction field an interesting series by Ray Cummings, who had on occasion done scientific detective stories in the past, ran in *Detective Fiction Weekly*. The first one, titled "Crimes of the Year 2,000" (May 11, 1935), was more a catalog of futuristic devices to be employed by crime fighters of tomorrow than a story: a bloodhound machine, electric eavesdropper, phonographic wrist voice recorder, helicopter air patrols, all contributing toward trapping a criminal bent on stealing $4 million in platinum from The Great Circle Flyer due from England. Gadgetry diminished in the second story, "The Television Alibi" (July 20, 1935), built around a triangle involving a female television entertainer. There were six stories in all, the last, "The Case of the Frightened Death," appearing in the July 24, 1937, *Detective Fiction Weekly*.

The first story in the series, while poor fiction, was on the right track as far as underscoring that crime detection of the future would involve a complex assortment of devices, not merely a single gadget which would serve as a criminal catchall. The later stories in the series strongly implied that advances in psychological knowledge would also play a role in tomorrow's criminology. Cummings, by 1935, had already gone into an almost hopeless storytelling and stylistic decline, but his work still contained useful lessons for the openminded writer.

As the Depression deepened in the 1930s, the most popular writers found their income sharply declining. While extremely versatile, doing some writing for the moving pictures and still managing to have an occasional book published, Arthur B. Reeve faced the reality that the popularity of his scientific detective, Craig Kennedy, had sharply fallen off. Craig Kennedy stories popped up in many magazines, as the editors found they could buy them just as cheaply as the works of any other pulp writer and wistfully hoped that a little of the magic might still attract the public.

With the date of January 1934, at the very depths of the Depression, Charles Spencer launched Fiction Guild, Inc., with the publication of two pulp magazines, *World Adventurer* and

World Man Hunters. Despite the services of Edgar Sisson, a former editor of *Cosmopolitan*, and Robert S. Ament, whose qualifications were not given, the magazines were a publishing disaster.

World Man Hunters had brought Arthur B. Reeve's Craig Kennedy back, but his performance, "Doped," in the February 1934 issue was far below par, concerning a crime which tied in the relationship of drugging horses to human addiction.

Later that year, Beacon Magazines, an alternate name for Standard Magazines, with Leo Margulies as director, introduced *Popular Detective* with the issue dated November 1934 and featured *Craig Kennedy Returns*, an action-packed novelette in which the villain is a neurotic robot. Leo Margulies asserts that Arthur B. Reeve was having great difficulty writing at the time, and he was paid a token fee to permit A. T. Locke to ghost-write that Craig Kennedy story for him and the others that followed in *Popular Detective*.

Arthur B. Reeve's path crossed that of a fantasy magazine when his novelette *The Death Cry* was the cover story of the May 1935 issue of *Weird Tales*. Otis Adelbert Kline was Reeve's agent, and Kline had been a contributor to *Weird Tales* off and on since its very first issue. He had sold Farnsworth Wright, the magazine's editor, on the possible appeal of a Craig Kennedy murder mystery with a weird note to it. Times were difficult, and *Weird Tales* was hoping it could attract the patronage of some of the detective pulp readers.

Reeve received $150 for the 16,000-word story of the strange murders committed by a sino-vampire-cat with poisoned fangs. Reeve had tried hard to give the story a weird note, even injecting as a character an old woman who believed in the supernatural. The trouble was that *Weird Tales* was the repository of imaginative talent the magnitude of H. P. Lovecraft, Clark Ashton Smith, C. L. Moore, Robert E. Howard, Seabury Quinn, Robert Bloch, and Henry Kuttner, and alongside of these, Arthur B. Reeve's best was pallid. The editor admitted that there was considerable criticism from the readers of the story, and said that future "detective" stories would be truly supernatural.

Reeve managed to get a novel published by Appleton-Century in 1936, *The Stars Scream Murder*, and having set up residence in Trenton, New Jersey, was apparently working in some capacity for a Philadelphia newspaper. Reeve was suffering acutely from asthma when he was assigned to cover the Lindbergh kidnapping trial in Flemington, New Jersey. The Sunday night before the end of the trial he got a cardiac asthma attack so bad that a priest gave him extreme unction at 2:00 A.M. Monday morning, after the doctor had left for a second time, he got up, shaved, and drove twenty-five miles to Flemington, to hear the summation of the trial and filed his story.

He went again on Tuesday for the Wilentz summation and filed another story. That night he received another severe attack that required opiates to ease the pain.

Wednesday, he dragged himself to the court room for the verdict. Then, in the penultimate act of his reporting career, he secured a major scoop on the Hauptman verdict that would have made Craig Kennedy proud. In a letter to Leo Margulies dated February 27, 1935, he wrote: "Meanwhile Red Gallagher and Frank Roughill and myself snipped a telephone wire that ran down outside my window in court. Drew in the live ends. Our wire upstairs, anyway. Clipped in. We had a direct wire from inside the court room to the city desk in Philadelphia! Bunched up under eagle eyes of state troopers and deputy sheriffs, after court doors locked when jury came in, Red and I whispered running story of verdict to Roughill under table. Slammed Associated Press fake report extras of Life Imprisonment, scooped all the other papers, Associated Press, News, with indoor wireless, everybody, one of big unprincipled scoops of modern news. Then I collapsed. Been in bed ever since. But what a time! I feel as if I had brought Craig Kennedy back with a bang."

Apparently he had been discussing the idea of a Craig Kennedy detective magazine with Leo Margulies, for in the same letter he wrote: "How comes the Craig Kennedy magazine idea? I think I've brought Craig back with a bang. Made plenty of friends down there too. Surely there must be something doing with the Craig Kennedy idea. I may go in the gutter but Craig isn't going in the gutter. No more. I believe there's a big chance."

The following year, August 9, 1936, asthma, a bronchial condition, and his heart killed him at the age of fifty-five.

Had he lived, Arthur B. Reeve would have continued to push Craig Kennedy, and there would have been further appearances on an ever-less-frequent scale. His character had outlived its popularity. The novelty of the gadgetry and the use of the scientific method to solve crime sufficed for a time, but Arthur B. Reeve, though he had a good story sense and could create an emotional drive as he wound his stories to a conclusion, was far too sparsely journalistic in style to have continuing reader acceptance. His stories did teach the lesson of the appeal of special devices and gimmicks to readers. In the years that followed these gadgets were to grow in ingenuity and imagination. Dick Tracy, the famed comic-strip detective started in 1931, utilized everything from a wrist-watch radio to a space ship. The futuristic gadget is also just as essential to an Ian Fleming espionage story as is the sex.

The value of Craig Kennedy's full supply of modern gadgetry was not lost on Ed Earl Repp, a science fiction writer discovered by Hugo Gernsback in 1929, whose "laboratory sleuth" John Hale carried with him in addition to a gun, a kit which included a spectroscopic pistol which "shot" defracted light onto a photographic plate, instantly revealing its elemental components, an electroscope for detecting radioactivity, one camera with fast film, and a second with infrared film and a thermometer which registered automatically both the high and low temperature of any object it came in contact with. He used all of these to solve the appearance of a low-temperature apparition in "The Scientific Ghost" (*Amazing Stories*, January 1939), created through the use of "frozen light."

John Hale was carried through five adventures in *Amazing Stories*, all competently written on a fast-action pulp level and all terribly hackneyed in plot but creditably imaginative scientifically. Their popularity, however, never rose above "filler" status in the eyes of the reader.

The issue that carried the initial John Hale story also carried "I, Robot," by Eando Binder, the mechanical "man" who provided inspiration for such masters as Isaac Asimov and Clifford D. Simak. The robot had appeared many times before as the agent of a criminal, but in a later story in the series, "Adam Link, Robot Detective" (*Amazing Stories*, May 1940), Binder used him for the first time in the tradition of Sherlock Holmes. Adam Link's attempts to bring to justice those who have committed the murders his metal mate Eve Link is accused of may have planted the seed in the mind of Isaac Asimov for the

154

creation of R. Daneel Olivaw, the highly involved robot sleuth of *The Caves of Steel* and *The Naked Sun.*

To many authors, the solution of crime in a science fiction setting was little more than a tongue-in-cheek literary toy. Malcolm Jameson, in "Murder in the Time World" (*Amazing Stories,* August 1940), has the murderer send the corpse into the future in a time machine to get rid of it and follows only to find the police of tomorrow will have laid a trap for him; John York Cabot (pen name of David Wright O'Brien), in "Murder in the Past" (*Amazing Stories,* March 1941), sends a man into the past in a time vehicle to kill a friend who will betray him on the basis that "prevention is better than vengeance."

An alien sleuth appears in "Oscar, Detective of Mars" by James Norman, which was published in *Fantastic Adventures* for October 1940. Inexplicably brought to earth by the conjuring of Hodar, a stage magician, is a Martian four-feet-five-inches tall, with a feathered bottom and a humanlike face except for a tulip-shaped nose. It is this last characteristic which makes him so effective at detection, because Martians converse by odor, and Oscar can read the odors of everyone he meets and the places he visits. Another powerful advantage is a skin so tough that bullets bounce off it. In the first story, he uncovers a plot by an industrialist to take over the country with the aid of a fear serum, and pins a murder on the man in the process.

In the follow-up story, "Death Walks in Washington" (*Fantastic Adventures,* March 1941), he solves the death of a Senator, killing a raft of zombies with silver bullets in the process. There were three other stories, all in *Fantastic Adventures:* "Oscar Saves the Union" (September 1941), "Oscar and the Talking Totems" (April 1942), and "Double Trouble for Oscar" (October 1942). The stories were extremely lightweight, tongue-in-cheek entertainment, but the series was a better almalgamation of the detective story and science fiction than most.

Frederick C. Painton created for *Argosy* a group of stories written about the exploits of Joel Quaite, time detective. A misfit in the year 2500, Quaite and seven-foot Tex O'Hara are sent back by time machine to unravel mysteries of the past. The stories are not crime stories, for in the first, "The World That Drowned" (May 4, 1940), the men are sent back to Atlantis; in the second, "The Golden Empress" (October 5, 1940), Quaite adventures in the Byzantine Empire; and in the final short novel *The Dawn-Seekers* (April 19 and 26, 1941), to the days of Neanderthal man. In each story he seeks to unravel the truth or falsity of history and legend. A unifying link is the girl Neith, met in Atlantis and discovered reincarnated in Byzantium.

The most remarkable group of stories to arise out of this experimentation were those built around John Carstairs, Botanical Detective. Whether it was in tracking down a diamond plant (which eats carbon and excretes diamonds), a denizen of Uranus, stolen from The Interplanetary Botanical Gardens in the United States in his first story "Plants Must Grow" (*Thrilling Wonder Stories,* October 1941), or using plants to capture criminals as in "Snapdragon" (*Thrilling Wonder Stories,* December 1941), all the cases contrived by author Frank Belknap Long involve his detective's speciality.

Six of the eight stories in the series, including the final novel *The Hollow World* (*Startling Stories,* Summer 1945), where John Carstairs strains his botanical talents to best an entire plant kingdom on the newly discovered twelfth planet, were collected into a book titled *John Carstairs, Space Detective* (Frederick Fell, 1949). Highly original conceptions of interplanetary plant life are thrown at the reader with a fecundity which is admirable. However, the stories were written at fast pulp tempo, and stretches of awkward writing (from a man who is generally a superior stylist), as well as careless plotting, tend to give the collection a teen-age cast.

One of the stories in this otherwise offbeat series, "Plants Must Slay" (*Thrilling Stories,* April 1942), in which John Carstairs must contend with an invisible plant that murders humans with a gun, was included in *The Saint's Choice of Impossible Crime,* ghost-edited for Leslie Charteris by Oscar J. Friend and published in paperback by Bond-Charteris Enterprises, Los Angeles, 1945. The collection, the first of its type, was an acknowledgement that random scientific detective stories were again arousing interest. Included, in addition to Long, was the inevitable Simon Templar novelette about a criminal who had a process for making synthetic gold and how the Saint, true to his title, resisted the temptation to appropriate the method, in *The Gold Standard,* by Leslie Charteris (taken from *The Saint and Mr. Teal,* Doubleday, 1933). Just as inevitably, the two best stories in the collection were not even crime stories, and only by a stretch of the imagination could it be said that a crime was even committed: "The Impossible Highway," by Oscar J. Friend, and "Trophy," by Henry Kuttner.

However, represented in the anthology was Frederic Brown, an outstanding writer of crime stories, with *Daymare*—"a mystery novel of the future" (*Thrilling Wonder Stories,* Fall 1943) —where Rod Caquer, of the Callisto police, solves a murder in the best modern tradition and in the process foils a plot to enslave the minds of mankind. This story presaged the entrance into the scientific detective field of a crack professional capable of homogenizing both the detective story and the science fiction story into an acceptable blend.

There would eventually be other anthologies of scientific detective stories revealing those whose interests straddled both fields. *The Science-Fictional Sherlock Holmes,* edited and published in hardcover by Robert C. Peterson, Colorado, 1960, contained stories by Anthony Boucher, Mack Reynolds and August W. Derleth, Poul Anderson and Gordon Dickson, and H. Beam Piper and John J. McGuire, all from science fiction magazines and all pastiches of Sherlock Holmes. A paperback collection, *Space, Time & Crime,* edited by Miriam Allen de Ford (Paperback Library, 1964), included good representation of science fiction that dealt with elements of crime and detection, all from science fiction magazines of the period 1949 to 1964. The intent of this collection was to publish a selection that would be equally at home in a science fiction or a detective magazine. All had a good blending of both elements, including authors as distinguished as Isaac Asimov, Fritz Leiber, Fred Pohl, Frederic Brown, and Poul Anderson, among others.

Hans Stefan Santesson carried the idea one step further and into hard covers in his anthology *Crime Prevention in the 30th Century* (Walker, 1969), which aimed at presenting stories of crimes of the future, using tools of the future and fought by methods of the future. Three of the stories in the volume were written especially for it. Several had strong elements of humor and there was a growing taste of sophistication.

Inspirator and godfather to the first two of the anthologies was Anthony Boucher. One of the nation's leading mystery story critics and a distinguished writer in that field, his remarkable mystery novel, *Rocket to the Morgue,* under the pen name of H. H. Holmes (Duell, Sloan and Pierce, 1942), dealt with the murder of the son of one of the world's greatest science fiction writers. The reading of this mystery by the noninitiate would provide an insight into the world of science fiction as well as an appraisal of the science fiction authors and their fans. The book was appropriately dedicated to "The Manana Literary Society and in particular for Robert Heinlein and Cleve Cartmill." Mack Reynolds would produce a mystery novel of a similar stripe for Phoenix Press in 1951, *The Case of the Little Green Men,* which contained a fascinating mélange of material about the science fiction world.

As might be expected with such influential enthusiasts, the scientific detective story began to appear with increasing frequency and more often than not was written with professional competence. What could not be anticipated was that its practitioners would actually achieve the "impossible," in this case, the creation of a valid detective story that was at the same time a true science fiction story. Boucher made references to this challenge in *Rocket to the Morgue* when he referred to an author he believes has succeeded in this task: "Don's John W. Campbell always maintained that a detective science fiction story was by definition impossible, but wait till you read that one."

Boucher would go on to edit *The Magazine of Fantasy and Science Fiction,* but ironically, it was Campbell who published the first of the great masterpieces that science fiction was to produce in this vein, *Needle,* by Hal Clement, a two-part novel beginning in *Astounding Science-Fiction* for May 1949. In that novel, an alien detective is chasing an alien criminal through space and both ships crash on Earth. The aliens are symbiotes that must live within another creature. The problem of the Hunter, the space detective, is to discover *which* of the billions of humans is host to his quarry. The plot and its development was then as unique to science fiction as it was to the detective story.

Still another competing editor, Horace L. Gold, was to reap the harvest of the seeds of Boucher's literary faith in a brilliantly written novel of murder in the future, *The Demolished Man,* by Alfred Bester (*Galaxy Science Fiction,* January 1952), based on a man who tries to get away with murder in a society where the law enforcement agents employ Espers who can *read minds.* The truly powerful theme, rendered in a verbal frenzy rhetorically as startling as must have been the first exhibition of the dance steps of the Charleston, created an instantaneous and deserved reputation for Bester.

The second achievement of *Galaxy* in the scientific detection of tomorrow was the most inspired of all. It was written by Isaac Asimov, who had previously built two reputations in science fiction, one with his robot stories and the three laws of robotics and the second with his Foundation series of the galactic empire.

The Caves of Steel (*Galaxy Science Fiction,* October-November-December 1953) is the supreme masterpiece to date of the detective story in science fiction, so much so that it has received mention in at least one important book on the development of crime fiction. As story background, eight billion people of earth live in steel labyrinths and fifty underpopulated worlds of the galaxy are attempting, unsuccessfully, to recruit colonists in face of an antiprogressive trend. In this setting, the detective Lije Baley, assigned the task of solving a murder with interstellar implications, is given as an assistant a robot, R. Daneel Olivaw, who he fears is out to replace him. Bizarre and novel, it is a fine job.

A sequel, *The Naked Sun* (*Astounding Science-Fiction*, October-November-December 1965), where the same pair solve an unlikely murder on a world where people are repelled by personal contact and conduct their business by television, presented a fascinating situation.

The detective in science fiction is broadening his range to the entire galaxy, affirming for the science fiction author the old axiom: "The difficult we can do right away, the impossible just takes a little longer!"

TEEN-AGERS:

Tom Swift and the Syndicate

If, as claimed, the link that holds the chain of memory together is association, many thousands of those viewing and even participating in a demonstration of the video telephone at the building of The American Telephone and Telegraph Company at The New York World's Fair, held during 1964 and 1965 in Flushing Meadows, must instantly have recalled *Tom Swift and His Photo Telephone.* Tom Swift was but one of over 300 separate series of low-priced books of adventure for boys which formed a conspicuous and nostalgic part of the literary scene in the United States from the turn of the century until the Great Depression.

Tom Swift and His Photo Telephone or The Picture That Saved a Fortune, by Victor Appleton, was first published in 1914 and was the seventeenth book to deal with the inventions of the youthful Tom Swift. By all odds it was also the most remarkable one. It is the longest single story ever written around the subject of a photo telephone, and it came to grips not only with the problem of image transmission, but of automatically photographing the party during a conversation, while simultaneously making a voice recording.

The Tom Swift books were published by Grosset & Dunlap by special arrangement with The Stratemeyer Syndicate. The Tom Swift books were but one of scores of juvenile series handled by this "Syndicate," run by Edward Stratemeyer with methods similar to those used by Alexandre Dumas. The writing was farmed out to other authors after a plot outline had been agreed upon. The authors were paid a flat sum for their work and signed a contract disclaiming all rights in the production, which then became the sole property of the Stratemeyer Syndicate. The stories were published under house names.

Normally the public was no more interested in the men behind these stories then they would be in determining who wrote the actual definition of any given word in a dictionary, or who phrased an entry in an encyclopedia (in fact it was claimed that revealing who the author was would destroy the series image), but the extraordinary ᵤ cess and influence of the Tom Swift series put them into a class by themselves.

Upon the death of Howard R. Garis at the Cooley Dickenson Hospital, Northampton, Massachusetts, November 5, 1962, at the age of eighty-nine, *The Newark Evening News* ran, as part of the obituary: "Besides the Uncle Wiggily books and stories, he wrote the Tom Swift and Motor Boy series under pen names . . ." Howard R. Garis was renowned as the author of Uncle Wiggily, a rheumatic twinkly-eyed old rabbit, who dressed in a full suit and top hat, hopped and limped his way through 15,000 stories, at one time syndicated to nearly 100 newspapers and collected into 75 books that sold into the millions.

Reaction was sharp from The Stratemeyer Syndicate in East Orange, New Jersey, now run by Mrs. Harriet Adams, a daughter of Edward Stratemeyer, and Andrew E. Svenson, an editor and writer with an interest in the firm. They felt that the newspaper story gave the impression that Howard Garis had originated the series and written them all, whereas the facts were that the series had been originated by Edward Stratemeyer and the inventions and plot outlines determined not only for Garis, but for other writers who worked on the series.

They had reacted similarly when *The Newark Evening News* had carried a report of the death of Mrs. Lilian Garis, wife of Howard R. Garis, in their issue of April 20, 1954, which stated that she had written a number of the early Bobbsey Twins series, also a property of the Stratemeyer Syndicate.

Yet, on the occasion of his retirement from *The Newark Evening News,* Howard R. Garis had been very specific in reporting on series he had authored and the number of volumes he had written in each. *The Newark Evening News* for October 1, 1946, said: "Among his creations are 35 Tom Swift books, 20 Motor Boys, 15 Bobbsey Twins, 6 Six Little Bunkers." The foregoing were under pen names, but under his own name he also seemed very precise as he recorded 7 in the Teddy series, 14 Curlytops, 5 Dick Hamiltons, 5 Two Wild Cherries, 5 Smith Boys, 5 Venture Boys, 14 Buddy Books, and 5 Jack Armstrongs.

The Stratemeyer Syndicate never denied that Howard R.

Garis had worked on the Tom Swift series; indeed it was acknowledged that he had written the majority of them. What appeared to be involved was forestalling even the shadow of a claim to legal proprietorship.

While Edward Stratemeyer obviously did not write every word of each book produced by his syndicate (over 800 in his lifetime), it was asserted that he did generally plot and outline each of them, and it was felt that at least the outlines of the first four, and possibly more, of the early Tom Swifts were completely his work.

What was the background of Edward Stratemeyer? Did it suggest that he was the father of the ideas and plot outlines of Tom Swift?

Edward Stratemeyer was born October 4, 1862, in Elizabeth, New Jersey, of German parentage. His father, Henry Julius Stratemeyer, returned from the California Gold Rush of 1849 to marry Anna (Siegel) Stratemeyer, the widow of his brother, and open a tobacco store. He was reputed to have written his first story by hand on brown wrapping paper, an 18,000-word adventure juvenile which sold to Street & Smith for seventy-five dollars. The story, titled *Victor Horton's Idea,* was serialized in four installments in the issues of *Golden Days* dated November 2, 1889, to November 30, 1889.

He did not immediately go into full-time writing, but opened up his own stationery, tobacco, and newspaper store on North Broadway in Newark, New Jersey. In between customers he pressed forward with his fiction. Impressed by his juveniles, Street & Smith hired him as editor-writer of *Good News,* a weekly boys' magazine which began publication with its issue of May 15, 1890. He edited the magazine under the house name of W. B. Lawson. This position gave him the financial stability to marry Magdalene Baker von Camp, a Newark girl, in March 1891.

Stratemeyer proved an extremely able editor, securing as regular contributors to *Good News* such famed names in the boys' field as Horatio Alger, Jr., Oliver Optic, Bracebridge Hemyng, Edward S. Ellis, and Harry Castlemon. He contributed prodigiously himself, writing not only under his own name and that of W. B. Lawson, but also as Arthur M. Winfield, Henry Abbot, "Frank," Harvey Hicks, and "Jack." Stratemeyer's toughest immediate competitor was the well-established *Boys of New York* which ran an excellent array of series that had become boys' favorites, not the least of which were those of Frank Reade, Jr., teen-age inventor extraordinary, whose mentor, Luis P. Senarens, managed to concoct an inexhaustible variety of ships, tanks, submarines, and robots for his young hero to invent in time to meet all deadlines unfailingly since 1879.

To counter Frank Reade, Street & Smith during 1891 had come up with a character of their own, Tom Edison, Jr., whose scientific exploits, as complete novels, had run in *The Nugget*. Stratemeyer secured one novel concerning his exploits, *Tom Edison, Jr. and His Air Yacht; or, The Wonderful Cruise of the Sky Witch*, which he serialized in his issues of October 24, 1891, to December 12, 1891. By a remarkable "coincidence" this series, Street & Smith's answer to the Frank Reade, Jr., stories, was credited to one Philip Reade. A still more unusual fact about the stories was that they were written in the second person.

The real identity of Philip Reade has never been satisfactorily established, but Emerson Bell, the author of the longest series of science fiction tales that Edward Stratemeyer ran in *Good News* [those featuring the achievements of Lad Electric, beginning with *The Electric Air and Water Wizard* (November 18, 1893, to February 3, 1894)], was identified as Gilbert Patten, who would become better known as Burt L. Standish, author of the Frank Merriwell series!

It was while editor of *Good News* that Edward Stratemeyer laid the foundations for Tom Swift. First in *Jack, the Inventor; or, The Trials and Triumphs of a Young Machinist*, published in *The Holiday*, edited by Edward S. Ellis (April 25, 1891, to June 3, 1891), in which he asserts a feel for the drama of invention, and then in *Good News* in his novel, *Shorthand Tom; or, The Exploits of a Young Reporter* (February 3, 1894, to April 21, 1894), where the lead character is named Tom Swift!

Edward Stratemeyer took at least one plunge into publishing with *Bright Days,* a monthly, selling for five cents, which in its thirty-one issues beginning April 1896 and concluding February 27, 1897 (it briefly went weekly), appeared to be in the major part filled with stories under his own name and his pen names, several of them "science fiction."

Stratemeyer's idol was Horatio Alger, Jr. Despite a difference of almost thirty years in age, they were firm friends.

Stratemeyer sought to emulate the Alger formula in his own fiction and succeeded when Lothrop, Lee and Shepherd, Boston publishers, issued his first hardcover juvenile, *Richard Dare's Venture; or, Striking Out for Himself,* in 1894. The book was the first of the "Bound to Win" series which were interchangeable with the books of Horatio Alger. Stratemeyer became Alger's unofficial heir apparent, and a year after Alger's death in 1899 gained possession of and completed eleven "unfinished" Horatio Alger manuscripts under Horatio Alger, Jr.'s name, with the addition of the line: "Completed by Arthur M. Winfield."

The series that for years Stratemeyer lavished the most attention upon and most of which he was alleged to have written himself was The Rover Boys. The first of these, *The Rover Boys at School; or, The Cadets of Putnam Hall,* was published under the pen name of Arthur M. Winfield and issued by Mershon, New York, in 1899. A wholesome atmosphere of school life, sports, and adventure pervaded these volumes and, until they began to badly date in the twenties, they led all series in sales. After their decline, Tom Swift became the pacesetter.

One year after he started The Rover Boys, Stratemeyer attempted to establish a boy's invention series with Mershon Co., with *The Wizard of the Sea; or, A Trip Under the Ocean.* This novel, which followed the tried and true dime-novel formula of the boy hero, a marvelous invention, and thrilling voyage and strange adventures, didn't take hold at the time. The story was published in book form under the name of Roy Rockwood, but originally had appeared under the pen name of Theodore Edison in the August 10, 1895, issue of *Young Sports of America* with the title of *The Wizard of the Deep; or, Over and Under the Ocean in Search of the $1,000,000 Pearl.*

Stratemeyer was convinced that science fiction or "invention" stories, as they were then termed, could enjoy a respectable sale in hard covers.

An example of this was John Trowbridge, a professor of physics at Harvard, who had been a contributor to the story papers of the 1850s and 1860s, and who had published in 1890 a juvenile entitled *The Electric Boy,* combining authentic Horatio Alger elements with the potential marvels of electricity, followed with *Three Boys on an Electrical Boat* (Houghton Mifflin,

1894). Five years later, the book had gone into its eighth impression.

The lead character, Edward Kingsley, was a boy inventor who escapes from a man who has raised him and his "cousin" since infancy and now intends to separate them. The escape is conducted in an electrically driven ice boat built by the boy, and the opening chapters had the pathos of Horatio Alger. The boys sign on aboard a mysterious U.S. Navy ship powered entirely by electricity, carrying a number of secret electrical weapons conceived by Old George, a shipboard scientist. A war with England is narrowly averted, and the two boys enjoy a happy ending as they discover that they are actually both sons of a British general they were about to attack.

Not quite as near to that dime-novel formula, but close enough, was *Through the Earth* by Clement Fezandié, an extremely well-done juvenile concerning a sixteen-year-old boy with an impoverished widowed mother, who nobly guides a "car" through a tunnel drilled from New York to Australia. The book, published in 1898 by the Century Co., after a much-condensed version had been serialized in *St, Nicholas*, January to April 1898, had done extremely well. Its author, Clement Fezandié, was a successful businessman and former New York physics instructor who had written it for a lark, and science fiction readers are familiar with him as the ingenious author of scores of Doctor Hackensaw's Secrets, a series of highly original short stories that ran in *Electrical Experimenter, Science and Invention*, and *Amazing Stories* from 1920 through 1926. He refused to accept any payment from Hugo Gernsback, returning all checks that were sent to him!

These examples prompted Stratemeyer to produce the first of what would become known as "The Great Marvel Series" in 1906. This series, placed with Cupples & Leon and published under the name Roy Rockwood, came to fruition in the period when Stratemeyer found himself so busy that he began to engage other writers to handle his assignments. The first story in the series, *Through the Air to the North Pole or The Wonderful Cruise of the Electric Monarch*, combines the Horatio Alger and Luis P. Senarens themes to perfection. Two orphan boys, pudgy Jack Darrow and Mark Sampson, sixteen and fifteen years old respectively, are cruelly buffeted from town to town until they are injured while leaping from a train. They are befriended by a kindly old scientist, Amos Henderson, and his Negro aide, Washington. The four embark on a trip to the North Pole in an electrically powered dirigible the old man has built.

A second book, *Under the Ocean to the South Pole or The Strange Cruise of the Submarine Wonder,* followed in 1907, and the series gained momentum. The 1908 story, *Five Thousand Miles Underground or The Mystery of the Centre of the Earth,* was more imaginative, involving a "negative gravity" device for the airship and a descent into a hollowed-out world in the center of the earth, inhabited by a strange race.

A friend of Amos Henderson, a Mr. Santell Roumann, has invented a mysterious propulsive agent which he calls Etherium. They build a space ship and journey to Mars in the volume *Through Space to Mars or The Longest Trip on Record,* published in 1910. They encounter an alien race, discover Cardite, an unusual material which seems to have radioactive properties, and return to Earth.

Stratemeyer had begun large-scale farming out of work to writers by 1906. It is probable that he did not actually form a corporation until 1910, at which time the name legally was made The Stratemeyer Syndicate, Inc.

It was the year prior to 1910 that he approached Grosset & Dunlap, who had been publishing reprint juveniles in hard covers for fifty cents each, and suggested that he could supply them with *originals,* especially tailored for their audience, that could be produced to sell at the same price. They took him up on it and he created for them the Tom Swift Series (also switching to them, among other titles, The Bobbsey Twins and the Rover Boy Series, which had already been established). The instantaneous success of the idea won Stratemeyer the title of "The Father of the Fifty-Cent Books."

It was customary to launch a new boys' series with multiple volumes. Five Tom Swift books appeared in 1910. They were *Tom Swift and His Motor Cycle, Tom Swift and His Motor Boat, Tom Swift and His Airship, Tom Swift and His Submarine Boat,* and *Tom Swift and His Electric Runabout.* There followed *four additional titles* in 1911, and all these piled on top of at least a dozen other series with new titles Stratemeyer was producing at the same time left little doubt that despite his prodigious capabilities he obviously had assistance.

The evidence seems to be overpowering that a major share of that assistance came from Howard R. Garis.

Howard Roger Garis was born April 25, 1873, in Binghamton, N.Y., son of Simeon H. Garis and Ellen A. Kimball. His family were practicing Catholics, and his early life was spent on a farm.

The first literary job he obtained was as editor on a mortician's trade magazine, appropriately titled *Sunnyside.* This background, together with his skills at shorthand, prompted editor T. Edward Burke to employ him as a cub reporter on *The Newark Evening News* at a starting salary of twelve dollars a week. His first day's work, on October 1, 1896, was almost his last. He was assigned to cover a speech at a political meeting which turned into a street battle, and he didn't file a story because nothing important was *said!*

At *The Newark Evening News* he met Lilian C. McNamara, who had taken a reporter's job a year before him. They were married April 26, 1900, at St. Michael's Church, Newark.

This was the start of a remarkable literary family. His wife quit work and eventually turned out forty-seven books between her domestic chores, including a number of Bobbsey Twins and titles in the Girl Scouts and Gloria books. She had one series known as "The Lilian Garis Books for Girls," revolving around the experiences of girls in school, and two of them were about her daughter, Cleo Fausta (*Cleo's Misty Rainbow* and *Cleo's Conquest*). Cleo would author *The Orchard's Secret,* as well as a number of girls' books. A son, Roger, wrote titles in the X-Bar-X Boys and the entire Outboard Motor Boat series. A play of his, *The Pony Cart,* dealing with a sexual psychopath in a small town, opened and closed at the Theatre De Lys, New York, September 14, 1955.

Howard Garis wrote his first book while assigned as a reporter to a Newark police station. It was an adult novel titled *With Force and Arms; a Tale of Love and Salem Witchcraft* (J. S. Ogilvie, New York, 1902). He attempted to write in the idiom of old Salem, and the result was awkward. Full of color and excitement, the novel was primarily a rousing adventure story. Its lack of success was nevertheless a deep disappointment to him.

He had been writing a series of juvenile stories for *The Newark Evening News* and these were collected and published as *The King of Unadilla, Stories of Court Secrets Concerning His*

Majesty (J. S. Ogilvie, 1903), with equally modest sales. *Ilse of Black Fire* (Lippincott, 1904) was a well-written boy's adventure story of the discovery of a mass of radium worshipped by natives on an uncharted island off the African coast. The science was excellent, but this book did not sell, either.

This turned him to short stories, and among the magazines he sold to was *The Argosy.* His earliest story was "The Joke Jim Bailey Played" (December 1904), about two Newark newspapermen mistaken for pickpockets at a political rally. His first science fiction was "An Evaporated Bank Burglary" (May 1905), revealing the secrets of the Johnson Annihilator, a liquid which, when sprinkled on paper, exploded after evaporation. The best of his science fiction was the whimsical Professor Jonkin's stories, and the best of that series was the delightful satire, "Professor Jonkin's Cannibal Plant" (August 1905), which indicated that Garis had read a number of stories in that vein, most likely "The Devil Tree of El Dorado" by Frank Aubrey (reputed to be the pen name of F. Atkins, a writer for *The Argosy,* and also alleged to be Fenton Ash, science fiction writer), which was still going into new editions since its initial publication in 1897. Another excellent example of Garis' special brand of humor was contained in "Professor Jonkin and His Busier Bees" (March 1906), where the good scientist crosses bees with lightning bugs so they can see to work at night. "His Winged Elephant" (March 1907) found Professor Jonkin breeding a mosquito the size of an elephant. As late as 1914, Howard R. Garis still occasionally turned out a magazine story, as evidenced by "Let Us Eat," involving social criticism of homes for the indigent aged (*The Cavalier,* February 28).

Garis resigned from *The Newark Evening News* in 1908 "to devote full time to the writing of juveniles."

The 1946 newspaper writeup on his retirement specifically stated that he had written twenty of the Motor Boys series. The Motor Boys series was the property of Edward Stratemeyer, and twenty-two novels had been issued continuously from 1906 to 1924. Previous to 1906, Stratemeyer's skill at planning and selling books had already exceeded his very considerable ability to write them. Garis lived at 12 Myrtle Ave., only five blocks from Stratemeyer's mansion-sized home at 163 North 7th St. in the Roseville section of Newark. There seems little reason to doubt that Howard R. Garis was writing the Motor Boys series for Edward Stratemeyer no later than 1906.

The very nature of the Motor Boys is especially noteworthy. They involved the adventures of three major characters, Ned, Bob, and Jerry, "in auto, boat, and airship." The striking similarity of approach to the first three Tom Swift books, involving a motorcycle, motorboat, and airship, becomes instantly apparent. The preparation of the Tom Swift books had to be done in 1909. Howard R. Garis not only was the logical writer to work with Stratemeyer, but it is probable that the opportunity to do five Tom Swift titles may have been the key factor in his resigning from *The Newark Evening News.*

It was in 1909 that Howard Garis also had published the first of six Dick Hamilton Series with Grosset and Dunlap, *under his own name.* Stratemeyer had not sold to Grosset and Dunlap up to that time and Garis may even have been influential in helping him secure the contact resulting in their agreement to publish Tom Swift.

There is another factor which lends weight to the assumption that Howard Garis began writing Tom Swift from the very first book. In 1909, Edward S. Scudder, publisher of *The Newark Evening News,* asked Garis for a daily children's feature for the newspaper. Recalling a dignified old rabbit he had seen in the woods of Verona, N.J., Garis innovated the Uncle Wiggily series of Bed Time Stories, a collection of which went into hard covers in 1910. The characterization of Wakefield Damon in *Tom Swift and His Motor Cycle* reads distinctly like something out of Uncle Wiggily: "'Why bless my top-knot!' exclaimed the odd gentleman. 'If it isn't Tom Swift, the young inventor! Bless my very happiness! There's my motor-cycle, too! Help you? Why, of course we will. Bless my shoe-leather! Of course we'll help you!'"

If Howard R. Garis wrote precisely the first thirty-five books in the Tom Swift series, that would have brought him up to *Tom Swift and His Giant Magnet, or, Bringing Up the Lost Submarine,* published in 1932. The year 1933 found *four* books from Howard R. Garis in the new Rocket Riders series from A. L. Burt. This group dealt with rocket-driven vehicles of various types (sleds, dirigibles, boats, and cars), and Garis made a strong case for liquid fuels being the only feasible ones for rockets, at a time when members of rocket societies were the only ones who understood the advantages. Garis' son, Roger, also had four

169

books in the Outboard Motor series from A. L. Burt the same year. It would appear that Garis shifted from Tom Swift at this period for purely business reasons.

In his biography of Howard R. Garis, *My Father Was Uncle Wiggily* (McGraw-Hill, 1966), Roger Garis states: "I know there was a series my father did which concerned space exploration. One of the books, which I still have, was *Through Space to Mars.*" This definitely pinpoints Howard R. Garis as the author of most, if not all, of the Great Marvel Series, the most imaginative of all Stratemeyer offerings. In addition to the stories previously mentioned in that series, a lunar field of diamonds was the prize in *Lost on the Moon* (1911); a piece of Alaska is flung into space in *On a Tornaway World* (1913) to become a satellite around the earth; a small nearby world, unseen because it rotates constantly in the shadow of Earth, is the locale of *The City Beyond the Clouds* (1925); the rocket principle is used to propel a ship from Venus to the Earth in *By Air Express to Venus* (1929); and improved rockets take Earthmen to Saturn in *By Space Ship to Saturn,* the last of the series, published in 1935.

The relationship between Edward Stratemeyer and Howard R. Garis had been a warm one. Stratemeyer's daughter Harriet recalls that Garis visited often when she was a small girl, and after she was presumably thought to be in bed, the two men would prance about acting out the ideas and scenes planned for their latest volume. "To me, Howard Garis *was* Uncle Wiggily," she recalls; "he was a kind, gentle man with a whimsical sense of humor and a wonderful way with children."

The onset of World War I in Europe edged the juveniles in the direction of conflict. A publishing firm as distinguished as Harper & Brothers, New York City, issued in 1914 *The Last Invasion* by Donal (sic) Hamilton Haines. A foreign army called The Blues invades Maine and Texas, and the United States rallies to repel them. Narrators of the story are teen-age boys. It is a modern war, fought in the air, and the boys are involved in a battle between an armored dirigible of the Blues and a fighting plane of the United States. The volume was illustrated and sold for $1.25. Haines had contributed "modern" army stories to leading magazines previously, including "Meachem's Ride" (*Pearson's Magazine,* August 1910), showing the superiority of wireless communications and aerial reconnaissance over older methods.

There was a second book featuring the youthful heroes, *Clearing the Seas; or, The Last of the Warships* (1915), in which the supremacy of airpower over seapower is predicted by Haines.

A most unusual war series, a precursor of the pulp magazine character, *Operator #5,* was "The Conquest of the United States Series," by-lined by H. Irving Hancock, which consisted of four volumes published in 1916 by Altemus. The Germans invade the United States, and each volume deals with the defense of another major city. The books read suspiciously like propaganda, possibly even inspired by the British (since the Germans were the invaders), calculated to impress the need for preparedness for war on the Americans. The author was a prolific producer of boys' books for Henry Altemus Company, Philadelphia. He had written for them The Motor Boat Series, The West Point Series, The Annapolis Series, The Young Engineers Series, Boys of the Army Series, the Dave Darrin Series, the High School Boys Series, the Grammar School Boys Series, and The High School Boys Vacation Series, all under his own name, and an unknown quantity of others under pen names.

The first volume dealt with *The Invasion of the United States, or, Uncle Sam's Boys at the Capture of Boston,* and, like all of the others, sold for one dollar. In that first volume, the German fleet sinks the American fleet and captures Boston, defeating a makeshift army of Regulars, National Guardsmen, volunteers, and boys from Gridley High School who experience the events. In *In the Battle for New York, or Uncle Sam's Boys in the Desperate Struggle for the Metropolis,* the Germans sweep down on New York, taking the metropolis and threatening Philadelphia. In *At the Defense of Pittsburgh, or, The Struggle to Save America's Fighting Steel Supply,* that vital bastion almost falls and the series culminates with *Making the Last Stand for Old Glory, or, Uncle Sam's Boys in the Last Frantic Drive.* Vast production of airplanes west of the Mississippi, a new submarine fleet, and support from the Brazilian army saves the United States in the showdown.

It seems most probable that the entry of the United States into World War I in 1917 was the cause of the termination of the series. It abruptly rendered the premise invalid and negated the need for propaganda to push the United States into war.

A promising series in the low-priced fifty-cent field like Stratemeyer's was The Boy Inventors, written by Richard Bonner and published by Hurst & Company, New York. There were six in all between 1912 and 1915, featuring the adventures of the scientifically minded seventeen-year-old cousins Jack Chadwick and Tom Jesson, working with the brilliant Professor Chester Chadwick. The first volume, *The Boy Inventors' Wireless Triumph,* used radio as a means of getting Tom Jesson's father, an explorer who is lost in the wilds of Yucatan, back to safety. In the process they employ a combination automobile and dirigible which they have invented, as well as a gas gun.

The same inventions reappear in the various stories, and in the second book, *The Boy Inventors and the Vanishing Gun,* in which a self-propelled antiaircraft gun is the focus of the plot. Possibly the most interesting of their inventions, featured in the sixth and last of the series, was a radio telephone. The pattern of the stories and the characters, even down to a Negro aide for comic relief, is almost identical with the Tom Swift books, but they did not sell nearly as well.

There is probably an untold story of competition in the simultaneous publication by Grosset & Dunlap and A. L. Burt of two series the same year (1922), *both* titled *The Radio Boys.* Grosset & Dunlap's was supplied by Stratemeyer under the house name of Allen Chapman. Burt's was credited to Gerald Breckenridge, and its title, *The Radio Boys Seek the Lost Atlantis* (1923), in which ruins and records of the sunken continent are discovered in the African desert, is by far the most fascinating of them all.

There were two other boys' radio series. One was written by A. Hyatt Verrill, who in 1926 would become a regular contributor to Hugo Gernsback's *Amazing Stories.* This very unusual group of stories issued by Appleton was called "The Radio Detective Series" and related the various ways teen-age boys could use "wireless" to help unravel crimes in widely spread adventurous areas of the world. Four volumes were issued in 1922.

The other series, called "Radiophone Boys Stories," was sponsored by Rielly & Lee, Chicago, the publishers of the Oz books, and five volumes were issued, all written by Roy Judeon Snell. Some of these stories may legitimately be considered science fiction, with titles like *The Sea-Going Tank, The Flying Sub,* and *The Invisible Wall.* The books appeared between 1924 and 1928, and like Verrill, Roy J. Snell was no house name, but a well-known prolific writer for the pulps and boys' magazines, and he had frequently done science fiction.

The phenomenal success of the Tarzan stories led Edward Stratemeyer to come up with *Bomba the Jungle Boy or The Naturalist's Secret* (1926), the first of twenty volumes carrying through to 1938 which appeared under the Roy Rockwood name. Cupples & Leon published them because Grosset & Dunlap marketed the low-priced editions of the Tarzan stories. But Stratemeyer, who in 1929 acknowledged that new titles in The Rover Boys series were no longer likely, would never live to see the Bomba series concluded. He maintained an office on the eighteenth floor of a New York building for his "Syndicate" and still commuted from his home on North Seventh Street in Newark where he died May 10, 1930, at the age of 67, from complications arising from pneumonia.

Despite its size and complexity, the Syndicate had been a one-man business. His two daughters decided that they would not let it die. They moved the offices to East Orange, New Jersey, and editorial management passed to Harriet Adams, graduate of Wellesley, class of 1914, and artwork to her sister, Edna C. Stratemeyer. When *Newark Sunday Call* feature writer Myra Montfort Thomas, sensing a human interest story, interviewed the two, she reported: "Both women guard the business details jealously. For instance, one may not look at a synopsis. Nor may one know what books, under what bylines, come from their 'factory.' "

The girls did not find it that easy. Times had changed. The Depression—the worst in the history of the nation—had set in. Fifty-cent books for the entertainment of teen-agers were a definite luxury. The pulp magazines had proliferated at ten cents and fifteen cents apiece, offering reading entertainment of the action-packed variety that children loved in every area of adventure. Radio provided an increasing number of daily teen-age serials, including such favorites as Buck Rogers, Tarzan, Fu Manchu, Tom Mix, Jack Armstrong, and Little Orphan Annie, all free for the listening.

Howard Garis and his family of writers had left them to write for other companies, and time began to badly date most of their best series.

For decades Edward Stratemeyer had created the ideas for the series, the characters, and the type of plots he thought would sell. He commissioned writers like Garis, who loved children and had the feel for what they would enjoy, to produce them for him, and then bought all rights, collecting all future profits himself.

Perhaps if he had lived, he could have continued to produce new ideas and series that would have carried him through the Depression. Perhaps he could not have: the Depression very sharply ended great careers in every aspect of business and art.

The highly successful Tom Swift series began to receive severe competition in the early thirties, not only from the "Rocket Rider Series" written by Howard R. Garis, but, more pointedly, the "Adventures in the Unknown Series," written by Carl H. Claudy and also published by Grosset & Dunlap.

Carl H. Claudy had been a regular writer for the pulp magazines during the 1920s, appearing in publications as widely read as *The Popular Magazine*, with adventure stories, and, as an outdoor man who loved sports, hunting, and climbing, he imparted an air of authenticity to those stories.

He had worked as a newspaper man and eventually wound up as executive secretary of a national association, headquartered in Washington, D.C. Early in 1931, science fiction written by him began to appear in *American Boy* and would continue to see print more or less consistently through the end of 1939. His first was a long novelette titled *Land of No Shadow*, published in the February 1931 issue. The story could have been printed in any of the leading science fiction magazines of the day—*Amazing Stories, Wonder Stories,* or *Astounding Stories* —and would have been judged a powerful, above-average adventure science-fantasy.

It tells of a scientist who builds a machine which can send men into the fourth dimension. Two young men—good friends —move into the fourth dimension where all is varying shades of grey, and gigantic, unapproachable humanoid figures, capable of walking through matter, provide a sinister menace. The writing was good, the story development sound, and the mood excellent. It was far above juvenile standards.

Claudy's second story, *The Master Mind of Mars*, was a novel serialized in *American Boy*, November 1931 to February 1932. The handling of the novel was more juvenile than *Land of No Shadow*, but the development of the plot, in which the characters gradually fathom the nature of the disembodied Martian "people" and their robot servants, was definitely cerebral. Revised and lengthened, Grosset & Dunlap put this novel into hard covers in 1933 as *The Mystery Men of Mars,* with a selling price of fifty cents. The lead characters were Alan Kane, an intellectual young student, and Theodore Dollivar, a redheaded physical giant. Both men in the hardcover editions are twenty-five years of age, though in the original magazine version they are thirty.

The third novel, *A Thousand Years a Minute,* is a time-travel story in which the two lead characters travel almost a million years into the past to the prehistoric ages, befriend a near-human primitive, and return, battered but thrilled by their exciting adventures. The book was greatly expanded from the novelette *A Million Years Ago* (*American Boy,* May 1932).

The Land of No Shadow was revised and lengthened for the third book, also published in 1933. In this extremely well-done novel, Alan Kane is killed and buried, but Theodore Dolliver somehow retains the faith that he still lives and will return.

Return he does in *The Blue Grotto Terror,* expanded from *X Mystery* in *American Boy,* October 1934, to engage in an adventure twenty miles beneath the surface of the earth and cope with an unimaginable and inimical intelligence. Published in 1934, it was the final story to go into hardcover, though Claudy contributed a score of other science fiction juveniles to *American Boy* and other publications, few of which were reprinted.

Claudy's books, as fiction, were the best in storytelling quality of any of the boys' books, including Tom Swift, up to their time. They could quite satisfactorily pass for light adult entertainment, and would be worth reviving and maintaining in print on a teen-age list.

A juvenile which deserves mention because of the fame of its character is *Flash Gordon in the Caverns of Mongo* by Alex Raymond, published by Grosset & Dunlap in 1936. Flash Gordon had been introduced on the Sunday pages of American newspapers January 7, 1934, and scored a success second only to Buck Rogers. The strip was the last flowering of the old scientific romances similar to those of the Munsey magazines, done in the tradition of Edgar Rice Burroughs, and the stress was on action, mystery, and romance. Unfortunately, the book had none of Alex Raymond's superb drawings. The plot concerned a race in the core of the planet Mongo who control, by telepathic commands, octopuslike monsters which threaten the civilization on the surface. Flash Gordon, after an appropriate series of adventures, frees the planet of this menace.

Evidence that early Stratemeyer books were dating surfaced in the middle thirties when Grosset & Dunlap permitted the leasing of titles they let go out of print to other publishers of low-priced juvenile fiction. One of them was The Goldsmith Publishing Co. of Chicago, which reissued three of the earliest Bobbsey Twins as part of their juvenile list in very cheaply produced hardcover titles which sold for as little as twenty cents apiece in variety stores.

Among their other titles were several newly developed science fiction stories, the best-selling of which was *The Moon Colony* by William Dixon Bell (1937), telling of a rocketship adventure to the moon. This book has some very good and some extremely bad science, and is brutally violent. On the positive side, Bell specifically mentions "Goddard's liquid rockets" as the power source for his space ships, certainly one of the earliest fiction writers to use the reference. At the very moment the book was being written, Goddard was working on large liquid-fueled rockets in Roswell, New Mexico, with funds provided by the Guggenheims. The attempts of a renegade scientist, Herman Toplinsky, to put water, air, and arable soil on the moon and establish a colony, provides the plot of the story. A population of gigantic intelligent crickets is encountered, who contest the colonization.

Bell wrote another book for Goldsmith published in 1938 titled *The Secret of Tibet*, which, while science fiction, was not as popular. During and after World War II, Goldsmith published several titles by Roy Snell, who had written the Radiophone Series, which could qualify as science fiction, specifically *Secrets of Radar* and *Destination Unknown.*

Further indications of lack of interest in Stratemeyer books came when Grosset & Dunlap permitted Whitman Publishing, Racine, Wisconsin, to take over seven of the later titles in the Tom Swift series. Harriet S. Adams, in an interview published in the April 4, 1968, *New York Times,* stated that it was the policy of Stratemeyer never to permit a character to marry, because "once, when a wedding occurred, readership dropped." She elaborated on this point in *The Newark Sunday News* for March 23, 1969, by specifying *Tom Swift and His*

House on Wheels as the offending volume, where Tom is married to his girlfriend, Mary Nestor, in the last paragraph. It may or may not be a coincidence, but that volume was published in 1929, the start of the Great Depression!

Harriet Adams had begun to write a series of girl detective stories concerning Nancy Drew for her father before he died, and as the years progressed she did an increasing amount of writing on that and other characters under the pen names of Carolyn Keene and Laura Lee Hope (The Bobbsey Twins). She wrote the last of the Tom Swift hardcovers, *Tom Swift and His Planet Stone*, published in 1935. Tom Swift discovers that seeds which have come to Earth on a meteorite will grow in hot houses, and their perfume has a curative effect, as has powder made from them when dried and crushed. He succeeds with this marvelous medicine in saving the life of baseball's home-run king when efforts of the nation's greatest doctors have failed.

Whitman was publisher of the Better Little Books, imitations of the Big Little Books, combining story and cartoon in fat little volumes sold through variety stores for ten cents. An intriguing selection of famous comic strip reprints, as well as originals derived from the moving pictures and radio, was available in these volumes.

Two Tom Swift originals were issued in this format.

The first, *Tom Swift and His Giant Telescope* (1939), relates the problems of building an advanced optical instrument that makes it possible to see the cities and inhabitants of Mars. When the *New York Herald Tribune* for April 14, 1946, headlined "Tom Swift Quit Inventing in '41; His Future Secret," they were referring to the second Better Little Book, *Tom Swift and His Magnetic Silencer*. Tom Swift went out of print in any edition in 1944. The Rover Boys had thrown in the sponge two years earlier.

Scarcely a year after the announcement, Grosset & Dunlap, finally able to get a more substantial supply of paper following the normalization of events after World War II, issued the first of The Rick Brant Science-Adventure Stories with *The Rocket's Shadow* in 1947.

Rick Brant's father owns an island off the coast of New Jersey, heading a group of scientists who work in laboratories there. In *The Rocket's Shadow*, they hit the surface of the moon with a

177

radar-controlled rocket. In the second book, *The Lost City*, they encounter a lost tribe of Mongols in the Himalayas, and in the third book, *Sea Gold*, work on an operation that extracts minerals from the sea. The series proved very popular and went into several dozen titles.

As television became more widespread, a teen-age program built around the adventures of *Tom Corbett, Space Cadet*, proved a hit in 1952. Grosset & Dunlap arranged with Rockhill Radio, producers of the program, to issue a series of teen-age Tom Corbett books. The first, *Stand By for Mars!*, appeared in 1952 and was credited to Carey Rockwell. Willy Ley, the renowned rocket authority, acted as "technical advisor" on all the books. Beyond that, the entire idea for *Tom Corbett, Space Cadet*, had been blatantly lifted from Robert A. Heinlein's juvenile *Space Cadet*, published by Scribners in 1948, causing some to claim that the books were really his. The titles of the books explicitly give their plots: *Danger in Deep Space, On the Trail of the Space Pirates, The Space Pioneers, Revolt on Venus, Treachery in Outer Space, Sabotage in Space,* and *The Robot Revolt.*

Robert A. Heinlein was, for a time, an extremely popular writer of teen-age science fiction, beginning with *Rocket Ship Galileo*, published by Scribners in 1947, a tale of three boys who journey to the moon with a scientist; continuing with *Space Cadet;* and then with *Red Planet*, "A Colonial Boy on Mars," in 1949; following through with *Farmer in the Sky* (1950); and on for eight other titles. While the first two books in the series qualified without reservations as juveniles, from the third on the elaborateness of invention, the integrity of the science, the quality of the writing, and the maturity of outlook left no question that these were adult science fiction with teen-age heroes.

Even after the first serialization of the novels began to occur in magazines like *Blue Book, Astounding Science-Fiction,* and *The Magazine of Fantasy and Science Fiction*, Scribners maintained the pretense that those were juveniles until the publication of *Starship Troopers* which, presenting the philosophy that no one be permitted to vote who had not in some way participated in the armed services of the country, convinced them they had to terminate the series and, by so doing, lost Heinlein to Putnam. In 1970, Robert A. Heinlein sold paperback rights to the twelve Scribner "juveniles" for an advance of $100,000 from Ace Books!

Harriet Adams had tried to pull the Stratemeyer Syndicate back together again in 1947, when she hired a *Newark Evening News* writer, Andrew E. Svenson, to help run the operation. For all intents and purposes, The Stratemeyer Syndicate had ceased to exist with the retirement of her sister, Edna Squier, in 1942.

Activity began immediately, but it wasn't until 1954, as Harriet Adams watched the continuing success of the Rick Brant, Tom Corbett, and the Robert A. Heinlein juveniles, that she decided it was time to take another flyer with Tom Swift. To obtain a completely fresh, updated outlook, the hero was to be the son of Tom Swift, Tom Swift, Jr. With an appropriate editorial instinct, Harriet Adams also updated the house name, Victor Appleton, on the new Tom Swift books, having them credited to Victor Appleton II!

Following the business techniques of her father, in 1954 Harriet Adams issued five of the new series simultaneously: *Tom Swift and His Flying Lab, Tom Swift and His Jetmarine, Tom Swift and His Rocket Ship, Tom Swift and His Giant Robot,* and *Tom Swift and His Atomic Earth Blaster.* The new books were far more imaginative, almost blatantly so. *Tom Swift and His Flying Lab* was concerned with a machine that could not have conceivably been constructed by a company smaller than Boeing Aircraft. It was intended to be used to conduct experiments in the earth's ionosphere and was powered by atomic energy, lifted and propelled by rockets, and carried a helicopter and a fighter plane as accessories.

The second book dealt with the use of a Jetmarine, a submarine powered by atomic energy, which activates a pump driving seawater out through pipes, forcing the vessel ahead as a result of the reaction. The submarine was painted with a material that made it sonarproof. In the third book, Tom Swift, Jr., built a rocketship capable of space travel.

The Tom Swift, Jr., adventures caught on, and new titles were issued at the rate of two annually. A new invention per book remained the basic formula of the series. It wasn't long before Tom Swift, Jr., had his own space station for medical research, radio and television relays. As the books progress, the reader

179

finds himself almost completely immersed in the whole retinue of Tom Swift's inventions, which are now carried over from story to story. By the time number twenty-four, *Tom Swift and His Polar-Ray Dynasphere*, is reached, the nature of the new invention has become unclear, though it seems to create a magnetic field powerful enough to draw power to it and slow down other spaceships. The twenty-seventh book in the series, *Tom Swift and His Subocean Geotron*, involved what was actually a greatly improved model of his Jetmarine.

Merchandising methods have changed much more radically than the plots. In 1966, the Tom Swift books, listed at $1.25, could be found on "special" at many supermarkets and discount stores throughout the country as low as sixty-nine cents.

The sales of the old Tom Swift books had always been greatly understated. By actual check, Harriet Adams now reports that the old series had sold, in all editions, the incredible total of twenty million copies. Bomba, the Jungle Boy, got to ten million before it was discontinued. The new Tom Swift, Jr., editions, which had sold a total of ten million copies by 1965 and were moving at the rate of two million a year, may have reached the twenty-million figure, and are among the best-selling juveniles in the world.

Harriet Adams still refuses to tell anyone who writes any of the stories, or even the names of the editors working for the company, which also still packages The Bobbsey Twins, Nancy Drew, and many other best-selling juveniles. She implicitly believes in her closemouthed business formula, as she does in her story formula, working on the basis that she must be doing something right.

When the Great Marvel and Tom Swift series were begun prior to World War I, there were no science fiction magazines, and there seems little question that they created thousands of fans for that type of fiction. After the science fiction magazines became part of the fiction scene, not only Tom Swift but the other boys' books employing adventure plots appeared somewhat pallid in comparison. At their best, they were derivative from the magazines. Tom Swift, Jr., today, reads like a juvenile adaptation of some of the stories written for *Amazing Stories* in the 1920s, particularly in the uses to which he puts his inventions. Like the comics and moving pictures which use science fiction themes, juveniles are a popular entertainment, apart and separate. They may take from the main body of science fiction, but offer nothing in return.

Despite this, when Tom Swift's stereotyped dialogue is so universally known that it can inspire a national craze for phrase-making called Tom Swifties, whose progress was only halted by legal action on the part of The Stratemeyer Syndicate when it became too risqué, it must be making some impact on our culture. And when a slice-of-life storyteller like J. D. Salinger writes a *New Yorker* story titled "Uncle Wiggily in Connecti-cut," because the woman in the story has stubbed her toe and limps like the rheumatic gentleman rabbit, perhaps it heralds a return to the age of sentiment.

WAR:

Warriors of If

"... I class with George Griffith as a purveyor of wild *'pseudo'* scientific extravaganza," H. G. Wells wrote novelist Arnold Bennett in 1902 in summing up the attitude towards his works in the United States. Six years later, in the opening chapter of the serialization of his novel, *The War in the Air,* in Britain's *Pall Mall Magazine,* he said of his lead character: "... Bert's imagination was stimulated by a sixpenny edition of that aeronautic classic, Mr. George Griffith's 'The Outlaws of the Air,' and so the thing really got hold of them."

Those two quotes summed up the strange hate/love attitude and ambivalent feelings of contempt, respect, and envy that H. G. Wells held towards his popular science fiction contemporary, George Griffith. The ironical part was that literally no one in the United States classed Wells with Griffith, for Griffith was unknown there. The anti-American feeling expressed in George Griffith's first best seller, *The Angel of the Revolution* (1893), made him a pariah whom publishers did not deign to pirate, even in those days of weak international copyright agreements.

In England it was another matter. Certainly during the years 1893 and 1894, George Griffith was the leading science fiction author in England. He lost that brief renown when H. G. Wells's *The Time Machine* appeared in hardcover in 1895, but still remained the best-selling science fiction author in England, at least until the tremendous success of *The War of the Worlds* in 1898.

Griffith was probably the most popular of all the future-war authors that multiplied after the success of "The Battle of Dorking" by George Chesney in *Blackwood's Magazine* for May 1871. Not only was a large part of his voluminous output future-war (probably no one wrote more novels on the theme), but the stress in most of them was air power. More clearly than any

182

author before him, he grasped the revolutionary role aircraft would play in warfare, at a time when there was not even as much as a powered lighter-than-air vessel in existence.

Wells, who was a contributor to *Pearson's Weekly* and *Pearson's Magazine* at the same time as George Griffith, was obviously greatly impressed by him. Even after Wells had gained ascendancy and a score of imitators of Griffith—William Le Queux, Fred T. Jane, Louis Tracy, M. P. Shiel, and Max Pemberton among them—flooded the pages of the periodicals and the bookstalls with future-war efforts, the George Griffith titles were reprinted in paperback and sold everywhere for only sixpence each.

Obviously, a writer as popular and widely read as was George Griffith is not only important because he reflected the attitudes of his times, but because he obviously helped shape them. Additionally, his early success could not help but be a major influence on an entire generation of British science fiction writers. Despite this, despite at least a half-dozen best-sellers, despite thirty-seven books, despite the fact that while living he made the *Who's Who*, he does not rate a single line in any broad literary history, past or present. Nor has there been a critique of his work published, the major exposition upon him being a 1,500-word essay in the British trade journal *Flight International* for December 22, 1966, based on a letter from and interview with his son, Alan Arnold Griffith, formerly chief research engineer for Rolls Royce, who is credited with originating the technology of the jet-lift for vertical takeoff of aircraft.

Does he deserve more?

Decidedly so.

George Chetwynd Griffith-Jones was born August 20, 1857, at Seven Wyndham Place, Plymouth, England, the son of George Alfred Jones, Ll.D., and Jeanette Henry Capinster. His father was born 1823 in Madras, India, son of George Jones, a colonel in the thirty-second Foot Company of the Honorable East India Company. He was educated at Bedford, England, and entered Trinity College, Cambridge, in 1840; he left the University without graduating.

The mother, daughter of John Louis Henry, "gentleman," had come from Bath and married George Alfred Jones, June 5, 1853. At the time he was living in Dawlish, South Devon, and gave his profession as Classical tutor.

He later reentered Cambridge and received his Ll.D. in 1857. His first position as a cleric was at Plymton in 1857, moving the same year to a better opportunity in St. Peter's, a relatively new church in Plymouth. George was baptized in that church on September 20, 1857.

Records show that his father performed baptisms at St. Peter's up to 1860, when he moved from Plymouth to Tring, and then in 1861 to Ashton-under-Lyne, a suburb of Manchester. In time he attained the position of senior curate. His final church was Mossley, a nearby community, where he was appointed vicar in September 1864, remaining there until his death, which occurred the evening of January 14, 1872, as the result of a "stomach haemorrhage."

In the obituary, published in *The Ashton Reporter* for January 20, 1872, he was described as "conservative and generous within his means." That his means were not too ample was attested by the fact that he left no will and that his monies and personal property totaled under 300 pounds ($1,500). The courts awarded all of this to his wife, Jeannette.

When his father died, George was fourteen years old. As the youngest of two sons, he got the least attention. His overworked father occasionally taught him some Latin and Greek. The National Schoolmaster would visit the parsonage on a hit-and-miss basis and teach him reading, writing, and arithmetic. Supplementing this were periodic lessons in French under his mother's tutelage.

The most fascinating education he obtained from his father's substantial library, which contained generous quantities of Sir Walter Scott, Bulwer Lytton, Charles Dickens, R. M. Ballantyne, and, most especially, Jules Verne.

On the death of his father he was sent off to a private school at Southport. It was there he discovered how uneven his education actually was. There were few better at Latin than he, but not many worse at the most simple arithmetical sums. He spent fifteen months in school and was the second top in his class when he left. He wrote: "Then I went to another school, or perhaps I should put it more correctly if I said that I matriculated in the greatest of all universities—the world. I went to sea as an apprentice on a Liverpool lime-juicer . . . In the seventy-eight days between Liverpool and Melbourne I learnt more of the world than I had learnt in fourteen years, but the methods of tuition didn't suit me. The learning was hammered in a little too hard, mostly with a rope's end and the softest part of a belaying pin, so I took French leave of that class-room and went to another; in plain English, I ran away from my ship and went up in the bush."

Without any further educational background, except for a period when he had tutored the son of an Australian settler for £2 10s a week, he secured a mastership at Worthington College, a preparatory school!

He got his own education at night and taught by day. He spent a year in Germany studying, and then he returned to teaching in England, starting at the bottom. To get the necessary diplomas, he continued working nights. He referred to the period as "seven years' mental penal servitude." At the end of that time he had achieved a salary of 120 pounds a year. "It was thus," he stated, "at the mature age of twenty-seven years and eight months, that my school-days happily came to an end."

His writing career actually started while teaching at Brighton, where he contributed stories to the local paper. In his biographical background, he claims to have written for an American newspaper a historical sketch called *The Cross and the Crescent.*

A collection of verse entitled *Poems* appeared in pamphlet form under the Lara byline in 1883, and a second collection, *The Dying Faith,* in 1884. At the time he wrote this material he was English and Modern master at the Bolton grammar school, under the headmastership of Reverend J. Hewison.

It was at Bolton that he met his wife Elizabeth Brierly, daughter of a grocer (born April 20, 1861; died August 18, 1933), and they were married February 19, 1887, at the Parish Church of Great Lever in that city; he twenty-nine and she twenty-five. He taught at Bolton at least through 1887, passing his College of Preceptors Examination in that year, flinging it in the face of the school board, and quitting teaching forever.

He began writing for a "local London paper in 1888, eventually becoming its editor." The going was rough, and he not only wrote most of the paper but helped set type. Eventually the owner turned it over to him, and he struggled along, but got involved in a political crusade that resulted in a series of libel actions. He disdained to use lawyers and defended himself in court. He finally was forced to close down his paper.

Eventually he was out on the street, with starvation literally threatening him. From a friend he secured a letter of introduction to Cyrill Arthur Pearson, publisher of *Pearson's Weekly*. Part-owner and editor of *Pearson's Weekly* was Peter Keary, who put him to work addressing envelopes for the many circulation-boosting contests sponsored by that publication at two pounds or ten dollars a week.

Pearson's Weekly was a tabloid-sized, sixteen-paged publication, printed in six-point type, three columns to the page, without illustrations, that made its introduction on the newsstalls on July 24, 1890, at a British one penny a copy, dated July 26, 1890. The covers of the first and all issues that followed were printed on red paper and made up of a variety of small advertisements. The paper was a blatant imitation of *Tit-Bits* (one of very many), a publication which was the basis of the George Newnes fortune, introduced with the October 22, 1881, issue. In fact, the twenty-four-year-old publisher and son of a cleric, C. Arthur Pearson, had been the business manager of *Tit-Bits* and his associate, Peter Keary, an editor.

Tit-Bits was entirely composed of items that normally would be human-interest fillers in magazines or newspapers, the closest thing to it in the United States today being *National Enquirer*, except that the British publication stayed away from crime, sex, and the horrifyingly grotesque.

Tit-Bits had boosted its circulation with an endless series of simple contests, and through including accident *insurance* as part of the purchase price. *Pearson's Weekly*, in its first issue, offered one thousand pounds ($5,000) to anyone killed in a railway accident with a copy of the publication on his person, *providing* he had mailed in his signature on a form from a purchased copy of the issue of the week he was killed. The same issue also offered an annuity of up to 100 pounds a year to clergymen or ministers whose names were sent in on forms printed on the first page of the magazine by the most people. These and other contests were carried perpetually, and it was to handle the opening, sorting, and addressing of mail in their connection that George Griffith had been hired by *Pearson's Weekly*.

Because of his well-traveled background, he was a fascinating conversationalist and had a more practical knowledge of the world than his flamboyant life indicated. As a result, editor

Keary got to like him and set him to answering readers' questions for a column titled "What Can We Tell You?" This ranged all the way from the difference between white and red wines, to the recommendation that a far-flung family maintain communication by a circular letter. Gradually he began to write special features as well as columns for the publication, and he continued this through to the turn of the century.

Pearson's Weekly ran at least one short story every issue, frequently the lead-off feature of the number. In 1890 tales of fantasy, horror, and science fiction began to make up part of the mix. The fascinating short story "The Singular Case of Jeshrun Barker," November, 29, 1890, tells of a man who can remember the future! Of particular significance was the inclusion under the title of "The Baron's Visitor" in the April 18th number of Edward Page Mitchell's little gem of a story, of a ghost *from the future* that haunts the past, "An Uncommon Sort of a Spectre," which originally appeared anonymously in the United States in the New York City Sunday edition of *The Sun* for March 30, 1879. The first work of pure science fiction, "From Silvered Locks to Feeding Bottles," was a translation from the Spanish of R. B. de Bengoa, trimmed to half its length, with the title changed from "An Animal Elixir." It is an extremely well-done tale of an old man who permits himself to participate in a scientific experiment, where as part of the therapy he receives the infusion of blood from a four-year-old child. He finds himself daily growing younger and dies a stillborn infant, eighty-five years later. "What Darkness Means," a short tale published in the issue of September 12th, tells of a man who subjects himself to absolute and utter darkness for twenty-four hours, delineating with considerable effectiveness the experiences he underwent and the psychological impact upon him. A paraphrase of the famous science fiction hoax "The Case of Summerfield," where the Northern California populace was scared out of its wits by the apparently documented story of a man who claimed to have discovered a means of igniting the oceans of the world and threatened to do it unless paid millions of dollars (*Sacramento Union,* May 13, 1871), was run in *Pearson's Weekly* for December 3, 1892, as "The Finger of Fire."

The biggest sensation in magazine serials then prevailing had run earlier in the year in a six-penny, elaborately illustrated, tabloid-sized, slick-paper weekly, *Black and White,* subtitled

187

"A weekly illustrated Record and Review." With its January 2, 1892, number, *Black and White* had commenced *The Great War of 1892*, a fictitious forecast of a World War utilizing the literary technique of telling the story in the form of telegraph cables, letters, interviews, newspaper accounts, and "special correspondents." Future-war stories had been common ever since "The Battle of Dorking" (1879), but as an elaborately illustrated serial told with such journalistic realism, it was a sensation. The next year it was placed in hardcover by Heineman as *The Great War of 189—: A Forecast*, and the author was revealed to be Admiral Philip H. Coloomb, with the assistance of Charles Lowe, D. Christie Murray, and F. Scudamore. There was just a tinge of futurism, such as a battle fought at night with the aid of giant electric lights, and bombs dropped from a dirigible in an isolated incident. It was an excellent job of merchandising to the middle class, and it paid off handsomely in circulation.

All publishers were aware of its success, but C. Arthur Pearson cast about for some way to profit from it. Peter Keary, in his book *Success After Failure*, told of a discussion among the staff of *Pearson's Weekly* about who could do a new serial. Griffith said he thought he could, even though he had never written one before. A novelette of his, *The Veil of Tanit*, about the voyage of Vikings to South America after the seige of Carthage, had appeared in the special Christmas 1892 issue of another of Pearson's magazines titled *Search Light*. Skeptical, the staff agreed to permit him to try when he brought in a synopsis of *The Angel of the Revolution* the next day. The synopsis was published complete in the January 14, 1893, issue of *Pearson's Weekly*, apparently making it unnecessary to read the story, except that the serial hadn't been written yet! Week by week, between his other editorial duties, Griffith ground out the chapters, altering and embellishing the plot so as to remove the onus of knowing what was coming next.

The January 21 issue ran a prologue 5,000 words long that never appeared in the book. It told of Alan Tremayne, holding the titles Earl of Alanmere in Yorkshire and Baron Tremayne in Cornwall, lost in the Hartz Mountains of Germany, who is guided by some mental power through a snowstorm to a cabin inhabited by one of the loveliest girls that he has ever seen, and by a man whose head, down to his mouth "was cast in a mould

188

of the highest and most intellectual manly beauty," but from below that point resembled "the mouth of a wild beast." Below the hips he was a "dwarf and a cripple." The crippled man is Natas the Jew! (Natas is Satan spelled backwards), otherwise known as The Red Terror, head of a worldwide brotherhood of Nihilists. Tremayne hears Natas's story of his crippling by the Russians because he is a Jew, and his non-Jewish wife who dies in white slavery in Siberia. He meets their daughter Natasha, whom Natas has trained to be one of the leaders of his revolutionary movement. Tremayne is placed under hypnotic control of Natas to place himself in positions of influence and power for the Cause.

In London, Richard Arnold, a twenty-six-year-old inventor, has built a model of a flying ship utilizing the helicopter principal and powered by an internal combustion engine, employing liquefied gases as fuel. Here Griffith had escaped from the trap of trying to adapt the heavy steam engine for air flight. It was Griffith who had interviewed Hiram Stevens Maxim, inventor of the machine gun, for the August 13, 1892, *Pearson's Weekly,* presenting an elaborate description of a flying machine with the fatal flaw of steam power. Maxim had described the necessity of building a light condenser, and Griffith's inventor, Richard Arnold, in *Angel of the Revolution,* makes a point of stressing how his internal combustion dispenses with the condenser.

A demonstration of the flying machine is given to the Red Terror Group. In arranging the experiment, Arnold credits the origin of the idea as follows: ". . . you see that she is a combination of two principles—those of the Aëronef and the Aëroplane. The first reached its highest development in Jules Verne's imaginary 'Clipper of the Clouds,' and the second in Hiram Maxim's aëroplane." Verne's source of electrical power remained obscure, and Maxim's engine was too heavy. By using the internal combustion engine and adapting Verne's helicopter concept, he had built a successful machine.

Visiting Russia for the terrorists, Arnold brings back the news that a functional powered balloon has been demonstrated there, and fifty are to be purchased by the government of that country. A secret spot in Africa, which they call Aeria, is selected by The Red Terror group and prefabricated, completely finished parts for the aerial fleet after the model of *Ariel* are delivered by boat and assembled.

The world situation deteriorates and France and Russia attack England. Germany aligns herself with Britain, and a grim effort is sustained to keep convoys of food and supplies from the United States and Canada from being sunk.

Natasha, who had been captured during the incursion into Russia and rescued by Arnold, falls in love with the young inventor. She also begins to display her extraordinary marksmanship with weapons and coolness in emergency situations.

The head of the American terrorists threatens to withdraw his support from the cause unless Natasha is made his bride. Natasha flies to America presumably to accede to his demand, but at the meeting draws a pistol and shoots the man dead.

The big money interests in the United States have devised a plan to invade Canada, and send their fleet to blockade British ports. Before they can do this, the five million terrorists in the nation strike, cutting all communications, transportation, and shipping. Their airships hover over all key military installations, and the President himself is arrested. The Constitution of the United States is plucked from its case and torn up. "There were few who in their hearts did not believe the Republic to be a colossal fraud," Griffith stated.

Back on the Continent, the Russians and French mass to invade England. All of Great Britain's fleet is in position to repel them, but then, in an almost brilliant anticipation of future warfare, George Griffith has the Russians soften British defenses by a merciless bombing from improved powered dirigibles. Then the British fleet is attacked by a flotilla of French submarines with torpedoes, wreaking havoc, and simultaneously, the dirigibles slow down so that they hover above the warships and drop bombs with uncanny precision.

England is invaded and most of its armies trapped around an encircled London. Famine and rioting break out in the city, and it is only a matter of time before the siege results in surrender. In this dark moment, an agent of the terrorists arrives to see the King, with terms from Tremayne that call for turning over the British government to the Anglo-Saxon Federation, and, in exchange, rescue will arrive in seven days. The King accepts, preferring to surrender to an Anglo-Saxon conqueror than to a Russo-Franco-Italian bloc.

A vast army, recruited from America and Canada, sets forth in oil-fueled ships which travel beneath the ocean except for their decks, main guns, and stacks. A secret army has been training in Scotland and in remote sections of England. This army attacks, troop ships land, and the terrorists' aircraft come to the aid of the besieged armies of London. Proximity fuses are employed to destroy close-grouped enemy dirigibles in the air.

Natas, in his moment of final triumph and vengeance, sentences the Tsar to hard labor in the mines of Siberia for life. A new order is imposed on Europe, mandating the elimination of armies and the rule of the Federation. Natas abdicates his position of power to Tremayne, but at a following meeting of the hierarchy of his terrorists, tells the frightful story of the fate of himself and his wife in Russia and catalogues the incredible planned brutality towards the Jews by the government of that country.

A world police force was set up to stop wars by force in areas not yet under the control of the Federation. Of course, Arnold and Natasha are married, and the story ends with a "black-eyed six-weeks-old baby nestling in her bosom."

The Angel of the Revolution ran in weekly installments from January 21, 1893, to October 14, 1893, totalling 150,000 words. The results were gratifying to Pearson. Circulation began to soar. Letters of praise poured in. Competitors began frantically searching about for writers who could do something similar.

The Tower Publishing Co., Limited, was a relatively new firm, and did not attempt a wide spectrum of books, but selected strong titles that they thought might have mass appeal. Tower books were thought to be involved with Pearson, but there was no substance to this. Tower books were particularly noted for their excellent printing, binding, and illustration, yet sold at reasonable prices. W. Laird Clowes of the U.S. Naval Institute had written a novel of a naval war between France and Great Britain, *The Captain of the Mary Rose, a Tale of To-Morrow,* originally serialized during 1892 in *The Engineer.* Tower published it in hard covers with sixty illustrations by Chevalier de Martino and Fred T. Jane, many from the original magazine publication. Of the illustrators, Jane was especially interesting. His specialty was drawings of naval ships, but he was not a very good illustrator. Second only to naval ships, he loved to draw science fiction, and hundreds of his inferior drawings were to be found in magazines and books dealing with fantastic themes. This passion for science fiction would later result in his authoring at least four science fiction novels, several of them achieving considerable popularity.

The Captain of the Mary Rose, while exciting, was rather parochial speculation of naval operations in a hypothetical war between England and France, but it caught on at its six shilling price (about $1.50), received excellent reviews, and would eventually go into at least seven editions. This convinced Tower that there was a volume market in the higher-priced area for future-war books, so they contacted *Pearson's* for book rights to *The Angel of the Revolution,* publishing it in October 1893. An advertisement which appeared in the October 14, 1893, *Pearson's Weekly* revealed *for the first time* the name of the author!

The hardcover was a raging success. By early September, the sixth edition had been sold out, and no one has ever ascertained how many editions and printings the book eventually went into, though advertisements announcing the eleventh of the hardcover did appear. It was one of the bestsellers of its time, possibly the best-selling future-war book of the nineteenth century. Griffith was instantly established as one of the most popular authors of the day. The publisher had no trouble assembling rave reviews which were quoted in *Pearson's Weekly,* in advertisements in backs of other books, and in companion magazines.

Whether the royalties from the bestseller were received by Griffith or C. Arthur Pearson is conjectural. As an employee, writing anonymously for hire, Griffith may have forfeited them. Either way, his entire life was changed. He made an agreement to write exclusively for C. Arthur Pearson's publications.

Children were now a blessing instead of a burden, and he would eventually have three, two boys and a girl. When a son was born during the serialization of *The Angel of the Revolution,* he named the boy Alan Arnold, after *Alan* Tremayne and Richard *Arnold,* two of the heroes of the book. The names seemed to have conferred good fortune, because the boy would become Dr. Alan Arnold Griffith, FRS, CBE, recipient of the Silver Medal of the Royal Aeronautical Society and the Blériot Medal, for his theoretical and practical services to aviation, including a paper for the Aeronautical Research Council in 1955 on *The Boundary Layer in Satellite Re-entry Problems.*

A several-thousand-word synopsis of *The Angel of the Revolution* was printed in *Pearson's Weekly* for December 23, 1893, under the title of *A Flight into the Future,* "An introduction to the sequel to 'The Angel of the Revolution.' "

Even as the sequel to *The Angel of the Revolution* was announced, Alfred Harmsworth's competing magazine, *Answers*, had begun serialization of William Le Queux's future-war story titled *The Poisoned Bullet* with its December 1893 issue. The results were as felicitous for *Answers* as Griffith's novel had been for *Pearson's Weekly*, as sales began to soar. Le Queux, then twenty-nine years old, was the son of a British mother and French father, who had been disowned. After wandering through Europe, he secured employment on such papers as *The Middlesex Chronicle, The Globe, The Times*, and briefly edited *Piccadilly*, a society sheet. He had sold a number of stories and was on very friendly terms with George Griffith, C. Arthur Pearson, and Peter Keary. His account was straight journalism, written like a dramatic history book, with virtually no lead characters, no love interest or sub plot, and no marvelous invention. When it was completed, George Griffith recommended that he send it to Tower, who had done so well with *The Angel of the Revolution*. Le Queux took his advice, and Tower issued the novel in 1894, in a handsome illustrated edition under the title of *The Great War in England in 1897.* Just as in Griffith's novel, the combined armies of Russia and France invade England, and almost bring her to her knees. This time the alliance with Germany and help from the United States and the colonies turns the tide. The public reception was almost a duplication of the Griffith book, and Le Queux had made his first big reputation.

The Syren of the Skies was an extraordinarily advanced work of science fiction, displaying an almost towering imaginative superiority by George Griffith over those who had preceded him or his contemporaries. Additionally, Griffith's ability to draw unusual characters, particularly underscored with his impressive depiction of Natas, the crippled superman in *The Angel of the Revolution*, was highlighted again in the sequel, in his rendering of Olga Romanoff, the beautifully ruthless woman whose genius is dedicated to the restoration of the power of the Russian Tsar.

Olga Romanoff is the granddaughter of Paul Romanoff, a 100-year-old descendant of the crown of Russia, who was born the day Natas died. The year is 2030, and for 125 years the world has been ruled by the Supreme Council of the Anglo-

193

Saxon Federation. The strength of this Federation rests in the air fleet of Aeria, now populated by the descendants of the terrorists.

The book is strongly influenced by Edward G. Bulwer Lytton's famous "utopia," *The Coming Race*, published by Routledge, London, in 1874. Bulwer Lytton wrote of an underground world that had discovered the secret of the irresistible force called "Vril." With a potency comparable to an atomic explosion, this force could destroy virtually anything it hit.

The Aerians have a force similar to this, and Alan Arnold, son of the president of that group of rulers, reveals to Olga Romanoff at an early meeting: "I had better tell you at once that we have realised, to all intents and purposes, the dream that Lytton dreamt when he wrote that book."

Olga Romanoff's father had rediscovered the secret of flight and even improved upon it some years past. He was betrayed and the Aerians destroyed him. Olga Romanoff has vowed to avenge him.

She gains control over Alan Arnold and one of the Federation's ships through the use of a will-destroying drug. With Russian money, she builds an air fleet in the covered cone of a giant volcano in the Antarctic.

Olga Romanoff forms an alliance with Khalid, the ruler of 700 million Moslems, whereby he will lend her his aid in the conquest of the world, and, in exchange, Olga Romanoff will see that Russia, which has abandoned religion, will embrace the Moslem faith.

After one year in which Aeria has allied itself with England and Eastern Europe, both sides have built enormous war potential. The Moslem fleet is virtually destroyed by the invention of two devices by Aerian Max Ernstein. One is an anticipation of sonar, whereby it is possible to detect the presence of other ships miles away. The other is a magnetic device which destroys the effectiveness of enemy "radar." Air fights commence at speeds of 600 miles per hour. Six Russian cities are entirely devastated. Land armies find that they can only fight in the absence of air powers.

Years past, through a code performed on a photo-telegraphy system, communication with the civilization on the planet Mars had been established. Mars has a highly advanced, far less emotional, civilization than Earth. They send a message now that an enormous incandescent mass of gas, the result of the collision of two bodies in space, will intersect the earth in its orbit and consume the surface in flame. All this had been prophesied by Natas. There is hope for the survival of a very few in deep caverns within the earth.

Aeria digs underground, permitting the rest of the world to be conquered by Olga Romanoff's air fleet and the Moslem hordes.

When the earth has been purged by flame, the remaining Aerians emerge from the caverns. They search out Olga Romanoff in her Antarctic retreat, and find her partially paralyzed and mad. The Khalid is dead, but she believes he is Alan whom she has always loved. While expressing that love, she dies of a stroke.

The novel, with all the faults inherent in its weekly serialization—leisurely writing at some points and compressed action at others—is a supremely rich mosaic, with strong invention, resourcefulness of situation, and excellent characterization. The soundness of Griffith's predictions on war in the air, under the sea, the use of something akin to atomic energy, devices resembling radar and sonar, command great respect.

In many of Griffith's books, certainly more than any author of his times, women were truly liberated. Natasha was the gun-wielding heroine of *The Angel of the Revolution;* Olga Romanoff was the beautiful, evil, female genius who conquers the world; and his short story collection *A Heroine of the Slums and Other Tales* (Tower, 1894) led off with a heroine. In life he was to set out to top a woman's achievement announced in the very first (July 26, 1890) issue of *Pearson's Weekly,* when C. Arthur Pearson, under the heading of *Around the World in 74 Days,* wrote: "One of the most marvelous traveling feats ever performed was accomplished between November 14, 1889 and January 30, 1890. On the first date, Miss Elizabeth Bisland, an American author of great popularity, and with a personality even more charming than her literary style, started on a tour round the world with the object of seeing by how long a time she could reduce the famous eighty days in which this journey was accomplished by Jules Verne's hero, Mr. Phineas Fogg."

As the title indicated, Miss Bisland had beaten Jules Verne's time by six days and had obtained worldwide publicity as a result. Now Pearson struck upon the idea of sending a veteran and experienced traveler like George Griffith around the world, with an itinerary that would eclipse Miss Bisland's record.

Griffith was aided by Cook's Tours in working out a schedule that would permit him to circumnavigate the globe in sixty-five days or less by conventional means of transportation. He started out 11:00 A.M., Monday, March 12, 1894, from Charing Cross, and arrived in Southhampton on May 16th, to complete his circle in London two hours after his landing in England.

The June 2, 1894, issue of *Pearson's Weekly* began the series of articles on *How I Broke the Record Round the World*, and it was published in fourteen parts in thirteen issues, concluding in the September 1, 1894, number with "The End of the Run." He had shaved forty minutes off his own schedule!

So sharply had Griffith's serials lifted the circulation of *Pearson's Weekly*, and so convinced was the publisher of the appeal of fantastic adventure, that he was determined not to gamble on losing some of his new-found readership because of the lack of a suitable serial novel. There were few adventure story writers more popular than H. Rider Haggard after the appearance of *King Solomon's Mines* in 1885 and *She* in 1887. The issue following the conclusion of *The Syren of the Skies, Pearson's Weekly* began the fine lost-race novel, *Heart of the World*, which ran from August 11, 1894, to January 26, 1895. It was an enthralling story of the attempt and failure by the descendant of an Aztec emperor to retake Mexico from the white man and how he finds The Heart of the World, the golden lost city of the Aztecs, with its population intact.

Short Stories was a weekly all-fiction magazine, selling for a penny, which C. Arthur Pearson had acquired beginning with the number July 11, 1893. It had been launched by brothers E. and H. Bennett with the issue of January 12, 1889, as *The Magazine of Short Stories*, carrying "anecdotes" and "recitations and readings" as well as "adventures" in its sixteen pages of small type unbroken by illustrative matter. Experiencing little growth, the periodical had to be sold.

Pearson immediately put illustrations into the magazine and began the special insurance promotions that had proven so popular with *Pearson's Weekly*. He also began to place more emphasis on *serials* and broaden the range of adventure material published. Finally, to give it the big push in terms of appeal, he decided upon a new George Griffith future-war serial to attract that author's following to this recent acquisition. He prominently publicized *The Outlaws of the Air* for a number of issues in *Pearson's Weekly*, to begin in *Short Stories* for September 4, 1894, as a story that was not only an adventure, but dealt with the current menace of the Anarchists and the Nihilists, bomb-throwing groups who believed that the fabric of civilization was fundamentally wrong, and that it had to be destroyed before it could be rebuilt.

The plot of *The Outlaws of the Air* was in many respects close to that of *The Angel of the Revolution*. A secret society in London is left a legacy to continue their work to change the governmental structure of the world, as well as the secret of a special aircraft designed by their benefactor before he died.

A group of defectors, led by Max Renault, steal the aircraft. They proceed to bombard London with high explosives, blowing up the Parliament, Scotland Yard, the Bank of England, and other landmarks. France and Russia declare war on England for harboring the Anarchists.

Maxim helps design a new aircraft which is believed to be superior in performance to the stolen vessel. The new craft is also built on the helicopter principle and is armed with cannon and machine guns. The enemy is now duplicating the ship they have stolen, and in an aerial encounter with three of them, Maxim's vessel sends one crashing to the ground and captures a second.

An internal struggle within the anarchist organization results in Max Renault being delivered to the British for justice, and most of the other leaders being killed. The Aerial Navigation Syndicate forces a peace after bombarding Paris and destroying the Tsar's air fleet, and a utopian country of Oceana is established in the Pacific.

The Outlaws of the Air is a hastily written, poorly organized novel, showing every evidence of meeting weekly deadlines with appropriate cliffhanger endings. Yet, the utter cynicism with which it depicts the motives of *both* sides of a great war reveals that George Griffith was a step above the average thriller writer.

Reaction to *The Outlaws of the Air* was muted by the hardcover publication of *The Syren of the Skies* under the title of *Olga Romanoff* by Tower in November. The book was dedicated "To Hiram Stevens Maxim, the first man who has flown by mechanical means and so approached most nearly to the long-sought ideal of aerial navigation. . . ."

An advance copy reviewed by *The Birmingham Chronicle* was praised with the generous statement: "Mr. George Griffith has within the last year made a bound into the first rank of novelists. He is the English Jules Verne. There is not a more imaginative writer on the press, and hitherto all his best work has appeared anonymously. Mr. Pearson (of 'Pearson's Weekly') discovered him." Sales began to soar, and Griffith was on his way to another best seller.

Heart of the World, by H. Rider Haggard, concluded in the January 26, 1895, issue and two-thirds of a column was devoted to Griffith's new novel *Valdar the Oft-Born:* "In the forgotten days of the Golden Age, and in Asgard of the Gods within the vanished Polar Paradise, the action will commence. . . ." The editor made certain to remind the readers that "Mr. Griffith writes exclusively for 'Pearson's Weekly' and 'Short Stories.' "

The truth was that *Valdar the Oft-Born* was to be an imitation of a tremendously popular novel that had appeared almost five years earlier, *The Wonderful Adventures of Phra the Phoenecian* by Edward Lester Arnold, initially serialized in *The Illustrated London News* in twenty-six installments, July 5 to December 27, 1890. Edward Lester Arnold was the son of the respected narrative poet Sir Edwin Arnold, who was best known for *The Light of Asia,* a book of verse on the teachings of Buddha, and as an interpreter of Far Eastern philosophy. He gave the novel his sanction by writing an introduction for it "in the garden of my Japanese home in Tokyo, April 14, 1890."

Phra was a young Phoenecian merchant who sailed to Britain, there to marry the half-savage princess Blodwen, but is killed when the Romans invade the country. He revives 400 years later with his terrible wound healed, and finds his long-dead wife had tattooed the story of her life on his body year by year while he was entombed!

The saga of a man awakening again and again from death sleep, to enter actively into events and to be able to recount the history of England in terms of everyday living, adventure, and romance down a time corridor of 1,000 years, had irresistible appeal.

Edwin Lester Arnold was born in Swanscombe, Kent, England in 1857, and was taken as an infant by his father to India. In that country, the older Arnold was to serve as principal of Deccan College, Bombay, through 1861. The boy studied agriculture on the large Scottish and Midland estates after returning to England. Before attaining his majority, he tried settling in tropical Travancore, but came down with malaria and had to rejoin his father, traveling with him for many years.

Sir Edwin Arnold had become editor of the *Daily Telegraph* in 1873, and he secured his son a situation on the paper in 1883. There was no question that the father was influential in getting the story placed with so prestigious a publication as *The Illustrated London News.* First book publication was with Harper's in 1890, which is not as unusual as it sounds. *Harper's Magazine* at that time published its magazines and certain of its books simultaneously in England and the United States.

Edwin Lester Arnold would use the theme again in his novelette *Rutherford the Twiceborn,* published in the May 1892 *The Idler,* where a ghost forces Rutherford to go backward into life after life to where, in a previous incarnation, he had killed and stolen the family fortune from another.

It was the popularity of Arnold's story that *Valdar the Oft-Born* was intended to capitalize upon, possibly encouraged by William Ingram, publisher of the *London Illustrated News,* who had a financial interest in *Pearson's Weekly.* The unusual thing was that *Phra the Phoenician* was science fiction, with an attempted plausible explanation for the bouts of suspended animation, but *Valdar the Oft-Born* from the "new Jules Verne" was dedicated in its hardcover form: "To those whose faith in the ages-old doctrine of re-incarnation will reveal to them something more than romance in the saga of Valdar, this dream of the changing ages is fraternally inscribed."

Valdar, an immortal from the Norse Asgard sentenced to mortality for a transgression, is in Babel and Nineveh when they are destroyed by earthquake; awakes 2,000 years later in the new Nineveh; is in Egypt with Cleopatra; dies at the foot of the cross during Christ's crucifixion; stands at the side of Mohammed during the period of disbelief; leads a band of Norsemen on the Crusades; sails for Queen Elizabeth against the Spanish Armada; fights against Napoleon at Waterloo; and during each new life finds a woman who is the incarnation of his beloved Brenda who has chosen to share his fate. When the story ends, Valdar still looks forward to his next awakening and to more romance and adventure.

Valdar the Oft-Born began in the February 2, 1895, issue of *Pearson's Weekly* and concluded in the August 24, 1895, issue, every installment liberally illustrated by Robert I. Patter. The writing, characterization, dialogue, action, and the inventiveness of the situations were all superior to *The Wonderful Adventures of Phra the Phoenician,* and the concept obviously provided a marvelous format for a serial. Yet, because it was so closely imitative, and because it was an outright mythological fantasy rather than science fiction, it does not enjoy the repute of Arnold's novel.

Griffith was constantly seeking travel assignments for *Pearson's Weekly,* and on February 13, 1895, he left for Peru. He was so conscientious and prolific that stories and chapters of serials continued to arrive in England on every boat. There were six stories under the Levin Carnac pen name published from April 6 to May 11, 1895, the last one, *The Gold Plant,* an excellent work, where plants literally absorb gold from the ground and become preciously metallic.

John K. Leys, a writer of boys' novels, was the only other author who had science fiction appearing in *Pearson's Weekly* during this time. "Dr. Monk's Experiment," a two-part story which ran in the March 16 and 23, 1895, issues, told of a man who succeeds in discovering an unknown element in the blood which is the life force and is able to extract it from others and extend his own span of years.

The Outlaws of the Air was the last book of Griffith's published by the Tower Publishing Company, appearing in June 1895. Though it enjoyed a good sale and press, it is quite probable that no royalties were ever paid on it. On the recommendation of George Griffith, William Le Queux had given his novels *The Great War in England in 1897* and *Zoiraida* to Tower. The first title in particular had been a phenomenal best seller, but Tower went bankrupt and Le Queux not only received no royalties, but his copyright was sold to another publisher!

Fred T. Jane's future-war novel, *Blake of the Rattlesnake,* implying that torpedoes would decide the course of the next war, was published by Tower in 1895 and got excellent readership, but undoubtedly he was among those who failed to get paid. In his case, since he also illustrated his own book, he took an additional loss.

George Griffith found himself in the middle of a revolution during his South American trip, to judge by a three-part article, *Election by Bullet,* which began in the September 7, 1895, *Pearson's Weekly.* He pulled no punches. Having entered South America with a series of revolutions going on, it was his opinion that virtually all of the uprisings seemed to be a battle for the right to steal. The victors became the new oppressors until the next revolution.

It should also be remembered that when Griffith took a boat trip to and from South America, there was plenty of time to complete a novel in the progress of the journey. On the way back, Griffith had begun a new novel titled *Golden Star,* inspired by what he learned of the Incas in Peru. *Golden Star* began in the September 7, 1895, *Short Stories* and told of Vilcaroya, Inca Prince, and his sister, Golden Star, who agreed to be placed in suspended animation in a sanctuary, custodians of the secrets of their civilization, anticipating that the Spanish would destroy their empire. They hoped to be revived at some future date with the knowledge to restore its glory. Three hundred and sixty years later, Vilcaroya's mummified body is discovered and taken to England, where he is brought back to life by Dr. Laurens Djama, a physiologist.

Vilcaroya returns to Peru and, recruiting twenty loyal pure-blooded Incas, locates the gold cache of his race. Finally, unearthing Golden Star, Vilcaroya unites the peoples of the South American nations behind him and with the aid of sympathetic countries restores it to Indian rule.

The novel was not one of Griffith's better efforts, and he lost the opportunity of making it an unusual future-war story by compressing the reuniting of South America to less than half a chapter in the book. The Golden City concept could also have owed something to Haggard's *Heart of the World,* run only a little earlier. Before its conclusion in the December 21, 1895, number, *Short Stories* was running other science fiction, pirating them with little identification from American magazines and books. The most famous was "The Diamond Lens" by Fitz-James O'Brien, telling of a tiny woman viewed in a drop of water under a microscope, which appeared under the title of "The Eye of the Morning" by J. O'B in the November 2, 1895, number. Even more unusual was "The Balloon Tree," credited to Richard Sibert in the December 14, 1895, number, but actually written by the great American newspaper editor Edward Page Mitchell for the February 25, 1883, *New York Sun*. This little-known masterpiece is a sensitive story of the discovery of a highly intelligent and airborne form of plant life in Australia.

Pearson, now thoroughly convinced that serials were the road to success for a general fiction magazine, announced the publication of *Pearson's Story Teller*, to appear October 9, 1895, a weekly penny magazine to be made up *entirely* of serials, *eight* of them starting in the opening number. One of them, *Behind the Barrier*, billed as "a story of mystery and peril in the Antarctic regions," was an early important science fiction title written by George C. Wallis, who would still be appearing in magazines like *Weird Tales* and *Tales of Wonder* in the 1930s. The other serial of special interest was a nonfantasy novel by George Griffith, *The Knights of the White Rose*, a vigorous historical adventure novel of the seventeenth century.

While Griffith was traveling all over the world, C. Arthur Pearson was discovering new talent in future-war serials, the type of story that drew readership. His new find was the thirty-three-year-old Louis Tracy, owner of a popular sporting paper, *Paddock Life*. Tracy, at eighteen, was the youngest man in the history of the British army to gain a captaincy. His family was well off, but a letter he wrote to a local paper got him the offer of a reporter's position. He had been resident in India as the editor of a newspaper there and founded his own newspaper back in London, which he eventually sold. In November 1895, feeling that the world was hostile to Britain, and encouraged by a generous cash offer from C. Arthur Pearson, he set out to write *The Final War*, of England against the world, which began in the December 28, 1895, *Pearson's Weekly*, and concluded in the August 1, 1896, issue. Each installment was written week-by-week as the magazine went to press.

The story took place in 1898, when an invasion attempt by France and Germany on England is repulsed. The Suez Canal is blown up to prevent the French from seizing it. America allies itself with England.

The final triumph over the French is brought about by an electric rifle which projects a light that travels in parallel lines —*a laser beam*—and the bullets remain within the perimeter of that light as it focuses upon a target, never missing!

Within thirty days after the novel had been completed, it was out in hardcover from Pearson's in England and G. P. Putnam in the United States, soaring into the best-seller ranks in both countries. Tracy, by the simple device of making America the allies of Britain instead of their enemies, had insured himself a market across the Atlantic. "A capital story and full of action," *The New York Times* enthused at the handsomely printed (about $1.75) edition, ". . . Such a vast topic . . . treated in the cleverest manner."

If there was the slightest doubt that Tracy had that objective in mind all along, it was dispelled by his article in the September 12, 1896, *Pearson's Weekly,* titled "Do the Americans Really Hate Us?" Tracy had returned from a trip to the United States, and he brought back the message that the Americans fundamentally liked England above all other nations, and in a pinch would actually prove their staunchest ally.

C. Arthur Pearson as a reliable, well-paying publisher was beginning to attract an increasing number of new and old authors of ability and now had the money to launch new enterprises. His most successful was a monthly quality magazine to sell at the equivalent of ten cents to go into competition with *The Strand.* He would call it *Pearson's Magazine,* and the first issue, dated January 1896, on sale December 12, 1895, sold 200,000 copies almost immediately. The size of today's *National Geographic,* it was printed on fine paper, with illustrations and photos on virtually every page, and with names as illustrious as Rudyard Kipling, A. Conan Doyle, and Bret Harte to eventually grace its pages.

Significantly, George Griffith was utilized more as a staff writer of fillers for this publication than as a major circulation booster. An article illustrated by Fred T. Jane, "War on the Water," in the February 1896 issue, gave Griffith's idea of what would happen in a battle between two ironclad fleets; "The Grave of a Nation's Honour" was a vicious anti-American article by Griffith in the March 1896 number, on the United States' role in carrying forth the building of the Panama Canal and how our Monroe Doctrine kept South America in bondage. The May 1896 issue had "A Peep into Penal Servitude," a chapter of a book Griffith would eventually complete as *Sidelights on Convict Life.* The June issue carried a short story under his pen name of Levin Carnac, "A Genius for a Year," where special pills make a man literarily brilliant for one year. There were other contributions by him, but all of a minor nature.

The truth was that C. Arthur Pearson felt he did not need George Griffith for science fiction in his new magazine. He was now able to buy the works of a brilliant young genius, H. G. Wells, whose *The Time Machine* was the talk of the literary world in 1895. In the July 1895 number he ran "In the Abyss," a short story by Wells of the discovery of intelligent manlike marine life, with an advanced culture, on the sea's bottom. Illustrating the story was Warwick Goble, whose inspired grease pencil may have made him the greatest science fiction illustrator of his day against formidable competition. Apparently aware of this, Pearson blurbed: "Mr. Goble's illustrations which accompany the story, are as brilliantly conceived as the story itself."

Making money from his phenomenal output, George Griffith was more interested in travel assignments than he was in assessing the implications of what was happening. When Pearson asked him to make a trip to South Africa, to appraise the situation there, and write a *near-future* war story of what might occur, he was ready to leave in three days.

Given carte blanche to travel at will, Griffith visited the Cape Colony, Natal, the Free State, the Transvaal, the Portuguese territory, and Bechuanaland. He secured an exclusive interview with President Kruger and other leaders of his government, and came away convinced there would be a showdown between England and the Boers. His introduction to *Briton or Boer?* appeared in the August 1, 1896, *Pearson's Weekly*, in which Louis Tracy's *The Final War* concluded. Each chapter was illustrated by the top-ranking artist Harold Piffard. The story, which ran through to January 9, 1897, was well done, thrill-packed, and exciting, involving intrigue, a naval battle with the Russians, and truly engrossing army campaigns across South Africa until the Boers are conquered. The real Boer War would commence October 11, 1899, when the Boers invaded Natal, and end May 31, 1902, when a peace treaty would be signed at Pretoria.

Though armored trains with cannon and machine guns were the most advanced technology employed in *Briton or Boer?* and though the probability of the war did not require brilliance, the book was both timely and readable, and would prove to be one of Griffith's most popular. The advent of the *real* war saw an eighth edition in May 1900, simultaneously with a cheap printing.

For reasons which have never become known, Pearson did not continue to publish Griffith's books. Perhaps *Valdar the Oft-Born* had proved disappointing relative to the outstanding sales of *Angel of the Revolution* and *Olga Romanoff*. Ironically, it was William LeQueux, whom Griffith had led astray by recommending Tower as a publisher, who returned a poor favor with a good one. At a dinner at the home of Peter Keary, editor of *Pearson's Weekly*, Le Queux introduced Griffith to F. V. White, a book publisher with whom he had enjoyed very favorable business relations. White was to publish the majority of Griffith's books until that author's death, beginning with *Briton or Boer?* in February 1897, and following it quickly with *Golden Star* under the title of *The Romance of Golden Star* in June 1897.

Pearson's policy on future-war stories specifically and imaginative stories generally was achieving phenomenal sales results for him. At a stockholders' meeting of the company held October 15, 1896, at Winchester House, London, *Pearson's Weekly's* sales were put at a half million a week and the sales of *Pearson's Magazine* were said to be gaining momentum. Advertising was so good that in certain cases they could not keep up with it and had to turn some away.

To keep the sales rising, they rushed into print Louis Tracy's new serial, *An American Emperor*, beginning with *Pearson's Weekly* for December 26, 1896, two weeks before the conclusion of *Briton or Boer?*, and to run through to July 24, 1897.

Though most of the war aspects were a battle between the French and Arabs, *An American Emperor* proved to be a startling success. An American billionaire, Jerome K. Vansittart, goes to France and puts into effect a scientific project to irrigate the Sahara with fresh water distilled from the oceans as part of a plan to secure a woman of royal blood.

Louis Tracy, writing week to week, had gotten sick once during *The Final War* and almost missed an installment. Possibly the same thing happened in *An American Emperor*, because he called in a friend, M. P. Shiel, to write chapter twenty-nine, which spanned the April 17 and April 24, 1897, issues.

205

Shiel was a struggling writer who the previous year had issued a small volume, *Prince Zaleski,* concerning a detective who was a weirdly gothic pastiche on Sherlock Holmes. Shiel's greatest reputation would come later with *The Purple Cloud.*

Pearson, at least temporarily, had assigned Louis Tracy as well as George Griffith to the second team. Already, Louis Tracy's new novel of a French doctor who uses Mesmerism for base ends, and who is done in by an amateur lady detective, was scheduled to begin in *Short Stories* the issue of February 16, 1897. Starting with the May 25, 1897, issue of that same publication, George Griffith would start a series titled *Men Who Have Made the Empire,* which in a jingoistic style would emerge as profiles of twelve great Empire builders from William the Norman to Cecil Rhodes.

The April 1897 issue of the monthly *Pearson's Magazine* perhaps underscored the cavalier attitude of Pearson towards his crack future-war writers, George Griffith and Louis Tracy. That issue featured the opening installment of the greatest future-war story of them all, *The War of the Worlds,* by H. G. Wells. The furthest in advance anyone had carried the future-war story up to that time was George Griffith in *Syren of the Skies,* where the civilizations of 100 years in the future fight it out while the earth is in process of destruction by a fiery comet. Both George Griffith and Louis Tracy had made it unequivocally clear in the dedications of their books and in interviews that C. Arthur Pearson had not only motivated the future-war stories, but even specified what continental cities were to be conquered and by whom. Pearson was paying top dollar for his stories and calling the shots. Previously, H. G. Wells, in a letter to Arnold Bennett, stated that he received the equivalent of seven and one half cents a word for the serialization of his novel *The Sea Lady* in *Pearson's Magazine* in 1901. Though Wells, in an introduction to a 4,000-word condensed version of *The War of the Worlds,* published in the February 1920 issue of *The Strand Magazine,* purports to have gotten the idea for the story from a conversation with his brother while walking through the countryside, it is almost certain that Pearson strongly suggested a future-war story to end all future-war stories, and H. G. Wells said as much in a letter to Elizabeth Healy, when he wrote, "I'm doing the dearest little serial for Pearson's new magazine, in which the earth is invaded by aliens from another planet."

The Time Machine had made Wells's reputation, but *The War of the Worlds* made him economically. The English public relished in the novelty of having the Martians devastate their countryside and turned his book into a best-seller. In the United States it was serialized by *Cosmopolitan* and published in hardcover by Harper's.

Since we know by Wells's own admission that he read and admired Griffith, and since we know he simultaneously was contributing material to the same magazine, is it unreasonable to conjecture that he may have been influenced by other ideas of Griffith beyond those in *Outlaws of the Air* which he openly acknowledges? *Olga Romanoff* had several important sequences about highly advanced Martians that communicate with the earth civilization of 100 years in the future. That could have been instrumental in making the origin of the invaders the planet Mars, instead of the Moon, Venus, or Mercury!

While *The War of the Worlds* (illustrated by Warwick Goble) was still running in *Pearson's Magazine, Pearson's Weekly* announced: "Mr. H. G. Wells' story, 'The Invisible Man'—which starts next week will be one of the most entrancing serials ever written . . . Tell everyone you meet that 'The Invisible Man' appears in next week's P.W." The penny weekly which had spearheaded Pearson's road to fortune with future-war novels written by a staff serial writer now could afford a masterpiece by an author who was probably the greatest science fiction writer of all time.

The Invisible Man, by H. G. Wells, began in the June 12, 1897, *Pearson's Weekly* and ran nine installments through August 7. None of the installments were illustrated, though short stories in the same issues carried numerous cuts. It was obvious that Pearson thought he had something out of the ordinary, for as it opened he blurbed: "Nothing so genuinely thrilling, so marvellously entrancing, so thoroughly out of the common, has been written for many a long year."

Pearson's got the book rights to *The Invisible Man* and published it at three shillings and six pence (about eighty-five cents) in September 1897. He promoted the book with an article, "Would You Like to Be Invisible?" in the September 25, 1897, *Pearson's Weekly,* sporting the same line drawing of an invisible man in a bathrobe drinking a glass of water which appears on the front of the first edition. He also ran an interview with

H. G. Wells, "The Story of a Story, or, How the Invisible Man Was Created," in the November 20, 1897, *Pearson's Weekly.* The book was lengthened and revised from the magazine, and later editions would carry an epilogue.

With H. G. Wells, Pearson found that he had a tiger by the tail. *The War of the Worlds* had put Wells in such demand that he could name his own price for fiction and pick his own spots. He was then, as he would remain throughout his life, eternally dissatisfied with publishers, shifting from one to another. No one owned Wells. Therefore, while Pearson could on occasion buy a Wells story in the future when he bid high enough, there wasn't a prayer of keeping him exclusively or even semiexclusively.

Wells was probably not the only important contemporary author influenced by the work of George Griffith. The circumstantial evidence is strong that both *Trilby* and *The Martian* by George Du Maurier derived elements from Griffith's works, *The Angel of the Revolution* and *Olga Romanoff.*

George Du Maurier, the renowned artist who interpreted British life for *Punch,* as a result of a conversation with Henry James, decided to write fiction and produced three fantastic novels, *Peter Ibbetson, Trilby,* and *The Martian,* all best-sellers. Further, he had probably met George Griffith. *Pearson's Weekly* was running a series of interviews titled *Workers and Their Work,* published anonymously, but it has been established that Griffith wrote number nineteen in the series in which he interviewed Hiram Maxim, the inventor. An earlier interview, number fifteen, was on George Du Maurier and ran in the December 12, 1891, issue of *Pearson's Weekly.* This interview, titled "George Du Maurier and Society Art," specifically mentions the novel *Peter Ibbetson,* which had just scored a success that year.

In *The Angel of the Revolution,* the Jew, Natas, through the power of hypnotism, forces the British noble, Alan Tremayne, to do his bidding in changing the course of world events. Like *Trilby,* Tremayne is helpless to resist and can only incompletely understand the consequences of his work. Natas has "bought" and married a Gentile girl.

The most powerful character in *Trilby* is the infamous Svengali, a Jew, who, through the power of hypnotism, forces a girl to perform his bidding and thereby accomplishes what he cannot do himself. The girl, Trilby, is helpless to match wills with him and only dimly understands his end objectives. Svengali also lusts after a Gentile girl, in this case Trilby.

Serialization of *The Angel of the Revolution* began in the January 21, 1893, issue of *Pearson's Weekly*. Serialization of *Trilby* began in the January 1894 issue of *Harper's Monthly Magazine*.

Olga Romanoff by George Griffith incorporated a method of the highly advanced, intelligent Martians communicating with us. The novel to which it was a sequel, *The Angel of the Revolution*, had as its heroine the brave, beautiful Natasha who is half Jewish.

In *The Martian*, a highly advanced intellect from the Red Planet comes to Earth in spirit and through automatic writing influences the life of her host. The "heroine" of the novel is Leah Gibson, a beautiful, brave Jewess.

Olga Romanoff was serialized as *The Syren of the Skies* beginning with the December 30, 1893, issue of *Pearson's Weekly*. *The Martian* was first serialized beginning with the June 1896 issue of *Harper's Monthly Magazine*, which was simultaneously published in the United States and England.

During the end of 1897, George Griffith was not giving a thought as to whether he had been influential in the plot directions taken by two such popular figures as H. G. Wells and George Du Maurier. He was grinding out fiction to satisfy the demands of the Pearson organization. His novel, *The Gold Magnet*, an undistinguished adventure story about the invention of a device that is attracted to gold the way a compass is to the North Pole, began in *Short Stories* for October 16, 1897.

Far more fascinating was a long novelette, *The Great Crellin Comet*, published in the Christmas Annual of *Pearson's Weekly* in November 1897. (It was the vogue during that time to publish an *extra* issue at a greater size and price to be given as a gift at Christmas.) A giant comet is about to hit the earth, and the danger is that its nucleus may be dense enough to cause a disaster. Giant cannon, like those of Jules Verne's *From the Earth to the Moon*, are built in both England and the United States to fire projectiles with a velocity of ten miles a second timed to explode on hitting the nucleus of the comet. The most interesting thing about the story is that an actual *countdown* from 10 to zero is used.

Needless to say the comet's center is destroyed, but preceding the collision, Griffith has British science fiction sales soar: "Every existing copy of the 'Journey to the Moon' was brought up within an hour; Camille Flammarion's wonderful story, 'The End of the World,' had already been translated into every civilized language and was selling by millions; while Mr. H. G. Wells's even more extraordinary 'War of the Worlds,' although it had no actual bearing on the great subject, was bought up in colossal editions with almost equal avidity."

Knowing that H. G. Wells was no longer within his reach, Pearson promoted Louis Tracy back to *Pearson's Weekly* with a sequel to *The American Emperor* titled *The Lost Provinces.* This standard future-war novel of a battle between Germany and France began with the January 1, 1898, number and ended June 11, 1898. Armored steam-driven tanks, coupled two together so that troops could be carried behind enemy lines and equipped with machine guns to decimate the German troops and bring a French victory, make their appearance.

By now, Louis Tracy had done more for his friend M. P. Shiel than get him a single chapter to write. He obtained for him a commission to write a future-war serial for *Short Stories. The Empress of the Earth,* which ran from the February 5, 1897, issue to June 18, 1897, brought the yellow menace to England (although the United States had "enjoyed" a number of stories of its own conquest by the Asians eighteen years earlier, the best known *The Last Days of the Republic* by P. W. Dooner, 1880). Under the direction of Dr. Yen How, the Yellow Hordes conquer all Europe up to the English Channel. The British drown 20,000,000 Chinese, and kill another 150,000,000 by germ warfare, and win the war. The book, published by Grant Richards as *The Yellow Danger* in 1898, was one of Shiel's better-selling volumes.

Shiel then got the commission to write a novel based on the Spanish-American War then in progress, to follow Louis Tracy's "The Lost Provinces" in *Pearson's Weekly.* Titled *Contraband of War,* it commenced in the May 5, 1898, issue and ended July 9, 1898. It projected the war between the United States and Spain, and at one point a powered balloon drops bombs on a battleship, but is shot down with a rifle. Torpedo boats enter into it, but even though the end of the war is not told, M. P. Shiel assures the readers that, since Americans are Saxons, they must inevitably defeat the Latins! Accompanying *Contraband of War* in the May 14, 1898, *Pearson's Weekly* was an article titled "Can the Yankee Navy Win?" predicting that the United States would have a tough time against Spain and only the Anglo-Saxon strain of blood present would see it through. The May 21 issue had a page and a half on "The Yellow Press" of the United States and the part it played in forcing the country into war.

Meanwhile George Griffith had been ordered to duty on Pearson's humorous penny weekly, *Pick Me Up*, subtitled "The Artistic Comic," to grind out a future-war serial titled *The Great Pirate Syndicate*, beginning with the issue of March 19, 1898, which evidenced many of his faults and a few of his good points. The United States, using a fraudulent set of Russian papers alleging that the original Alaskan border was five degrees further east, claims gold of the Yukon territory. The greatest scientists of the western world join to produce the weapons to bring this predatory power to bay. They create an air vessel with helicopter lift that can sail on the ocean and fly in the air, and which is housed on an *aircraft carrier* powered by turbine engines, making it the fastest ship on the sea; aerial torpedoes which can fly five miles and descend vertically on their target; and a radio device that can turn all ship's metal brittle and, through polarization at both ends of the vessel, eventually explode its powder magazine. Despite all this hardware, the problem is solved by buying up "The Yellow Press," which they assert forced the United States into the Spanish-American War, using it to influence Congress to pass laws forming an Anglo-American alliance.

It was obvious that the future-war story had been reduced to a formula and was standard hack fare as a circulation-builder of Pearson magazines specifically and many other British magazines generally.

Exempt from this criticism was a long novelette, *Hellville, U.S.A.*, by George Griffith, which appeared complete in the Double Summer Number of *Pearson's Weekly* for August 6, 1898. Griffith has some 30,000 revolutionaries and criminals forcibly relocated in a newly created city in Arizona and permitted no intercourse with the outside world. The results are the creation of a new Sodom with Gomorrah thrown in for good measure. Finally, the wife of the President, with the backing of the clergy, decides that after all, these people have souls and

211

there are many women among them. She leads a band of reformers into their midst and is never seen again.

In portions of this story the satire is good, and it clearly precedes in concept the much more famous Robert A. Heinlein story, "Coventry" (*Astounding Science-Fiction,* July 1940), where a similar situation is developed much more thoroughly. The low opinion in which Griffith held Americans seemed to intensify with time, probably aggravated by the fact that future-war writers like Louis Tracy had their novels published and enjoyed excellent sales in the United States, but his own were completely ignored.

Aware that he was not making it in a literary sense, Griffith tapped his impressions of South America to produce for book publication in April 1898 *The Virgin of the Sun,* a fictionalized version of Pizarro's conquest of Peru. Pearson would not serialize the story, though, strangely, he was willing to publish it as a book. It was almost as though he owed Griffith this chance. Probably to promote the novel, he ran just the prologue under the title of *The Line of Fate* in the April 23, 1898, *Pearson's Weekly,* and in an introduction to the excerpt, said: "It . . . is the most ambitious piece of work Mr. Griffith has yet done. He wrote it, as he told me recently, with the intention of getting in the first rank of living romanticists."

Griffith's next and last serial for a long while for *Pearson's Weekly* was a vigorous and colorful action story of the fall of Babylon, *The Rose of Judah,* replete with the colorful names of Belshazzar, Nitocris, Miriam, and Daniel, which ran from October 8, 1898, through to January 23, 1899. Considering that M. P. Shiel's serial *Cold Steel* which began in the December 31, 1898, *Pearson's Weekly* to May 6, 1899, was a historical swordplay story, it might be thought that Pearson was getting away from the idea of the future-war story. To the contrary, beginning in *Short Stories* for August 6, 1898, he *reprinted* Louis Tracy's *The Final War.* The following year, beginning with July 8, 1899, *Short Stories* reprinted George Griffith's *The Angel of the Revolution.*

Griffith, who had been living in Kensington, London, by 1899 had moved to Norfolk Cottage in Littlehampton, predominantly because of his love of sailing. He soon became a live wire in the community, rising to Commodore of the local boating club.

Abruptly, Griffith was off again for Australia, the precise purpose of his trip unknown, except that he said he wished to revisit scenes of old adventures. It almost sounded as though the wanderlust had seized him, and he departed *at his own expense,* instead of on the company expense account. The number of trips he made and when he made them is not clear. It was his claim that he had been the first to discover the source of the Amazon. This exploration could have occurred while he was in Peru. Along about 1896, he drifted in a balloon across the channel from London to Agincourt. He first made the British *Who's Who* for 1899, and after his death when he was listed in the British *Who Was Who, 1897 to 1916,* his quoted remark about his Agincourt exploit noted "that he was the last Englishman to fall there."

While on his Australian trip, George Griffith wrote one of his most engaging novels, *A Honeymoon in Space,* which started with the invention of a spaceship, the *Astronef,* powered by the secret of antigravity, whose inventor marries the girl he loves before the takeoff on an interplanetary voyage of exploration and has the distinction of the first honeymoon in space.

No science fiction novel by Griffith had ever run in *Pearson's Magazine,* so the decision to break *A Honeymoon in Space* into a series of six short units for that purpose was a pleasant surprise for him. In doing so, they had to eliminate the honeymoon portion entirely, so they retitled the series *Stories of Other Worlds,* and in the January 1900 issue in which the first, *A Visit to the Moon,* appeared, they ran almost a full-page synopsis of what had been cut, which comprised fully twenty-five percent of the novel. A tour is made of Mars, Venus, Jupiter, Saturn, and the asteroid Ceres.

The idea of a honeymoon in space may very well have come from the publicity stunt performed by famous astronomer, science popularizer, and science fiction writer Camille Flammarion (whose name Griffith specifically mentions in the text of his story *The Crellin Comet*). Flammarion spent his honeymoon aloft in a balloon and wrote an account of it for a London magazine.

By early 1903, no identifiable Griffith material was appearing in any of the Pearson magazines. It seemed probable that he had come to a parting of the ways with the company. Confirmation of this was implied in the 1903 assignment he received

213

from the *London Daily Mail* to cover Joseph Chamberlain's trip to South Africa, following the end of the Boer War. His last science fiction for Pearson's may have been the short story "The Raid of the Le Vengeur" in the February 1901 *Pearson's Magazine,* about foiling the attempt of a French submarine to enter the Thames River. One of his series of *Sidelights on Convict Life* was published in *Pearson's Magazine* as late as November 1902.

Hardcover books continued to appear, but a number of them never had any magazine publication at all. In 1901, three fantastic novels were published: *The Destined Maid* (February), in which the villain, shot in a duel, literally turns into a skeleton before his opponent, Chetwynd; *Denver's Double* (April), "a story of an inverted personality," dealing with identical twins, astral occupation of another's body, and hypnotism; *Captain Ishamel* (October), an extraordinary novel of a man doomed to wander deathless through the ages, who several times meets *the* Wandering Jew, and in the end invents long-range guns with explosive shells, in a "world of if," long before anyone else. Griffith, who embraced no religion, seemed to have strongly swung to the occult in 1901, something he had occasionally done in the past.

The books seemed to pour out in his last few years, and a substantial number of them returned to the theme of future war. Among the better known was *The Lake of Gold,* "A Narrative of the Anglo-American Conquest of Europe," published in 1903 by F. V. White. An inventor who takes his girl on a honeymoon in his new aircraft sees the glow from a lake of gold while flying over Patagonia at night, and uses the money to seize control of the American stock market and to form a syndicate which forces peace on Europe through an advanced fleet of airships and submarines. A good part of the story involves itself with American stock operations, and because Griffith is kind enough to permit the Americans a positive role in saving the world, he was rewarded by serialization of the novel in *The Argosy,* running in eight installments from December 1902 to May 1903. It was the only story by Griffith to appear in a magazine edited and published in the United States. No book of his was ever be published in America during his lifetime.

The World Masters, also issued in 1903, told of an enforced peace on the world through an invention which makes all met-

214

als too brittle to use. *The Stolen Submarine*, published in 1904, was a tale of the Russo-Japanese War, involving a superexplosive and a submarine. Ironically, Griffith did not know that the first submarine ever produced by a commercial manufacturer, The Electric Boat Company of the United States, was sold to Russia for use in the Sino-Russian War. When it was put on a flat car and shipped across the Trans-Siberian Railroad, it was found it could not be passed under the bridges, so bridges were rebuilt or circumnavigated all the way to Vladivostok. When the submarine got to Vladivostok, it was discovered that no one had thought of ordering torpedoes. By the time the order for torpedoes went through, the war was over—*and lost!*

After 1904, royalties on Griffith's books began to decline and so did his health. He looked around for a place to keep his family where the pound might stretch further. He selected Port Erin upon the Isle of Man, a large island, then boasting about 35,000 population, set in the middle of the Irish Sea, somewhat northeast of Dublin and northwest of Liverpool. He was virtually bedridden when his novel *The Great Weather Syndicate* appeared from F. V. White in May 1906. This time, instead of planes and submarines, Griffith's International Cartel used control of the weather to roast or freeze the world into an end to war.

The last story he ever wrote was "The Lord of Labour," which languished in manuscript until released by F. V. White February 11, 1911. An editor's foreword to that story gives some revealing insights into his last days: "Strange though it may seem, this strongly militant story was dictated by the author on his death-bed. He lay—'A waterlogged derelict,' as he merrily termed himself—and worked with such persistence, in spite of the orders of his medical adviser and the entreaties of his family, that he carried this novel to its end. His commanding voice rang out as he warmed to his subject, amazing all who knew his extreme physical weakness. With the exception of slight clerical errors, no alteration has been made in the story, and it is now published for the first time as the 'Swan Song' of George Griffith."

The discovery of a radium mine off the coast of England provides the hero with the wherewithal to work on his radium rifle, whose explosion kills all nearby through heart shock and those a little more distant are disabled with a nervous breakdown. Utilizing the explosive in the radium guns in guided aerial torpedoes which only have to detonate within the area of a target to destroy it, an invading German army of three million is first demoralized and then defeated. Virtually to his dying gasp, Griffith continued to dictate war after war, each to end all wars.

George Chetwynd Griffith died June 4, 1906, at The Retreat in Port Erin on the Isle of Man at the age of 48. The cause of his death, certified by James Harold Bailey, M.B., of the Victoria University, was cirrhosis of the liver. Malaria, which Griffith had suffered from in Hong Kong, can cause a condition similar to cirrhosis, and so can hepatitis. However, Griffith's quoted statement that in the end he was "a waterlogged derelict," seemed to indicate that liquor was the primary cause of his demise. In his later books, drinking becomes more prevalent, and in at least one of his novels, he refers to the equivalent of an Alcoholics Anonymous in London.

New hardcover titles by Griffith would continue to be issued up until 1911. Of special interest was *The World Peril of 1910,* published by F. V. White (July 1907), which combined his typical European war dominated by aircraft and submarines with the menace of a comet about to hit the earth. In a sense, this had been done in the writing of *Olga Romanoff,* but in *The World Peril of 1910* he literally incorporated thousands of words from *The Crellin Comet,* which had previously been gathered in a short story collection, *Gambles with Destiny* (F. V. White, 1899). There was some revision, including lengthening the countdown from ten to twenty seconds, eliminating the name of Crellin, and other changes. Segments of *The Crellin Comet* were dropped into place sporadically throughout the midst of a straight full-length future-war novel.

The six-penny Griffith reprints to which H. G. Wells refers proceeded to be issued in a veritable flood in the years before his death. Six pence was about equivalent to ten cents, so these were the low-priced paperbacks of their day.

The last issuance of any Griffith edition before the end of World War I was the future-war novel *The World Masters,* from John Long in May 1914.

World War I was in progress. Most future-war stories were instantly dated. Even if they had not been, any appetite the

British public had for vicarious thrills of this type was sated by reality.

It is a legitimate question to ask of psychologists what did the seemingly endless torrent of future-war stories between 1871 and 1914, with Griffith only one of the perpetrators, indicate about human nature? Basically, did the people of England crave such a war? Did they masochistically enjoy the endless procession of catastrophes and defeats they suffered in most of the stories before final victory? Just as the Germans wanted to be told that the Aryans were the super race, did the British really want to read, over and over again, that Anglo-Saxon blood was inherently superior to all others and would always win out?

To stretch the matter one step further, for those who earned enough for survival in England at the turn of the century, was life such an endless bore that the dire perils projected in future-war stories provided some of the excitement that the ordinary course of living denied them? What part did these novels play in readying the country for a conflagration that their leaders knew impended?

The early novels alleged to be written to warn England of the pitfalls of unpreparedness, but the later ones obviously pretended to do no more than satisfy the appetite of the masses, and make some profit for the publishers and writers. There was no outcry from the pulpit against the flood of such novels, yet the clerics were not loath to rage and rant against the "penny dreadfuls" read by children and teen-agers, with their "soul destroying" stories of the Wild West, crime detection, and violent or exotic adventure. Did this lack of criticism indicate that future-war novels were actually "approved" literature in political circles?

George Griffith was obviously a popular, admired, and influential writer in his era. He has not survived his times because his literary output was for the most part a reflection not a shaper of the feelings of the period. He danced to the beat of the nearest drummer.

UNEXPLAINED PHENOMENA:

Lo! The Poor Forteans

Mostly in this book I shall specialize upon indications that there exists a transportory force that I shall call *Teleportation*. I shall be accused of having assembled lies, yarns, hoaxes and superstitions. To some degree I think so, myself. To some degree I do not. I offer the data.

That paragraph, the last in chapter two of *Lo!* by Charles Fort (Claude Kendall, New York, February 9, 1929), was taken out of context to open the serialization of that book in *Astounding Stories*, April 1934, which thenceforth ran for eight installments. The author had died only two years earlier, May 3, 1932, in a Bronx hospital, so he did not live to see the widest publication any of his works had ever received. *Astounding Stories* had at that time a circulation between 45,000 and 50,000. *Lo!*, the most successful of Fort's books in three printings, had reached a total audience of about 3,000.

F. Orlin Tremaine, editor of *Astounding Stories*, had taken over editorship of the bottom magazine in science fiction with its revival in October 1933, and the publication of *Lo!* was merely one step in a drive for field leadership (which he achieved in less than one year). His tool was "thought variants" or offbeat, fresh, original ideas, and his publication of *Lo!* was prompted more to supply his writers with new concepts than with the hope of enthralling the readership. Fort projected a multitude of far-out theories and notions, a few of which had not been previously used in science fiction.

"Here is the most astounding collation of factual data ever offered to a large audience. This book has been read by three thousand people—mostly writers seeking plots! We can offer it to the one group in America which can digest it," Tremaine told his audience in a dynamic opening blurb.

"*Lo!* is the natural inheritance for a thoughtful audience. So we bring it to you. It opens the door to controversial discussions in 'Brass Tacks.' Read it all. And you will believe that super-science is real," Tremaine concluded.

The first chapter was devoted to newspaper accounts of falls of frogs, fish, periwinkles, snakes, eels, crabs, red worms, and lichen from the skies. The second chronicled falls of coins on Trafalgar Square, the walls of a house that exuded oil and paraffin, scarlet rain, bleeding statues, strange animals, and possible sea serpents.

So it went for eight installments. At first the readers were politely appreciative of the "interesting" or "fascinating" accounts. Then they began to complain of boredom. Finally, they did not mention it at all.

There was literally no controversy in the reader's department (Brass Tacks). There were only a few stories in the year following that by any stretch of the imagination could have been attributed to ideas from Charles Fort. Among these were "Set Your Course by the Stars" by Eando Binder (*Astounding Stories,* May 1935), where the first rocket takes off from earth with its navigation instruments lined up on certain stars and then is forced to return when it is discovered that space is white instead of black; and "Exiles of the Stratosphere" by Frank Belknap Long, Jr. (*Astounding Stories,* July 1935), involving an advanced race with lighter-than-air metals that dwells in the upper strata of the air, sending only outcasts to the earth's surface. Even these were not directly attributable to *Lo!* but to theories in an earlier book of Fort's, *The Book of the Damned* (Boni & Liveright, 1919).

"Fortean concepts" were not unknown to the more serious collectors and authors of science fiction, even then. When *Lo!* was reviewed in the July 1931 *Amazing Stories,* its critic, C. A. Brandt, displayed an obvious familiarity with the author.

"In this book as well as in 'The Book of the Damned,' there is an oft-occurring reference to mysterious rainfalls causing the appearance of frogs, fishes, worms, etc. The generally accepted explanations have never satisfied Mr. Fort, so he must attack any and all explanations of any and all phenomena as totally incorrect and absurd.

"He is an expert mountain-maker. Given the tiniest molehill, he will make the Himalayas hang their heads in shame. His views on astronomy are somewhat peculiar and astounding: The stars are about a week's travel away, to him, the earth is pancake shaped. And it seems to rile him that scientific bodies do not welcome improved theories or explanations with open arms. . . ."

That C. A. Brandt's assessment of Fort's attitude was incontrovertibly valid was attested to by Edmond Hamilton, one of the early important specialist science fiction writers to transform Fort's ideas into fiction.

Hamilton worked up a correspondence with Fort by sending him some clippings involving inexplicable happenings. "I once asked him," Hamilton recalls, "what he would do if the Fortean system were taught in the schools as right and proper. He wrote back, 'Why, in that case I would propound the damnably heterodox theory that the world is round!' He was a born rebel."

The life of Charles Hoy Fort, particularly in his maturity, was in some respects as bizarre as his theories. Most of what is known of his early youth is derived from remaining portions of his unpublished autobiography, *Many Parts,** written in 1901. He was born in Albany, New York, August 9, 1874, son of Charles Nelson Fort and Agnes Hoy Fort. His father was the son of a wholesale grocer, apparently involved in the business and moderately well off, and his mother's family was engaged in the sale of plumbing equipment and supplies. He had two younger brothers, Raymond and Clarence, and his mother died in 1878, less than a month after the birth of her last son. The father hired a housekeeper to take care of them, finally remarrying in 1887, this time a young woman named Blanche Whitney.

The three boys were subjected to sometimes brutal disciplinary measures, and there was ample evidence that it was in part deserved. The youngest brother, Clarence, was institutionalized at the age of ten as emotionally disturbed, and Charles was in a constant state of revolt.

Charles's major interest as a boy was in the living things of nature, but he had no "reverence for life," cold-bloodedly killing, dissecting, or preserving whatever creatures were unfortunate enough to stray across his path. At that time, his desire was to be a naturalist.

*Quoted extensively in Damon Knight's book, *Charles Fort, Prophet of the Unexplained* (Doubleday, 1970).

The baroque sense of humor which was to manifest itself so frequently in his books was much in evidence during his high school days. His grades were deplorable, but he was learned, gleaning much information from the library of his paternal grandfather, Peter V. Fort. He showed writing ability in high school, enough so that his maternal grandfather, John S. Hoy, introduced him to a friend on the staff of the *Albany Democrat*. He did well on special reporting assignments, though suffering constant criticism for his difficult-to-read handwriting in an era when typewriters were not yet common. His experience at covering every type of assignment found him in 1891 selling brief featurettes and fillers to the *Brooklyn World* and probably to other markets. These items were rarely over 200 words long and frequently were humorous in nature.

Headstrong and willful, he smashed the glass in the front door of his house when, arriving home late one night, he found himself locked out. He got into further arguments with his father and ended up living with John Hoy. Shortly, he left for the Big City and a job on the *Brooklyn World*, which paper had been purchasing his filler material. He briefly edited a suburban weekly, the *Woodhaven Independent*, established by several men from the *Brooklyn World*. When that collapsed, he decided to bankroll the twenty-five-dollar-a-month legacy left him on the death of his paternal grandfather, Peter Fort, as the basis for seeing the world. Physically a shade under six feet tall and weighing close to 200 pounds, he was more than a stripling when he sallied forth.

During the two-year period centering around 1893 and 1894, he claimed to have traveled 30,000 miles, sopping up the essence of "life" needed to prepare him to be an author. He journeyed as far as South Africa and spent a substantial amount of time in the southern United States and in various parts of England. His travels were centered most heavily on English-speaking countries, and through all of this he worked very little, surviving on the twenty-five dollars a month sent to him (in a day when a working man was glad to get one dollar a day for a twelve-hour stint, the amount was equivalent in buying power to at least $200 today).

When he became ill from an unspecified disease he had picked up abroad, an English-born girl he had known in Albany since the age of thirteen, Anna Filing, befriended him. The result was their marriage on October 26, 1896. He was only twenty-two at the time, and she was four years older.

His family did not approve of his marriage, feeling that Anna Filing was beneath him socially. Intellectually they had little in common. She was extroverted, devoted herself to the kitchen, knew everything about all her neighbors, and regularly attended the motion pictures for diversion. He was introverted, frequently buried in some sort of research or literary endeavor, concerning the nature of which she knew far less than even his few correspondents. They had no children, but there seems to have been great devotion between them their entire married life. She put up with his many idiosyncrasies and he would accompany her to the motion pictures that held little personal interest for him, and their terms of reference to one another were unquestionably warm.

Writing sales were being made, but they were of the most humble type. Jokes and anecdotes were sold to the comic supplement of *The New York Sunday Journal,* tongue-in-cheek fillers to *The New York Herald,* an occasional quip to *Judge,* all of these bringing in from one to ten dollars apiece and usually published anonymously.

There were periods when his wife as well as he was seriously ill, and when everything that could be pawned and sold went to put food on the table. Fort's greatest ambition was to sell fiction, but no one seemed to be buying any.

Fort made few friends in his lifetime, but those he did make proved to be influential. The most important was Theodore Dreiser, whom he supposedly first met as a newspaperman in the nineties.

The melancholy and complex man who had authored *Sister Carrie* had been a contributor to *Ainslee's* since 1898, a magazine that was Street & Smith's first attempt to leave the dime-novel field and compete with popular general magazines like *Cosmopolitan, Munsey's,* and *McClure's.* He had made a friend of Richard Duffy, the magazine's editor, who helped him secure a position at Street & Smith editing dime novels.

One of the most influential men at Street & Smith was Charles Agnew MacLean, editor of *The Popular Magazine,* which was then challenging *The Argosy* for circulation leadership in the all-fiction adventure pulp magazine field. MacLean was much impressed by Dreiser, even using some of his poetry in *The Popular Magazine*. MacLean bought back the plates for *Sister Carrie* from Doubleday, paying $500, and planned to publish the book with Dreiser. When Street & Smith decided to publish an all-fiction pulp magazine aimed at women to be titled *Smith's*, MacLean recommended Dreiser as editor.

It was there that Charles Fort approached Dreiser with his short stories, probably because he had known him from his former newspaper days.

Dreiser, who would popularize the vogue of naturalism in fiction, became excited when he found Charles Fort's techniques far ahead of his time in composing slice-of-life vignettes, faithfully realistic interpretations of life in New York, all presented in an avant-garde stylistic method. Afraid to use him initially in *Smith's*, which still had to establish itself as a women's magazine, he introduced him to Charles Agnew MacLean with such an enthusiastic buildup that four of Fort's offbeat stories were accepted for use in *The Popular Magazine*.

He did not stop there. Theodore Dreiser's brother, Paul, had changed his last name to Dresser and was building a reputation as an actor and a songwriter. (He is best remembered for *My Gal Sal* and *On the Banks of the Wabash*.) Dresser had collaborated with Robert H. Davis, the fiction editor of the Munsey magazines, including *The Argosy*, on a play titled *Boomerang*. Dreiser sent Fort over to Davis, who also bought several of his stories.

When Richard Duffy left Street & Smith's in 1905 because they wouldn't give him an interest in *Ainslee's*, he took a job as managing editor of *Tom Watson's Magazine*, "The Magazine with a Purpose Back of It," a monthly, printed on book paper, featuring serious articles on international and national affairs, political cartoons, as well as fiction. Dreiser did such a good selling job on Duffy that seven issues in 1906 ran a short story by Fort, and most of them were his works of stark realism and avant-garde writing. Arthur Sullivant Hoffman, later to become the editor of *Adventure*, was then assistant editor of *Tom Watson's Magazine*.

For *Smith's* magazine, Dreiser got Fort to write the more sentimental type of tale that would appeal to female readership.

Only about two dozen Charles Fort short stories with place of publication have been so far established; twenty-two of them appeared in an eighteen-month period in magazines dated June

1905 to February 1907. The majority of those stories have never previously been examined for elements that might have provided the genesis of the later nonfiction works that were to create his reputation, or for a basic appraisal of his early writing skills.

He had submitted a 2,500-word story titled "Is This Earth Alive?" to *Tom Watson's Magazine* which was published in the March 1906 issue as "A Radical Corpuscle." The story is a brief satire which might be considered science fiction. The leucocytes, red corpuscles, and white corpuscles have a civilization in the human bloodstream, which culture numbers philosophy as one of its sciences. There are debates as to whether the host they inhabit is actually a living thing, and Fort draws parallels to the earth.

"Pursue your analogy!" cries a rival philosopher. "If we populate a living creature, then the creature inhabited by Man itself must be a corpuscle floating in the system of something inconceivably vaster. We are leucocytes to Men; Men are to the Earth; then hordes of Earths are to a Universe? You speak of many Men. Are there hordes of Earths?"

"How can these many independent bodies be part of a solid?" it is asked.

"Only comparatively are they far apart," is the reply, "as to a creature microscopic enough, the molecules of a bit of bone would seem far apart and not forming a solid, at all. To the molecules nearest to him he would give names, such as Neptune or Mars; like men, he would call them planets; remoter molecules would be stars."

Attempting to puncture that logic another corpuscle responds: "That a myriad worlds like your fancied Earth are molecules to an ultimate creature? But there can, then, be no ultimate creature; he, in turn is but a microscopic part of—Beware of him and don't listen to him, my friends!"

An angry mob finally shouts: "And he says that we, with our great warriors and leaders, our marvellous enterprises, our wonderous inventions, are only insignificant scavengers of this Man we inhabit? Down with him! Or, if we're too civilized to tear him apart, put him away where he belongs!"

As the philosopher barely escapes with his life into a tiny vein he hears the parting shot: "He says we were made for Man!" jeered the few leucocytes who gave the distasteful doctrine another thought. "But we know, and have every reason to know, that this Man was made for us!"

This satirical story is the earliest example so far uncovered of a line of thinking that would gradually lead Fort to the concepts expressed in *Book of the Damned.* It was also in *Watson's Magazine* that stories appeared which indicated that there might be some hope for Fort as a stylist and interpreter of human affairs.

This commendable outpouring of saleable short stories was to end with the appearance of "Mickey and the 'Collegemen' " in the February 1907 issue of *Smith's.* With Dreiser's departure for a top-drawer job at *Broadway Magazine,* sales were over at *Smith's,* and as a result of a falling out over publication of *Sister Carrie* with Dreiser, Charles Agnew MacLean also terminated sales at *The Popular Magazine* for Fort.

Watson's Magazine, doing poorly, was sold to an Atlanta, Georgia, firm with its January 1907 issue, and the name changed to *Watson's Jeffersonian Magazine.* Richard Duffy departed, to eventually find a post on *Literary Digest.* Not only did Fort lose the market at *Watson's Magazine,* but they never paid him $155 they owed him, which conceivably could have been the total amount for all seven stories!

Theodore Dreiser had invested in the B. W. Dodge & Company, book publishers, and had gotten them to reissue his book, *Sister Carrie.* It was a critical success. He was hailed as a literary doyen, called a "genius," interviewed by *The New York Times.* On the crest of this acclaim, he was offered a job as editor of *Delineator,* a women's magazine devoted to fashions, homemaking, cooking, patterns, and society, with some fiction and articles. He shifted from *The New Broadway Magazine* to *Delineator* with its July 1907 issue, and the former market closed on Charles Fort and there was no place for him in the latter. Dreiser, as a matter of special interest, took Arthur Sullivant Hoffman from *Watson's Magazine* to serve as his managing editor.

By the end of December, Fort was in an utterly desperate position. He had no markets, he was unable to sell the house left him by his grandfather, his belongings were gone, and there was no money left.

How he survived the following year is not clear. There is a possibility that his wife went to work. There is no record that he sold a piece of fiction to any magazine from 1907 to 1910.

Brief subjects with titles like "The Cow That Passed the Regents," "His Face Now Another's," "The Day of Two Sunsets," and "Ignatious Cassidy in a Greenhouse" had been verified as sold to *The New York Herald* and other newspapers in 1904. There was strong evidence that he continued to write these fillers, jokes, and anecdotes all along, and through them eked out a pitiful existence.

His passion for spending hours on end in libraries making notes of odd events that he came across was originally not an eccentricity. The notes were initially intended to provide source material for newspaper and magazine fillers. As economics grew worse, the library also became an avenue of escape from the grim realities without, and eventually an obsession in his lifelong search for strange phenomena.

It was Theodore Dreiser who in 1908 again came to Fort's help. He asked him for a *novel* to be published by the Ben W. Dodge Company in which he owned an interest and from which he drew a salary. Whether this was the spark that encouraged Fort to virtually go berserk and write novels totalling 3,500,000 words from 1908 to 1917 is not known. What is known is that the one solicited by Dreiser was the only one ever published, and all the rest were allegedly destroyed.

The title of his published novel, *The Outcast Manufacturers*, issued in hardcover by Dodge, New York, in 1909, sounds as though it may contain plot substance similar to the material in his later books, but the word "outcast" proves to be an *adjective*. It refers to the Universal Manufacturing Company, a New York firm that manufactures nothing, but is actually a mail order "business" operated by a man who stocks no merchandise, sending the orders he receives to be filled to companies that do, after deducting his profit.

The "hero" is a young boy from New Jersey who answers an advertisement for an advertising and promotion manager. Upon arriving in New York, he soon finds himself amidst a cast of characters who not only are like something out of Dickens, but which are *patently copied from Dickens*. He has deliberately come to New York to *fail* in business, because his rich uncle, whose operations he may inherit, believes that no one can be a success until he has failed at least once.

Upon abysmally "failing" six months later, he writes his uncle, telling him he is now ready to be welcomed into the family business, having fulfilled the requirements. The punchline comes in his uncle's reply: Since the boy started out to fail in the first place, and has accomplished his objective, he has *succeeded*, and so has *not* fulfilled the required conditions.

Fort could write, but he couldn't plot. This was true of all his short stories, as well as his novel. His idea for *The Outcast Manufacturers*, paper-thin for a short story, is lost in pages of Dickensiana. This weakness suggests a stylistically gifted writer desperately in search of a plot, later researching mountains of unusual evidence to formulate a hundred and one bizarre theories, unable to shape them into a cohesive whole, to remain all of his life no more than an excellent reporter with a unique style. He was frustrated by those who *could* see some pattern in the universe. Fort was a style in search of a story.

Only a single phrase in *The Outcast Manufacturers* hints at the later Fort, and that is when one girl twice repeats to a friend the term "telepathic realization," which was certainly an unusual expression to be used by a first-generation Irish girl in the slums of New York.

Whether Fort was invited to contribute anything to the four issues of the magazine *The Bohemian*, which Theodore Dreiser secretly owned and published September to December 1909, has not been established. Nothing under his name appeared. He is believed to have had a short story in the difficult-to-locate and short-lived magazine *1910*, titled "Had to Go Somewhere," since galley proofs of the story exist.

It is sometimes said that Charles Fort was not familiar with science fiction. Such statements are blatantly ridiculous. Many of the short story markets he solicited ran science fiction regularly, including those he had sold to like *The Argosy, The Popular Magazine, The Black Cat*, and *Broadway Magazine*. At the age of twenty, he was thrilled by the best seller *A Journey in Other Worlds* by John Jacob Astor (Appleton, 1894), Richard Ashby in *The Reincarnation of Charles Fort (Borderline*, January 1964) asserts. It was the antigravity unit making possible interplanetary travel in the story that intrigued Fort the most, and this concept appears in his later books. His short story "A Radical Corpuscle" was satirical science fiction.

In reading endlessly at the library, and making an interminable number of notes, it is inconceivable that Fort did not examine the leading periodicals of the day, particularly those that frequently published material on unknown phenomena. Fort is credited with creating an entire school of science fiction, the concept of Earthmen prey to or "owned" by superior creatures, the mysteries of sargasso seas and blood rains from the skies, grappling hooks coming down from the heavens and scooping up "samples" for analysis, teleportations, the movement of material objects for no apparent reason, and similarly provocative subjects. It must now be said, with considerable emphasis, that the influence of Fort may have helped *popularize* such topics, but there was science fiction precisely on such themes before he ever wrote his controversial books. *To take it one step further, circumstantial evidence is strong that he became infatuated with those concepts from reading several works of science fiction.*

The most significant was *Up Above* by John N. Raphael, initially published in the December 1912 issue of the British *Pearson's Magazine*. Some fifty-one pages, six of illustration, were occupied by the novel, which was later to appear in expanded book version from Hutchinson, London, in 1913. It was the major item in the annual Christmas issue of the magazine and was subtitled "The Story of the Sky Folk." The following credit was carried beneath the story: "The central idea and some of the details of this story have been borrowed by permission from 'Le Péril Bleu,' by Maurice Renaud."

Maurice Renaud was a misprint for Maurice Renard, a French science fiction writer whose *Le Péril Bleu* had been issued by Louis Michaud as a 372-page novel in 1911. Renard had previously appeared in translation and condensation in *The London Magazine* for September 1910, with the story *The Fixed Flight.* Its original appearance was earlier the same year from *Mercure de France* as a 247-page novel titled *Le Voyage Immobile; suivi d'autres histories singulières.* The story told of a whistling meteorite that passes over a ship at sea several nights in a row, following showers of shooting stars, and on its last appearance explodes, depositing a man into the sea. Upon being fished out of the water and becoming rational, the man reveals that he has invented an antigravity device that permits a ship to remain motionless in the upper atmosphere, while the earth revolves beneath it. The tale was published in 1932 by Hugo Gernsback as number fourteen of his "Science Fiction Series" (a group of eighteen twenty-four-page brochures sold through the mail) as *The Flight of the Aerofix,* and ran only 10,000 words. Maurice Renard would later gain fame for *The Hands of Orlac,* which in 1925 was made into a film in Germany, starring Conrad Veidt, under the title of *Orlacs Haende* by Robert Wiene, the producer of the classic *The Cabinet of Dr. Caligari.* The story was screened again by MGM as *Mad Love* in the United States in 1935 and introduced Peter Lorre to the North American audience. The plot deals with the grafting of a criminal's hands onto the wrists of a pianist who has lost his. The criminal, brought to life, seeks to regain his hands.

Americans had previously been offered Renard's novel *New Bodies for Old* from Macauley in 1923, whose theme, derived from *The Island of Dr. Moreau* by H. G. Wells, tells of the transference of a bull's and a man's brain, strange combinations of animals, and even the linking of the brain of a man to an automobile!

The digression concerning Renard is essential, for he will emerge as a most likely source of some of Charles Fort's basic ideas.

On the same basis, John Nathan Raphael, Maurice Renard's intermediary in the transference of his ideas to English, must also be considered. He was born in 1868 and died in 1917. When remembered at all, it is for his dramatization of *Peter Ibbetson* by George Du Maurier, the play in which a man and a woman live an entire life together when asleep, which was put into an actor's edition by Samuel French only as recently as 1934. There was at least one other book about the stage by Raphael, *The Callaux Drama,* published in an expensive illustrated edition by M. Goschen in England. He may have become acquainted with Renard through a mutual interest in the theatre, for Renard had published a book, *Theatre of Cherbourg,* in 1909.

Another French fantasy, *The Re-Appearing (Il Est Ressuscité)* by Charles Morice, dealing with the second coming of Christ, was translated for Hodder & Stoughton, London, in 1911. He was a prolific contributor of cultural articles and sentimental short stories to such publications as *Harmsworth's Magazine, The London Magazine,* and *Cassell's Magazine* since the turn of the century.

In *Up Above,* the reader is hit first by a rash of disappearances, beginning with the Prime Minister of England, continuing with an elm tree pulled up by the roots, an invalid woman in bed from the wreckage of a collapsing house, the town pump, the sign from outside the Blue Boar Tavern, a gilt-edged weathercock from the top of a church, a ewe and a curly-horned ram, climaxing with the story of a man who claims to have been picked up by some invisible force "making a grating sound" and dropped some distance away.

The natives of the region attribute the aerial disappearances to "Sky Folk," and when Professor Henry Tellurin arrives to investigate, his theories are similar.

"Has it ever occured to you [he asks the narrator, Rawlinson,] that if the fish at the bottom of the sea be thinking creatures they must have regarded the sudden disappearance from their midst of deep sea trees, of deep sea coral, and of their friends, their relatives, and enemies, very much as we here on earth regard the curious disappearances from Chalford? Imagine yourself for a moment to be a fish at the bottom of the ocean . . . imagine a huge shadow, the shadow of a gigantic submarine, flying over the land at the bottom of the sea. Out of this great shadow descend cables with huge grappling hooks attached, and suddenly landmarks from the bed of the ocean, seaweed, plants and corals, which, to the creatures at the bottom of the sea, are as much landmarks of their daily life as were the great elm and the village pump in Chalford, disappear up above. . . . Imagine how much more terrified and how much more puzzled they were when nets came down from the same mysterious shadow and took up fish from the ocean bed.

"Imagine then a race of people, let us call them Sky Folk . . . who live in what we call a vacuum—in air which is so rarefied that to the creatures who live in it the air we breathe must seem as thick and unbreathable as water appears to us. . . . But let us suppose that this race of Sky Folk has the same curiousity about the earth and the people on it as we have about the creatures at the bottom of the sea.

"Isn't it plausible that having this curiosity, and having at their disposal scientific methods, of which, for the present, we can know little or nothing, they should endeavour to discover more about us? How would they try to obtain information?"

Shortly after his expression of opinion, an opaque outline of an immense pincer descends from the skies and carries off a young man in front of the girl he has been picnicing with. *A fortnight later, Chalford is horrified by a light fall of red rain from the skies, which proves to be real blood.*

"If we were fishing and the fish were small," Professor Tellurin asks his friend, "what should we do with them?"

"Throw them back," is the reply.

Several nights later, a party of twenty picnickers are horrified when the decapitated head of a gorilla falls into their midst. Shortly afterward, the body of the man who disappeared falls into a lake from the sky, partly skinned.

The dead man has kept a diary. After he was picked up, he was kept in a room whose walls were transparent on all four sides, suspended in the air. The other human beings and animals who had disappeared are all in nearby cubicles, plainly visible. While they can see one another, sound cannot pierce the transparent barriers. They are fed vegetables periodically and "rooms" are temperature and pressure controlled. Even quantities of dirt, rocks, and seawater are held on display, in what is obviously a combination museum and zoo. He feels he is inside a gigantic invisible ship suspended over the atmosphere. He hears the squeaking of the Sky Folk, but never sees them. Once the air supply fails and he falls unconscious, but they restore it before he dies. "I suppose they look upon the birds which they have caught much as we look on shallow-water fish, and that us and the animals they must consider as we consider shellfish and heavy deep-sea creatures."

He observes them beginning their dissection experiments on creatures, including the gorilla whose head fell to earth. He straps the book of notations to his body, knowing that it will soon be his turn.

Finally, the big alien ship suspended above the clouds develops power trouble and settles, invisibly, in Trafalgar Square, creating havoc. The Prime Minister of England, who had disappeared, can be seen apparently sitting in midair. A tremendous effort is made to cut into the hull of the transparent ship and reach him. The outside of the vessel is like diamond-hard ice, but eventually a hole is drilled through it. The squeaking of the ship's masters can be heard. With the drilling of a second hole, the squeaking stops. The entrance of air and the change in pressure had killed the "aliens."

As they get the prime minister out, the "sub-aerine" literally

231

begins to *melt* into water. As the story ends, the thought is expressed that the "aliens," whoever they are, "will not send down another expedition."

It would seem strange if Charles Fort had not read the British edition of *Pearson's Magazine,* since 1896 one of the leading magazines of the English-speaking world, circulated and kept by many libraries in the United States. He had meticulously examined newspapers and obscure scientific journals going back more than a century, literally page by page.

Only a month earlier, in *The Popular Magazine* for November 1912, the late Jacques Futrelle's (he went down with the *Titanic* on April 15, 1912) short story "The Flying Eye" stressed similar plot material. Futrelle was already internationally renowned as creator of The Thinking Machine, a detective character that still is regarded as a classic in the genre. He had written a new series titled *The Secret Exploits of Paul Darraq,* which was running in *The Popular Magazine,* and "The Flying Eye" was the third story featuring that detective character, and it is unquestionably science fiction. Futrelle had written science fiction before, most notably a short novel titled *The Diamond Maker,* whose title is self-explanatory, published by Bobbs-Merrill in 1909.

The young detective, Paul Darraq, "investigates" a gigantic eye which appears daily over a New Jersey lake, and then disappears from sight. He brings companions with him, and, as they view it, the body of a man hurtles out of space and splashes into the water. Then, with no apparent aid, the man ascends from the water into the air and disappears into nothingness. Darraq states he has been searching through encyclopedias to find if in the past any natural phenomena similar to the appearance of a great eye has occurred, but can find none. Abruptly one of Darraq's companions suddenly is lifted by an invisible force and disappears into the sky. Darraq himself, in responding to a request for a meeting, dissolves into the air over Central Park, New York City. Over New York Bay, flying seagulls suddenly hit something invisible and fall to the ground. A bag of sand drops from nowhere onto the bridge of a battleship.

The problem is solved when it is revealed that a paint has been developed which makes an airship invisible, except for the port through which the pilot sees, which resembles a gigantic eye. A special hoisting apparatus is used to whisk individuals from the ground into "nothingness," and Darraq, who knew it all the time, has actually been acting as a government observer and tester before they buy the patent from the inventor.

The Popular Magazine had then a circulation of about 400,000 twice a month, and was one of the world's leading all-fiction magazines. It was also the same magazine to which Charles Fort had previously sold four stories.

The cover of the November 14, 1914, issue of *All-Story Cavalier Weekly*, illustrating the first of four installments of George Allan England's *Mystery of the Sky*, "The Empire of the Air," would have been enough to attract Charles Fort's attention even if Munsey had not been a market that he had sold several stories to previously. It showed a pulsating yellowish globe from which wriggled six pseudoyps with "eyes" on their ends, and it floated weightlessly in the air in front of an elderly savant. Paul Kramer has disappeared in the air after breaking the altitude record for the airplane, in sight of friends with high-powered binoculars. An observer, photographing through a twenty-four-inch telescope, watched the plane whisk from sight, and a series of photographs establishes the time within seconds.

The floating globe shown on the cover comes to the scientist's laboratory and conveys a message from Kramer: "If you can imagine a deep-sea fish instantly transported to a mountaintop, and there endowed with human intelligence and powers, you can form some faint conception of the indescribable transmutation which has overtaken me." He warns of deadly peril and human annihilation.

Kramer speaks through a girl in a coma from captivity in the fourth dimension, where the aliens are tangible to him and where they, for reasons not explained, cannot kill him. The aliens are intergalactic marauders who wish to reduce the earth to a gaseous state wherein it has nutrient value to their race. Directing the battle plan from the fourth dimension, Kramer has five men ascend in aircraft to be whisked into the other plane to assist him. Dust from Krakatoa, the giant volcanic explosion of 1833 which killed 30,000 people, still floats in the upper atmosphere, producing the frightening red sunsets seen on occasion. Polarization of the dust produces a field of negative energy which destroys the other-dimensional invaders and the story ends. But inherent in it were the Fortean concepts of disappearances into the air, moving balls of energy, unidentified flying objects, and superior beings to whom we are less than insects. Fort may well have read it.

It was in the period following the appearance of these stories that Charles Fort's "novels" turned from "humanistic" themes such as characterized *The Outcast Manufacturers* to theories and ideas that were definitely science fiction and were precursors of *Book of the Damned*. At least two such novels were written, one titled *X* and the other *Y*. Theodore Dreiser strove with might and main to sell them. He was particularly enamored of *X*, which he described as having as its theme the Martians projecting a ray upon the earth which brings into existence Man and other life, much like a photo is developed on a film. Allegorically, life is nothing but a motion picture with the substance of reality. Dreiser wrote his one-act play *The Dream* entirely based on Fort's concepts in the novel *X*.

The information about *Y* is more tenuous. It is said to have had an Antarctic locale. A character is Kaspar Hauser, who is described in detail in *Lo!* as the mystery boy who wandered into Nuremburg in 1828 with two letters, unable to read, astounded by the simplest things as though he had seen them for the first time. In *Y*, he is actually an emmissary from an unknown civilization. The use of the Kaspar Hauser material in *Y* dates the research on portions of *Lo!* to at least as far back as 1915.

How Fort existed from 1910 to 1916 is anyone's guess. He may have been assisted by Dreiser, and if so, at considerable sacrifice. Dreiser, in 1910, became infatuated with the seventeen-year-old daughter of a widow who worked as an assistant editor at Butterick. He threw over his wife, but the mother of the girl exposed his intentions towards the girl to the higher echelon of the company and he was fired. B. W. Dodge & Company, in which he owned an interest, went into receivership. In the years that followed, he made his living by freelancing, chronically in debt. During World War I, his outspoken sentiments in favor of Germany, as well as the "salaciousness" of his material, made him less than welcome in many markets.

In 1916, Charles Fort's economic situation took a dramatic turn for the better. When Fort's father died, he was left nothing, but the death of an uncle on May 28, who had received part of his father's legacy, emancipated him, for an estate was settled on the three boys. The death of the youngest brother, Clarence, saw a division between Charles and his remaining brother, Raymond. There was no indication of affluence, but he now had enough to live on without working. He could spend all his time in the library gathering data to write the kind of books that satisfied his sense of achievement.

Fiercely loyal, through bad times and good, Dreiser continued to try to sell Charles Fort's work. Finally, he was shocked to learn that Fort had destroyed all of his novels, including *X* and *Y*, but was sending him *The Book of the Damned*, the first volume of strange phenomena, for possible sale. Horace Liveright of the publishing firm of Boni & Liveright, had been cultivating Dreiser, hoping to get a "big" book from him. Dreiser took *The Book of the Damned* to Liveright and made the outrageous demand that either he publish it, or the firm could forget about him in the future. Liveright capitulated, and a small first printing appeared December 1919, to be followed by a second printing February 1920.

The question might be legitimately asked, why was Dreiser so interested in Fort's far-out, superscientific material. His enthusiasm for Fort's earlier works of realism was more understandable. The truth was that Dreiser found fascination in science, particularly theories on the creation of life, and there is multitudinous evidence that he read a great deal on the subject. Beyond that, he was interested in mysticism, one of his favorite books being Mark Twain's *The Mysterious Stranger*. In 1916 he published a volume of plays for reading titled *Plays of the Natural and Supernatural*. Among the plays in this volume was *In the Dark*, where an entire repertoire of spectral creatures influence the uncovering of a murder; ghosts from different ages of mankind hobnob in *A Spring Recital*, with cordons of mythical and near-mythical things; a locomotive and a shadow, handled as living forces, collaborate to kill a strange child in *The Blue Sphere;* and in *Laughing Gas*, the anesthesia itself is a "Power of Physics," and sundry shadows participate in dramatizing the situation of a physician undergoing surgery.

One of Dreiser's short stories is generally considered a masterpiece of supernatural horror; titled "The Hand," it was originally sold to *Munsey's* in 1919 for $300 and published in the May 1919 issue, then frequently reprinted, once as the featured story in the June 1929 issue of *Ghost Stories*. In that story, Davison, a prospector in the Klondike, kills his partner, Mersereau, when he catches him stealing a diagram of a new gold field. As Mersereau expires he reaches out toward his killer with his huge right hand as though he were praying for the strength to throttle him. Long after leaving the Klondike, Davidson continues to see that hand on the ceiling of his cabin or in the smoke of rooms, and finally in a tuberculosis sanitarium insists that his partner in the spirit world is trying to catch him weakened and asleep to finish him. This actually happens, and Dreiser, disdaining the double entendre or the psychological death-wish, has the ghosts speaking to each other as they choke Davidson to death!

The Book of the Damned was defined by Fort this way: "By the damned, I mean the excluded." The bypassing by the scientific community of reports of rains of blood, objects dropping from the skies, whether stones, living creatures, fish, gelatinous matter, or vegetation. He deplored the interpretation of the red sunsets being attributed to the explosion of the crater Krakatoa on August 28, 1883. He reported on many carcasses of "unknown" sea monsters. He theorized that we were being visited by intelligent beings from another planet, who dredged us up from the atmosphere, as we net fish from the sea. He speculated on another land or a Sargasso of the air up above. He listed scores of magazine, newspaper, and book references to all those and many similar events. When scientists accepted a phenomenon, he questioned their judgment. If they did not accept a phenomenon, he mercilessly excoriated them. Sometimes he had written to the source of the clippings for further information. If his book was any criterion, he rarely was able to get any worthwhile additional information or confirmation. He admitted to doubting the veracity, interpretation, or accuracy of many of the stories he used as "evidence," yet insisted that cumulatively they added up to something. He literally never was able to make the facts speak for themselves. He merely listed events and then would throw in a gratuitous theory. Only a brilliant journalistic style made the books readable, and only the uniqueness of his suggested explanations made wading through the volume worth the effort.

He believed "that our whole quasi-existence is an intermediate stage between positiveness and negativeness or realness and unrealness.

"Like purgatory, I think."

Fort's forte for cultivating few friends, but those few of only the highest caliber, evidenced itself again. Ben Hecht, a young reviewer for the *Chicago Daily News,* was given *Book of the Damned* for appraisal. Hecht, then penniless and desperate, took an idea from the book and sold it as a short story. He gratefully repaid his debt in an essay titled "Phantasmagoriophobia" on Harry Sell's Wednesday Book Page, where he coined the term "Fortean" as meaning a disciple of Fort. Lines from his review have been quoted ever since as endorsements of the author, concluding: "For it is written that the theory he has hurled into being is destined, like some phantom gargoyle, to perch itself astride every telescope and laboratory test tube in the land. For every five people who read this book, four will go insane."

Hecht was not the most important convert made by *The Book of the Damned.* Booth Tarkington read a copy while recovering from influenza (he thought it was a murder mystery) and dashed off an enthusiastic letter to *The Bookman:* ". . . what is a fevered head to do with assemblies of worlds, some shaped like wheels, some connected by streaming filaments, and one spindle-shaped with an axis 100,000 miles long?"

When George Allan England read *The Book of the Damned* and saw there incorporation of a half-dozen concepts identical with "Empire of the Air," he concluded that great minds think alike and proceeded to write "The Thing—from Outside," published in the April 1923 issue of Hugo Gernsback's *Science and Invention,* a well-done horror tale of a party of three men and two women, abandoned by their guides in the ice of the Hudson's Bay Area of Canada, who one by one turn into mindless idiots, "possessed" by some unseen, intangible "thing" lurking nearby.

"I tell you," insisted Jandron, "there are forms of life as superior to us as we are to ants. We can't see 'em. No ant ever saw a man. And did any ant ever form the least conception of a man? These Things have left thousands of traces, all over the world. If I had my reference books—"

"Tell that to the marines!"

"Charles Fort, the greatest authority in the world on unexplained phenomena," persisted Jandron, "gives innumerable cases of happenings that science can't explain, in his *Book of the Damned.* He claims this earth was once a No-Man's Land where all kinds of things explored and colonized and fought for possession and he says that now everybody's warned off, except the Owners."

George Allan England believed!

Since the story was reprinted in the April 1926 issue of *Amazing Stories,* the first issue of the first science fiction magazine introduced Fort to formal science fiction! "The theme of Mr. England's story is unusual and extraordinary," the blurb stated.

When Boni & Liveright scheduled Fort's second book, *New Lands,* for 1923 publication it was Booth Tarkington who wrote the introduction. Tarkington, a fine humorist himself, richly enjoyed Fort's obvious sense of frolic. Fort had his tongue in his cheek about many of his theories, but *not* about those in *New Lands,* which zeroed in most heavily on astronomy. For him the scum of the earth were astronomers. There was not a competent one to be found among them, and scarcely an error-free observation in the misspent lives of all of them. Literally nothing they had ever published was right.

The essence of his true belief was expressed in the book's opening lines:

> *"Lands in the sky—*
> *That they are nearby—*
> *That they do not move."*

As early as 1920, secure in his legacy, and launched on a writing career, Charles Fort had decided to take up residence in England. His primary motivation was that he had used up the resources of the main library at Forty-second Street and Fifth Avenue, New York City (one of the world's greatest), and felt it was time to begin working his way through the files of the British Museum. While there, another partially successful try at publishing some of his humanistic material was made, again through the auspices of Theodore Dreiser.

One of Dreiser's greatest supporters had been Frank Harris, frequently described as a "scounderel" and a "rogue," best known today for the authorship of the "pornographic" *My Life and Loves,* but with some outstanding editorial and literary achievements to his name. Harris, who had conducted most of his activities in England, secured the ownership of the American *Pearson's Magazine* with its October 1916 issue.

Stories and articles by Theodore Dreiser appeared in the magazine in 1918. Largely because he was pro-German like

238

Harris, as well as forthright, most magazines wanted no part of him. It was from the August 1919 issue, carrying Dreiser's short story "The Mayor," that Charles Fort quoted in *Lo!* references from the article "Ambrose Bierce" by Joseph Lewis French. There were changes of ownership in *Pearson's Magazine* and lapses of publication, but when it was started up in its new incarnation in 1923 as *The New Pearson's*, with Frank Harris now contributing editor, it incredibly scheduled serialization of *The Outcast Manufacturers!* The story began in the May 1923 issue. With the second installment in June, illustrations by the renowned cartoonist William Gropper enhanced its presentation. The story broke off, uncompleted, in the October 1923 number, even though the magazine continued publication. At no time was anything but the initials "C.F." used to designate the author and there was evidence that some revision had been done on the work.

Charles Fort worked at the British Museum until the small type and bad light made him blind. All purpose in remaining in England ended and sometime in the late twenties he returned to New York City, where gradually his sight returned. This was a bond Fort would have in common with Booth Tarkington. Both of them would go blind from excessive reading and regain only limited vision.

Booth Tarkington induced Henry Leon Wilson, famed author of the *Ruggles of Red Gap* (with whom he collaborated on the play *The Man from Home*, produced in 1907, which ran for six years), to read Fort. The result was explosive. Wilson's subsequent novel, *The Wrong Twin*, found a philosophic tramp printer spouting Fort's wildest theories at the drop of a hat throughout. Perhaps Wilson should have been suspect when he wrote *Bunker Bean* in 1912, a book in which the lead character buys a mummy which he claims was himself in a previous incarnation.

Barton Rascoe, highly respected critic of the era, found that the price of getting the information he needed for a biography of Theodore Dreiser was forced reading of Fort. He converted and became a rabid acolyte.

With such an accretion of coreligionists it was inevitable that a church would sooner or later be established, and that hallowed institution took the form of The Fortean Society, founded January 26, 1931, at a Savoy Plaza, New York, banquet by a charter group of celebrities which included Tiffany Thayer, J. David Stern, Ben Hecht, Booth Tarkington, Aaron Sussman, Barton Rascoe, Alexander Woollcott, John Cowper Powys, and Henry Leon Wilson.

It had twelve major aims, the first and last of which comprised the heart of its aspirations.

The first: To put the books of Charles Fort into the hands of as many people as can possibly be prevailed upon to read them.

The last: To perpetuate dissent.

Initial financing of the movement was provided by J. David Stern, newspaper publisher.

The High Priest of Fortean belief was Tiffany Thayer, a militant athiest anarchist, who gained reputation for his racy novel *Thirteen Men* (1930). He also wrote novels with elements of fantasy and science fiction; one of them, *The Greek* (1931), was completed at the time of the founding of the society and published by Fort's original publisher, Boni. *Doctor Arnoldi* (1934) and *One Man Show* (1937) would appear later. He had been in correspondence with Fort since 1923, and was therefore elected secretary of the association.

At first the efforts of the association were confined to getting Fort's remaining works into print. *Lo!*, the third book, was issued February 9, 1931, and the organization of the Fortean Society timed only two weeks earlier was, in good measure, a publicity stunt to help the sale of the book. The excellent newspaper and magazine publicity attendant it were in a good measure responsible for a total of three printings in six weeks (including a plug in advance of the meeting in the February 23, 1931, *Time*). The sale of the volume did not survive the echoes of the promotion. To benefit from the publicity, Liveright issued a third printing of *Book of the Damned*, February 1931.

The chief target of Fort's books had been the astronomers. His abuse of their efforts had been cruel, uncalled for, and vindictively unfair. His alternatives to their theories were so far-fetched as to be either a mass of satire or outright ignorance and stupidity.

The seemingly unexpected windfall of the publication of *Lo!* was a tremendous endorsement by a prominent leading popularizer in writing and lecturing of astronomy. This was the closest Fort ever came to a victory over science. Maynard Shipley's review "Charles Fort, *Enfant Terrible* of Science" was printed in the March 1, 1931, issue of *The New York Times.* He took Fort sharply to task for obtuseness regarding the scientific method employed in astronomy, but complimented him upon his documentation, called him a writer of "nonfictional thrillers," and incorporated a wealth of superbly quotable quotes, the most repeated of which was the closing lines of the review: "Reading Fort is to ride on a comet; if the traveler return to earth after the journey he will find after the first dizziness has worn off, a new exhilirating emotion that will color and correct all his future reading of less heady scientific literature."

The result was another printing of *Lo!* on March 23, 1931.

What the readers *didn't* know was that Shipley, in his own fashion, had been a Fortean for ten years! He was introduced to *Book of the Damned* in 1921 by his wife, Miriam Allen de Ford, later a frequent contributor to science fiction and fantasy magazines (a short weird tale of hers, "Ghostly Hands," appeared in the January 1929 issue of *Tales of Magic and Mystery*). Disagreeing with some of Fort's facts, he wrote to the book's publisher, eventually got an answer from Fort, then living in England, and a correspondence ensued which carried through to Fort's death.

Fort's last few months of life were, therefore, destined to be relatively happy ones, considering the unprecedented recognition and serious consideration of his theories. A large, puffy-faced man, with a grotesque mustache and thick-lensed, out-of-date glasses, he looked like a comedian made up for a silent film. Semi-reclusive, he entertained himself with a self-invented game of Super-Checkers, alleged to be played on a board of 7,000 squares with 1,000 units. His death on May 3, 1932, at the Royal Hospital, Bronx, was attributed to an enlarged heart. He was not quite fifty-eight. Anna Fort died five years later, August 25, 1937.

There was a most unfortunate situation after Fort's death which virtually eliminated Theodore Dreiser's support. Whatever Fort became, in either a literary sense or as a provocative figure because of his ideas, he owed to Theodore Dreiser. It seems almost absurd to believe that anyone would have ever published Fort's books were it not for Dreiser, and except for that man he might have abandoned all literary pretensions long before World War I and never been heard from again. Dreiser had written to Fort on August 27, 1930: "You—who for all I

241

know may be the progenitor of an entirely new world view-point: you whose books thrill and astound me as almost no other books have thrilled and astounded me . . ." In December 1931, when Fort's health was failing, Theodore Dreiser came to his apartment and gave him $100 for Christmas. In those Depression days, that sum was enough to keep two people going for six weeks. There is no way of knowing how many other times Dreiser contributed financially to Fort. Perhaps the mystery of Fort's financial survival before he received his bequest can somehow be traced to Dreiser. Yet, Fort gave Tiffany Thayer a letter which permitted him to take the 40,000 or so accumulated notes and possibly other letters and papers after his death, and Dreiser, who had initially been a founder of the Fortean Society, was understandably furious. He felt he had at least earned the right to examine Fort's material and he refused to have anything more to do with Tiffany Thayer or the Fortean Society, and requested that his name not be associated with it in any respect.

Dreiser had seriously considered writing Charles Fort's biography, but it never materialized, possibly because of this incident. After Dreiser's death, December 28, 1945, Tiffany Thayer reported in the Summer 1946 issue of *Doubt,* The Fortean Society magazine, that Mrs. Theodore Dreiser had agreed to send him all of the Dreiser-Fort correspondence except two letters in exchange for a life membership in The Fortean Society. Actually, thirty letters were withheld and photostats sent in their place, and some letters had already been contributed to libraries. Beginning with the twenty-first issue of *Doubt,* Theodore Dreiser's name appeared for the first time as a deceased founder of the Society on the membership applications.

Fort's immediate monument was his last completed volume of data, *Wild Talents,* concerned largely with teleportation, rushed into print by Claude Kendall in 1932. Without the carefully staged publicity and prearranged promotion accorded *Lo!* it proved a failure. The Fort "boom" collapsed.

Fort had gained at least one valuable supporter in the science fiction world, the popular author Edmond Hamilton. "The Space Visitors" by Edmond Hamilton in the March 1930 *Air Wonder Stories* carried a blurb by David Lasser, its editor, stating: "That such things may have actually come near the earth, is asserted forcibly by Charles Fort in his amazing book,

'The Book of the Damned,' in which he brings forward evidence to show that over a period of the past 150 years there has been evidence of strange extraterrestrial activity, presumably from sentient beings."

In "The Space Visitors," a "colossal scoop" descends from the atmosphere and carries away portions of villages, fields, and even a segment of the city of Chicago. The world is in terror, and civilization begins to dissolve. In desperation, thousands of air mines are manufactured and sent aloft, and eventually the space ship of the aliens, taking "samples," strikes them and is destroyed.

Replying to a letter from Forrest J. Ackerman in the readers' column of the May 1930 *Air Wonder Stories,* the editor indicated reader reaction by stating: "Edmond Hamilton's seems to have received universal commendation. More letters have poured into this office praising his originality than we have received for any story in a long time."

Hamilton had taken his story ideas from *Book of the Damned,* where Fort had said: "I think we're fished for. It may be we're highly esteemed by super-epicures somewhere."

From the same book Edmond Hamilton took lines which have since become the most famous of all of Fort's writings, as the plot for "The Earth Owners" (*Weird Tales,* August 1931).

In these lines Fort answers the often-asked question, "If we have been visited by extraterrestrials, why haven't they attempted to communicate with us?"

"I think we're property.

"I should say we belong to something;

"That once upon a time, this earth was No-man's Land, that other worlds explored and colonized here, and fought among themselves for possession of, but that now it's owned by something:

"That something owns this earth—all others warned off."

"The Earth Owners" finds this planet raided by black clouds of gas which suck the life-force from humans. All is saved when globes of light, the "owners" and protectors of this planet, chase off the raiders.

The story, despite its provocative theme, made absolutely no impression on the readership whatsoever.

That event had to await the coming of an irreverent Irishman, residing in England, named Eric Frank Russell, who initially read *Lo!* as serialized in *Astounding Stories,* without as much as raising an eyebrow. Then, when he ran across *Lo!* again (it was the only one of Fort's volumes ever published in England) in a secondhand book store, it inspired him with a missionary's zeal; he became Great Britain's counterpart of Tiffany Thayer.

When Tiffany Thayer turned out, at his own expense, the first issue of *The Fortean Society Magazine,* dated September 1937, Eric Frank Russell's notes from abroad became a regular feature of the magazine.

Russell had submitted fiction to F. Orlin Tremaine of *Astounding Stories* and had sold him four stories in 1937. When John W. Campbell assumed editorship, Russell found the going more difficult and rejections began to pile up. He searched Fort's books for an idea that might make a strong story and came up with the line, "I think we're property." He then wrote the story as a novel under the title *Forbidden Acres.* Rejected because the last half was too weak, Russell surprised himself and Campbell with the revision known as *Sinister Barrier.*

Street & Smith was about to launch a new fantasy magazine, *Unknown,* and it was felt that the novel epitomized what they wished to publish. It was the lead-off story in the first, March 1939, issue of *Unknown,* and in a long introduction to the story, Russell acknowledged his debt to Charles Fort and The Fortean Society, then went on to give a 50,000-word blow-by-blow report of the discovery that the earth is controlled by aliens and the desperate battle to defeat them. The reader approbation given the story turned Eric Frank Russell into a major science fiction figure overnight. Beyond that it was *the* major breakthrough for popularization of Fortean material in science fiction. A significant part of the stories in *Unknown* could thenceforth contain a Fortean flavor, notable among them "None But Lucifer," by H. L. Gold and L. Sprague de Camp (*Unknown,* September 1939), a powerful and ingenious unraveling of the secret of who really causes the miseries of the world by a man who inherits the job of perpetrating them, and "Darker Than You Think," by Jack Williamson (*Unknown Worlds,* December 1940), where latent genes tending towards lycanthropy are revived in certain members of the human race.

Russell himself stayed pretty much away from the Fortean notions in his later fiction because he feared a duplication of the charge brought against him that *Sinister Barrier* had been a deliberate remake of Hamilton's *The Earth Owners*. However, in nonfiction he carried on the faith with a Fortean mélange of "inexplicable" newspaper reports of strange phenomena in "Over the Border" (*Unknown,* September 1939) and "Spontaneous Frogation," telling of the mysterious arrival of thousands of frogs in a small lot in the middle of the city of Liverpool.

The Fortean Society's greatest coup was arranging the publication of all four of Charles Fort's books in an omnibus of 1,125 pages by Henry Holt & Co. in 1941. It was said that Thayer himself guaranteed any losses on the volume. What was not said was that the editor at Henry Holt was William Sloane, the inspired novelist of *To Walk the Night* (1937), where a man discovers that the woman he is married to is actually a nonhuman alien, and *The Edge of Running Water* (1939), in which a machine opens the door to another dimension. He was scarcely an unsympathetic party.

The review by John W. Campbell of the books of Charles Fort in the August 1941 *Astounding Science-Fiction* most heartily recommended it as a source book for plots. This advice was not only followed by his authors but after some years was suggested to them by Campbell. At first the adaptations were subtle and of the same high order of originality as "The Space Visitors" and "The Earth Owners." A prime example was "The Children's Hour" by C. L. Moore writing under the pen name of Lawrence O'Donnell (*Astounding Science-Fiction,* March 1944), a poignant tale of a man who discovers that the girl he loves is an immature member of a superior race and he is but one step in the progress of her education.

This turn of plot added width to the base of science fiction. However, the trend was to take a different turn as evidenced in Robert A. Heinlein's "Waldo" (*Astounding Science-Fiction,* August 1942) where a rocket drive is repaired and operated by *witchcraft.* The implications were that man's technical progress had blinded him to the fact that there are other directions he might have ventured in.

Actually, more of Fort's work is devoted to exploring the possibility for a basis in teleportation than in any other subject. Simply stated, teleportation is the ability to move objects by merely an exertion of the will. The poltergeist reports could all be clarified if men had such power. In fact, Fort explains thousands of unusual falls of objects by this "wild talent." "Burning Bright" by Robert Moore Williams, writing under the pen name of John S. Browning (*Astounding Science-Fiction,* July 1948), concerned, in part, a man who could levitate and make objects vanish as a result of high radiation dosage. By far the most masterful story ever written concerning levitation was "What Thin Partitions" by Mark Clifton and Alex Apostolides (*Astounding Science-Fiction,* September 1953), telling of the ability to levitate objects by a frightened little girl, and how it was usefully harnessed.

We find stories based on a single reference of Charles Fort, such as "He Walked Around Horses," by H. Beam Piper, which proceeds from an 1809 incident of a British envoy in Prussia who stepped out of sight while examining his horses and was never seen again. The story has him appear in an alternate world where Napoleon never gained power and the colonies lost the revolution (*Astounding Science-Fiction,* April 1948).

Campbell greatly encouraged Fortean concepts through the promotion of "psionics," a term for natural phenomena for which we have not yet discovered the scientific base. He promoted water-dowsing rods, dianetics, the Dean drive (a machine thought to defy gravity), and many other plainly crackpot devices. In the process, the science fiction authors followed a rash of "wild talents" among its literary protagonists which would never have been tolerated earlier, and which put Superman to shame.

Science fiction has attracted many crackpots in the past who thought its readers would be fertile ground for their particular obsession. The rejection of cultist, mystical, or irrational notions has been almost total whether it was the absurdity of heroes living in caverns under the earth or the "truth" behind the flying saucers. Charles Fort and the Forteans, promoted by editors and authors but never eagerly embraced by the science fiction readers, are destined for the limbo of Richard S. Shaver and the flying saucers.

The justification for Charles Fort has always been that he rocked the complacency of scientists by presenting them with thousands of happenings which logic could not explain. The explanation by his devotees that his stories were documented is a fraud. *The source of publication of the stories was documented, not the events the stories relate.* Fort collected 40,000 unusual reports in twenty-six years (some place the figure as high as 100,000). No one really believed that he interviewed or wrote concerned parties to verify any substantial portion of these stories.

It is a pretty obvious fact that no man can be right *all* the time. Neither can a man be *wrong* all the time. Fort came closer to being wrong all the time than any living human being of record.

A partial look at that record:

The earth is almost pancake-shaped and not round.

It does not revolve at all, or, if it does, only once a year.

The earth is surrounded by a shell of matter.

Stars do not exist, they are merely holes in this matter which twinkle because the canopy ripples.

There are frozen masses of earth, vegetation, and animal matter suspended above which occasionally are shaken down.

The planets are only a few thousand miles away.

Maybe he was the greatest humorist of all time, but even a satirical crank can occasionally be right. The discredited Immanuel Velikovsky in *Worlds in Collision* made a couple of right guesses which have revived his book. Fort, never.

To the contrary, everything that has happened since Fort died verifies that *he and his Fortean followers* were *wrong*, and science was right; particularly right were the astronomers whom he berated the most.

The rockets, probes, and satellites in space, and moon landings, are *adding* immeasurably to knowledge, but they would never have been possible if the scientific theories had not been fundamentally correct. Every new probe that goes up is another nail in the coffin of Forteans who feel that there was any honest value in contrariness for contrariness's sake. Had Fort succeeded in gaining more attention, he could only have *retarded* progress. There is no incident where reading Fort unfettered the mind enough to contribute as much as a metal clamp to civilization.

If there is any doubt that his viewpoint leads to *wrong thinking,* rather than clear, one need only survey the career of the official organ of the Fortean Society, titled *Doubt,* after its tenth issue, and read the views presented.

Fort initially started out to be the "gadfly" of science, but *Doubt* ranted and raved against the pope, Jesus Christ, conscription, vivisection, vaccinations, Wasserman tests, and Einstein.

The Fortean organ had the unique distinction of being against *both* science *and* religion. A cartoonist who drew for *Doubt,* named Art Castillo, did his best work lampooning Albert Einstein and Jesus Christ.

The climax came when Russia announced the launching of Sputnik in 1957, and this finding was confirmed by scientists of the rest of the world.

What was the Fortean reaction to this news? Tiffany Thayer wrote:

> Now asinine gullibility—internationally has reached a new apogee, and we are being asked to believe the most preposterous lie since the invention of virgin motherhood. Untestable theories, utterly incapable of proof, are being put forward as established facts by the heads of the world's great institutions of learning and the Chiefs of States, who do not even bother to keep their faces straight for the cameras . . . My subject you will have guessed is Sputniks I and II, and following here is a documentation of the writer's charge that the laymen of the world are victims of a fraud and a hoax perpetrated by politicians and scientists in international collaboration . . . Dr. Kilian of MIT is the only God and Willy Ley is his prophet . . . Whipple and Hagen and Kruschev make a strange trio of backslappers, don't they? After all the ink that has been spilt to make us hate Krushy, he tells the biggest lie of his life and these two pillars of free enterprise swear to it.

These rantings and ravings go on for about 15,000 words in which Thayer "proves" no earth satellites were ever sent up or could be sent up or will be sent up.

The launching of the earth satellite was the death blow to Forteanism. Its foundation had rested on debunking astronomical findings and the successful rockets completely, utterly, and without hope of resurrection wrecked Forteanism. The Society did not survive Thayer's death in 1959; neither did the bulletin which terminated publication with issue sixty-one the same year.

Lo! The poor Forteans.

ART:

PORTRAITIST of PRESCIENCE

Yet here upon a page our frightened glance
Finds monstrous forms no human eye should see;
Hints of those blasphemies whose countenance
Spreads death and madness through infinity
What limner he who braves black gulfs alone
And lives to make their alien horrors known?

H. P. Lovecraft penned these lines to Virgil Finlay after having been thrilled by the exquisite stipple and line technique which exposed the monsters of Robert Bloch's *The Faceless God* in almost photographic clarity to the readers of the May 1936 issue of *Weird Tales*. Lovecraft's enthusiasm was in concert with the times. No illustrator, in the history of fantasy magazines, had ever been greeted with so uniformly appreciative a chorus of reader approbation.

"Honor and festivals are due whatever gods were responsible for sending artist Virgil Finlay to you," wrote Robert W. Lowndes to Farnsworth Wright, editor of *Weird Tales*. "He is truly unique, that one; reminiscent of the classic illustrations in high-priced editions of Greek and Roman masterpieces."

To visualize and transfer to the illustrating board a camera-lens quality of the bizarre otherworldly mythology of H. P. Lovecraft, Clark Ashton Smith, and Robert Bloch required a creative imagination of the highest order; this Virgil Finlay possessed, and this the readers of first *Weird Tales* and then the science fiction magazines recognized and appreciated.

Virgil Warden Finlay was born to Warden Hugh Finlay and Ruby Cole, July 23, 1914, in Rochester, New York. His father was half-Irish and half-German and his mother English Protestant, from a religious colony that had landed in the United States in 1643, leaving England for the freedom to observe the sabbath on Saturday. His father was a woodworker, who at one

249

time supervised a shop of 400 men when wood finishing was a construction art. Changing times and the Depression found the father scrabbling for a living in his own business, to die disheartened at forty, leaving behind a daughter, Jean Lily, four years younger than Virgil.

In high school, the short, muscular Virgil was an all-around athlete, starring in boxing, soccer, and attaining championship caliber in pole vaulting, with jumps of 11.8 feet, a respectable height before the days of the plastic poles. To his schoolmates he appeared an athletic extrovert. At home evenings, his passion was writing poetry. The only sample ever seen by fantasy enthusiasts was "Noon Mist" (illustrated by Finlay) published in the final, September 1954, issue of *Weird Tales*, though others exist unpublished.

Despite the poetic muse, art was never far from the young Virgil's mind. In grammar school he had sketched, with a stylus on stencil, drawings for a mimeographed paper (a few still survive). As early as the age of fourteen his wash drawings of human figures were exhibited at the Memorial Art Gallery in Rochester.

At high school professional instruction was available, and he took advantage of it by taking as many art courses as could be fitted into his schedule. The first piece of scratch board he ever worked on was a result of classes with his instructress, Gertrude Bottsford. This drawing surface was to have a pivotal influence on the direction of his career. Ordinarily scratchboard is inked in black, and a sharp tool in the hands of the artist scratches a white line on a black surface. Finlay drew directly on the white surface as though it were ordinary paper, adding brushwork in black as required. He achieved his middle tones by working from white to black and from black to white in the same drawing.

Refinement found him eventually drawing directly on scratch board with a 290 lithographic pen, an instrument with a point so incredibly fine that most artists eschew it. To achieve his much-admired stipple, he dipped the pen in India ink and allowed only the liquid to touch the paper. The point was then wiped and re-dipped for the next dot. A lifelong exasperation was testing his scores of pens until he found one that permitted the ink to flow properly.

The stipple technique by which he achieved a graphic quality

250

in his black-and-white drawings, with their precise groupings of tiny black dots, was a technique which had been more common at the turn of the century. Few contemporary illustrators were willing to master the time-consuming art, which was to make Finlay a standout.

During his last year in high school, Virgil Finlay's father, who was teaching construction supervision at Mechanics Institute, made it possible for his son to take free night courses there. These courses continued following graduation and when the WPA (Work Projects Administration) inaugurated art projects during the Depression, he took advantage of the opportunity to take classes in anatomy, landscape, and portraiture.

He became a fine portraitist and was eventually able to command $300 a painting for what assignments were to be had during the Great Depression. This served as one of his major sources of income during a period when he gratefully accepted jobs on a radio assembly line, in a stock room, with woodworking shops, and as a prelude to his artistic career, actually held a card as a master housepainter!

Though his preference was for fantasy and the supernatural, the first magazine he bought with any regularity was *Amazing Stories* in 1927, because it was the closest thing to fantasy he could find. A year or so later, he encountered *Weird Tales,* and it was love at first sight.

The one thing he disliked about *Weird Tales* was its interior illustrations; he felt confident that he could do better. Six sketches were mailed off to editor Farnsworth Wright for consideration in the summer of 1935. Wright took only one as a test, because he doubted if the fine line and stipple work would reproduce on the cheap paper of the magazine.

Reproduction proofs run off on the pulp stock showed that while the drawings lost a great deal, they still printed with considerable effectiveness. For the record, that first illustration was of a reclining nude Medusa, and Wright used it to fill a space at the end of a Paul Ernst story, "Dancing Feet," in the December 1935 *Weird Tales.* In the same issue he was the artist for "Chain of Aforgomen" by Clark Ashton Smith and "The Great Brain of Kaldar" by Edmond Hamilton.

Farnsworth Wright didn't have to wait for reader reaction to know that he had stumbled on a good thing. Finlay was the key to a special project he had in mind. All his life Wright had been a lover of Shakespeare. It had been his dream to publish Shakespeare in low-priced magazine format. When Max Reinhart and William Dieterle produced *A Midsummer Night's Dream* as a moving picture for Warner Brothers in 1935, with a banner cast including James Cagney, Olivia de Havilland, Mickey Rooney, Dick Powell, Joe E. Brown, and Hugh Herbert, he felt this might be the spark to light a popular Shakespeare revival. He would produce Shakespeare's *A Midsummer Night's Dream* as the first of a series of Wright's Shakespeare Library, similar to *Weird Tales* in size, but on better paper, to sell for thirty-five cents. It would be an illustrated edition, with twenty-five drawings by Virgil Finlay, which, together with the fact that *Midsummer Night's Dream* was a fantasy, would supply the motivation for support from readers of *Weird Tales.*

The financial failure of both the film and Wright's Shakespeare Library were far removed in order of magnitude, but in each case they were a disaster. The effect on Wright was multiplied by the fact that in order to finish the twenty-five drawings for *A Midsummer Night's Dream,* Finlay would fail to appear in three consecutive issues of the economically-none-too-stable *Weird Tales,* risking the ire of impatient readers who clamored for more of his work.

By all odds, one of the most enthusiastic of all of Virgil Finlay's supporters was H. P. Lovecraft, who asked Farnsworth Wright to forward his fan letter to the artist's home. "I have for many months been an enthusiastic Finlay-fan," wrote Lovecraft on September 5, 1936. "Around last December I began to notice some art headings in *Weird Tales* which didn't need quotation marks around the word *art.*" That was the opening of the first of five letters Lovecraft wrote to Finlay, totaling about 12,000 words.

Lovecraft, in one of his letters, had high praise for *The Science-Fantasy Correspondent,* an outstanding, neatly printed publication that had included in its first issue for November-December 1936 Lovecraft's poem "Homecoming." The magazine was edited and published by Willis Conover, Jr., and Corwin F. Stickney, two teen-agers of precocious talent. Conover would eventually become a radio disc-jockey, as well as a participant on "Voice of America" broadcasts, and Stickney would enter the printing business.

Because of their mutual correspondence with H. P. Lovecraft, Willis Conover visited Finlay in Rochester, and on the basis of friendship talked him into doing a number of very fine line drawings for *The Science-Fantasy Correspondent* at no charge. The first appeared on the cover of the January-February 1937 issue and showed a pensive girl with a skull on one side of her and a statuesque bust of a giant cat on the other. An autobiography of Virgil Finlay to be called *Monstro, Baron of Kohl* (a "nickname" given him by H. P. Lovecraft) was scheduled to appear in the March-April 1937 issue but never did, probably because Willis Conover and Corwin Stickney parted after a disagreement and the publication was carried on by the latter. However, the cover was again repeated on that issue.

H. P. Lovecraft died March 15, 1937, and the May-June 1937 issue of Stickney's publication with a new title, *Amateur Correspondent*, was dedicated to him. The cover was Finlay's now-famous, frequently reproduced likeness of H. P. Lovecraft, dressed like an old English gentleman, quill in hand and the hazy outlines of some of his horrors behind him. No single illustration better symbolized Lovecraft. When August Derleth and Donald Wandrei collected the memorial volume to Lovecraft, *The Outsider and Others*, in 1939, Finlay drew a montage of Lovecraftian monsters for the jacket which has since become so integral a part of the book that without it, the sales price is substantially reduced.

Weird Tales paid Virgil Finlay eight dollars for a black-and-white illustration. It took Finlay three days to a week to execute one in his style, depending upon its complexity. Taking a practical approach to the entire matter, Finlay rationalized that since in 1936 and 1937 it was virtually impossible to find work, and if you did, fifteen dollars a week was considered a fair starting salary, the choice was fundamentally between drawing for *Weird Tales* at a pittance and being termed a master or doing nothing and being called a bum.

One way to give Finlay more money without hurting the slim *Weird Tales* budget was to permit him to do a cover. The problem was that for three years almost all the covers had been done by Margaret Brundage, a Chicago housewife who specialized in bright pastel nudes. Wright felt that his covers required the promise of sex to justify his high price of twenty-five cents. Brundage paintings had first appeared on *Weird Tales* with the cover of the September 1932 issue featuring *The Altar of Melek*

Taos by G. G. Pendarves. Eventually she had crowded even the famed Tarzan illustrator, J. Allen St. John, master of anatomy and action, from that spot.

Readers had for years raged unavailingly against her scenes of flagellation, suggested lesbianism, sadism, conclaves of concubines, and gaudy harems guarded by eunuchs, which promised far more than the stories delivered. Wright experimented with bringing J. Allen St. John back for a few covers and the reaction was so positive that he decided to go even further, and in the December 1936 issue, he wrote: "We have received many letters asking that we also use Virgil Finlay for one or more covers. We are happy to announce that Mr. Finlay will do the cover design for a new Seabury Quinn story, which will be published soon. If it is as good as his black and white work, then it should be something to talk about."

There could scarcely have been more reader excitement if Wright had come up with an unpublished Edgar Allan Poe story. Finlay's cover for "The Globe of Memories" by Seabury Quinn (a tale of a love that survives many incarnations) appeared on the February 1937 *Weird Tales* with the same realistic intensity and full confrontation of horrors that he exhibited in his black-and-white drawings. Henry Kuttner summed up the readers' feelings in a letter which read: "Just got the February *WT*. That Finlay cover is a knockout! And so is Virgil's illustration for Owen's yarn. In the name of Lucifer, let's have a Finlay cover along the lines of his extraordinary illustration for Bloch's *The Faceless God*."

What readers didn't know was that the cover for "The Globe of Memories" had to be redone. Finlay, due to his inexperience, had not allowed enough room for the cover lettering. In order to qualify for the assignment, Finlay had painted a sample cover for Farnsworth Wright identical with his scene for "The Medici Boots" by Pearl Norton Swet in the August-September 1936 *Weird Tales*. In it is shown a little demon emerging from a glowing brazier on the left, with an old witch in the center and a beautiful woman of the Medici on the right. The lovely boots of this Medici woman transmit to the wearer the murderous bloodlust of their original owner. The cover was never published, though of good artistic quality. This painting eventually would appear on the cover of the Summer 1973 *Weird Tales* when it was briefly revived by Renown Publications.

Virgil Finlay received $100 for his cover, which was a princely sum in 1937, and about twice as high as most pulp magazines of that period paid for full-color art work. How did this compare with the other top-drawer artists working for *Weird Tales?* It was slightly more than Margaret Brundage received for her pastel nudes, since her rate was $90 a cover. The popular J. Allen St. John, with immense appeal to the lovers of Edgar Rice Burroughs for his classic portrayals of Tarzan in action, also got $100 for covers and $8 for interiors.

Most of Virgil Finlay's black-and-whites were half-page, but when he did his magnificent series of full-page illustrations, each based on several lines from famous poems, he was paid $11 each.

Finlay became a cover regular and might have replaced Brundage immediately, except for a letter he received at his Rochester home, which changed the direction of his career. Dated November 26, 1937, it was addressed to him at 302 Rand Street, and read: "As a reader of *Weird Tales,* I have been interested in your illustration. There might be an advantageous opening on *The American Weekly* at the present time for you. I do not know whether you have thought of changing your town or whether you would want to come to New York. If you can do what we want someone to do, it would probably mean living in N.Y."

The letter was signed in pencil: A. Merritt.

Merritt was one of the great elder gods of the fantasy world, exalted author of *The Moon Pool, The Ship of Ishtar,* and *Dwellers in the Mirage;* the penultimate creator of escape fantasy, whose popularity would sustain itself long after his death. He was also editor of *The American Weekly,* the newspaper supplement to the Hearst papers which claimed the largest circulation in the world.

The salary offer was $80 a week. During a period when a man could support a family on $30, and anything above that lifted its earner into a comfortable middle-class strata, it spelled heady success.

In the Big City, the twenty-three-year-old Virgil Finlay immediately ran into trouble. He was the youngest man on the working staff of *The American Weekly* and the cocky prodigy of A. Merritt. His talent was great but his inexperience colossal. He was not a trained illustrator and was ignorant of publication

255

production and the terminology of the trade. The stipple and line technique which Merritt so admired was a laborious process and it took days to produce an illustration, something which made the art director twitch nervously.

Finlay was fired after six months for taking two-hour lunch periods, a temptation in New York City where cliques of office workers tend to try a different restaurant each day. For about four months he was put on a picture-by-picture basis, then Merritt had a change of heart and sent a note to hurry back, that all would be forgiven if he mended his ways.

Merritt was no easy man to work with. He would have a story conference with Finlay in which the sketches would be decided upon. When they were finished, Merritt frequently had mentally rewritten the story and wanted an entire new set of sketches. Story conferences with Merritt were physically difficult. Periodically Merritt would take off in a chauffered car, rounding up exotic cheeses from gourmet shops. He would bring them back to the office and forget about them or use them for cheese rarebit prepared on a little electric stove. Either way, as the odors were anything but exotic, they made spending any length of time in conference with Merritt an ordeal.

A psychological block prevented Merritt from continuing to write the marvelous fantasies which had made him famous. The nature of that block he eventually confided to Finlay. Essentially, it boiled down to the fact that he could no longer make literary transitions. A sword battle ended in a room and Merritt found himself stymied as to whether to permit the hero to exit through a door, window, or secret passage; to leave with sword in hand or in scabbard. He was afraid the wrong choice would destroy the poetic rhythm of his prose.

Finlay learned that magazine illustrating permitted certain liberties. When unable to find an illustrative scene for *The American Weekly's* serialization of John and Ward Hawkins's novel *The Ark of Fire,* which began April 3, 1938, he *wrote one in.* Not only was there no complaint from the authors, but when the novel of the earth plunging towards a fiery death in the sun was reprinted in the March 1943 *Famous Fantastic Mysteries,* the added scene remained intact!

There might have been seven million people in New York in 1938, but Virgil Finlay was still lonesome. Among his correspondents was Beverly Stiles, a Rochester girl he had known, and who had in common the same birth date. Her cousin, a friend of Finlay's, introduced them when Virgil was twelve and Beverly eleven. She had repeatedly refused his proposals of marriage for religious reasons, as she was Jewish. He had been born a Presbyterian, lost faith teaching Sunday school, tried the Lutheran church, then the Unitarian. When he agreed to convert to Judaism they were married November 16, 1938, in New York by Rabbi Dr. Clifton Harby Levy, a salaried consultant on religious matters for the *American Weekly* since 1899, a friend of A. Merritt, and a leader of the Jewish Reform movement.

The Finlays set up housekeeping in a one and one-half room apartment at 1800 E. Twelfth Street, Brooklyn. One of their early guests was Henry Kuttner, who had been in correspondence with Finlay from the West Coast and whom he finally met by arrangement in a bar in the Times Square area. Kuttner, having conquered his personal terror regarding subways, visited the Finlays during Easter, 1939, and brought with him Jim Mooney, an aspiring West Coast artist who boasted the distinction of having sold one illustration to *Weird Tales,* May 1937, for Henry's story "The Salem Horror." Because it was Easter, Kuttner brought Beverly a stuffed rabbit as a gift.

Employment at *The American Weekly* was anything but "regular." Virgil was laid off and hired back repeatedly. During his layoffs, he would be given work on an assignment basis. Layoffs were sometimes for abusing company rules, performing his work too slowly, but most often they were due to the perverseness of his benefactor, A. Merritt. Riding a high-pressure job, Merritt would change his mind about an illustration, berate Finlay for doing the "wrong" scene, and fire him.

It was during a layoff in 1938 that there was a turn in the fortunes of *Weird Tales* which influenced Finlay's economics. After years of marginally profitable publication, a period when the magazine was primarily controlled by the printers, the title was sold to Short Stories, Inc., headed by T. Raymond Foley and W. S. Delaney, and the editorial offices moved from Chicago to New York. Farnsworth Wright, who had a small interest in the publication, also came to New York with his family to continue its editorship.

The first issue under the new ownership appeared in November 1938, and Margaret Brundage was gone from the covers and Finlay from the interiors. The cover rate was dropped to

$50 and the first under the new ownership was painted by A. R. Tilburne. The interiors, done by Joseph Doolin, were paid for at the rate of $5 each.

Finlay interiors returned with December, and he had the cover for the January 1938 issue illustrating Cyril Mand's story "The Fifth Candle." He was paid only $50 for this and following covers, though his rate of $8 was maintained for the interior drawings. On "liberty" from *American Weekly* he proceeded to do the covers every month from that point on, crowding Brundage from that spot.

In later years, visitors to Margaret Brundage found that she was still furious at Finlay for usurping her cover primacy. Actually, *Weird Tales* was no longer willing to pay her $90 for the covers, and she was in Chicago while Finlay was in New York. The quality of Finlay's covers deteriorated almost immediately, though many of his black-and-white drawings were up to his old standard. He had taken the heavy monthly assignment from *Weird Tales* at a lower rate as an economic necessity, but his primacy there was to voluntarily end.

A change in mood by A. Merritt was documented in a letter now in the files of Gerry de la Ree dated March 1, 1940, which read: "Dear Virgil, Your work is all right and getting better. The main trouble was slowness, but I think you have overcome this. Of course, putting you back on the payroll means you will have to keep office hours. I am making the change effective as of the payroll of next week, starting Monday—and at $70. Good luck to you Virgil. Yours, A. Merritt."

During one of his hiatuses at *The American Weekly,* his friend Henry Kuttner urged him to switch to science fiction, which was a growth field. He introduced him to Mort Weisinger at *Thrilling Wonder Stories,* who was receptive to his work. A single illustration by Finlay done in a technique which vested a silvery sheen to the art work for "Experiment" by Roscoe Clarke, R.R.C.S., a grim tale of a man who turns into a living rat cancer, in the April 1939 *Thrilling Wonder Stories,* brought an immediately favorable reader response. As a result, Finlay also began to illustrate for *Startling Stories* and *Strange Stories,* companions to *Thrilling Wonder Stories.*

Of all the people he worked with in the fantasy field, Finlay was fondest of Kuttner. Finlay was best man at a civil ceremony at which Henry Kuttner married C. L. Moore, at the New York

City Hall, the morning of June 7, 1940, and his wife, Beverly, was the matron of honor. Finlay paid the justice of the peace and bought the bride and groom breakfast.

The closeness of this friendship is best expressed in Henry Kuttner's story "Reader, I Hate You!" (*Super Science Stories,* May 1943), written around a Finlay cover and depicting a puzzled giant holding a spaceship with a defiant little man on top, in one hand. The two lead characters are Henry Kuttner and Virgil Finlay searching for a science fiction fan, "Joe or Mike or Forrest J.," who accidentally carried the wife of a superman off in a chartreuse crystal.

From the standpoint of professional advancement, A. Merritt was Finlay's best "friend." In a photograph of himself he gave Finlay he inscribed: "To Virgil Finlay who illustrates stories just the way I like them." And he meant it! At that very time *Argosy* was reprinting *Seven Footprints to Satan* and Merritt arranged with the editor, G. W. Post, to have Finlay illustrate all five installments, beginning with the June 24, 1939, issue. Finlay would remain an *Argosy* illustrator, including many covers, until its change to large-size slick by Popular Publications with its September 1943 number.

When The Frank A. Munsey Co. began the issuance of *Famous Fantastic Mysteries* dated September-October 1939, dedicated to reprinting great science fiction and fantasy classics from its files, it was Merritt again who induced its editor, Mary Gnaedinger, to use Finlay to illustrate the serialization of *The Conquest of the Moon Pool* (November 1939). It was in this magazine and its companion, *Fantastic Novels,* that Finlay achieved a new pinnacle of popularity. The colorful old classics of A. Merritt, Austin Hall, George Allan England, Victor Rousseau, and Francis Stevens, with their rich imagery and strong symbolism, were made to order for Finlay's talents. The result was an offshoot almost unprecedented in pulp publishing, when *Famous Fantastic Mysteries* offered in its August 1941 issue a portfolio of eight Finlay drawings from the magazine, each on an individual sheet of high-grade glossy paper, suitable for framing. The portfolio sold for sixty cents or in combination with a one-year subscription to the magazine for one dollar. A second portfolio of eight was sold for the same price in 1943, and a third of eight for seventy-five cents in 1949.

Both Standard Magazine's *Thrilling Wonder Stories* and

Strange Stories paid better than *Weird Tales*, in fact, substantially better. Particularly well-paying was *Famous Fantastic Mysteries*. Standard Magazines paid roughly $15 a half-page and $25 a full page or two-page spread. *Famous Fantastic Mysteries* paid about $20 a half-page and $35 a full page.

Virgil Finlay eased off his drawings for *Weird Tales*. These stopped altogether when Farnsworth Wright was released as editor of that publication in January 1940.

With his *American Weekly* job back and all the outside work he could handle, Virgil Finlay appeared to be in good shape, but his genius for graphically depicting the nightmarish finally proved his undoing. Whipping all of his considerable talents into line he turned out an imaginative interpretation of the Sargasso Sea for *The American Weekly* that was so nauseous that a telegram arrived from William Randolph Hearst, Senior, to "Fire Finlay!" This time Merritt could not save him, though three weeks later he did again receive the first of a number of small free-lance assignments from Harry Carl of that publication, predominantly for the food page.

John W. Campbell, editor of *Astounding Science-Fiction*, had come into considerable criticism for the unsatisfactory cover work of Graves Gladney during early 1939. So it was with a note of triumph, in projecting the features of the August 1939 issue, that he announced to his detractors: "The cover, incidentally, should please some few of you. It's being done by Virgil Finlay, and illustrates the engineroom of a spaceship. Gentlemen, we try to please!"

The cover proved a shocking disappointment. Based on Lester del Rey's "The Luck of Ignatz," its crudely painted, wooden human figures depicted operating an uninspired machine would have drawn rebuke from the readers of an amateur science fiction fan magazine. The infinite detail and photographic intensity which trademarked Finlay were entirely missing.

No one was more sickened than Virgil Finlay. He had been asked to paint a gigantic engine room, in which awesome machinery dwarfed the men with implications of illimitable power. He had done just that but the art director had taken a couple of *square inches* of his painting, blown it up to a full-size cover, and discarded the rest. The result was horrendous. A repetition of it would have seriously damaged his reputation, so

260

Finlay refused to draw for Street & Smith again.

Virgil Finlay had begun to receive assignments from Raymond A. Palmer, editor of *Amazing Stories* and *Fantastic Adventures,* two magazines published in Chicago. His first work for them appeared in the January 1942 issue of *Amazing Stories* illustrating Frank Patton's "The Test Tube Girl." The story led off the issue and proved a wonderful showcase for Finlay. Originally titled "The Clorophyll Girl," it was actually written by Raymond A. Palmer and was probably the best story of his writing career, with a highly original plot of the human race doomed by the death of most women and the attempt to convert the remaining females into semiplants to create a race that could survive. Palmer handled the theme with considerable sensitivity. Finlay, utilizing his best technique, scored impressively with the readers.

When *Amazing Stories* reprinted Stanley G. Weinbaum's novel of a mental superman from hardcovers (Ziff-Davis, Chicago, 1939), they commissioned Finlay to illustrate it. *The New Adam,* serialized in the February and March 1943 issues of *Amazing Stories,* carried several full-page illustrations that had tremendous reader impact. A superbly executed nude of Vanny, the girl whose love meant disaster to the superman (February), surrounded with floating skulls instead of discreet bubbles, was offered on smoothly finished stock at fifteen cents a copy to the readers of the magazine. A full-page illustration for the second installment, symbolizing the superman as a naive and optimistic baby striding bravely forward in a world of malevolent horrors, led off the Virgil Finlay brochure produced by Nova Press in 1953. These were again reprinted in reverse order to illustrate installments of *Mandark* by Richard S. Shaver in Volume II, nos. 3 and 4, of *The Shaver Mystery Magazine,* published in 1948.

With work coming in from Ziff-Davis (which at the end permitted Finlay to send in any scene he cared to draw at will, and Palmer would have one of his staff writers do a story around it) Finlay was in good shape even without the full-time job at *American Weekly.* Even that situation resolved itself when Finlay was unexpectedly commissioned by A. Merritt to do a double-page spread in black and white with a red overlay. The subject was a Mayan temple and goddess. Merritt was thrilled at the results and paid Finlay $300 for it and said he would use him often at this price. That was the last the two were ever to see each other. Virgil Finlay was welcomed into the all-embracing bosom of the U. S. armed forces on June 2, 1943, just three days after he delivered his assignment to Merritt. On August 30, 1943, A. Merritt died of a heart attack at Indian Rock Beach, his Florida second home.

After three months' training as a combat engineer at Fort Belvoir, Virginia, Finlay was made a corporal. He spent two years in the United States, training at Camp Clarbourne, Louisiana; Camp Reynolds, Pennsylvania; and Marysville, California. Following a stint at Hawaii he was sent to Okinawa in April 1945, where he stayed until March 17, 1946. There he was made a sergeant (T-4) and served as chief draftsman to the Surgeon General, Brigadier General Maxwell.

His stay there was no sinecure. He was an engineer scout, involved in three battles, and frequently headed patrols of up to ten men, several times returning as the sole survivor. In these forays he was wounded by a knife-wielding Japanese soldier and grazed by a bullet from a Japanese tank. Fans used to write Finlay asking if his monsters were created from nightmares. His wife claims that he never had any nightmares until his return from the army.

The induction of Finlay into the armed forces created a crisis at *Famous Fantastic Mysteries*. His illustrations had been without question one of the periodical's major drawing cards. Without them many of the "classics" they reprinted took on the aspect of creaky period pieces.

Desperately, editor Mary Gnaedinger and Alden H. Norton who had used Finlay in *Super Science Stories* cast about for a replacement. Their one dim hope was an old man named Lawrence Sterne Stevens who illustrated for *Adventure*, a magazine owned by their company, Popular Publications. Stevens had been in the business so long that in his youth he had considerable training in the fine-line and crosshatch techniques.

"You've been asking for more work," he was told; "if you can make like Finlay, we'll turn *Famous Fantastic Mysteries* over to you lock, stock and barrel, covers as well as interiors."

Stevens was offered the opportunity because in the November 1942 issue of *Super Science Stories* he had done the opening spread to Henry Kuttner's "We Guard the Black Planet," of a man and a woman with wings, in superbly delicate line.

Stevens's first job was the cover and interiors for the novel *Three Go Back*, by J. Leslie Mitchell (*Famous Fantastic Mysteries*, December 1943), telling of three moderns thrust back in time to the era of the cavemen. His approximation of the Finlay techniques was remarkable. While inferior to Finlay in creative imagination, anatomy, and in the fine nuance the stipple could bring to the illustration, he did invest in his pictures a quiet charm, painstaking and pleasing detail, and the gracious feel of the era in which the story was set. Very quickly he created his own well-deserved following and eventually *Famous Fantastic Mysteries* would issue two portfolios of his work.

The old veteran Frank R. Paul, who had been doing some of the most outstanding black-and-white drawings of his fascinating and imaginative career for *Famous Fantastic Mysteries*, entered war work, and the magazine, covers and interiors, was virtually turned over to Lawrence.

When Virgil Finlay was released from the armed services, he found that art assignments were plentiful but housing was virtually nonexistent.

Plans were afloat to build Levittown, New York, and as a veteran, Finlay found he could get on the waiting list to rent one of the new homes for $100 deposit, so he signed up. In 1950, Levitt announced the building of homes for sale to veterans. The terms were no money down and $55 a month in mortgage payments. Since the rental homes cost $75 per month, with no equity, they could not afford to lose the opportunity. On November 7, 1950, Virgil Finlay moved into 55 Cobalt Lane, which was to be his home for the rest of his life.

As far as work was concerned, Mary Gnaedinger called him in Rochester to welcome him back to *Famous Fantastic Mysteries* with enthusiasm. With the February 1947 issue he was back in *Thrilling Wonder Stories* and within a short time his work was again appearing in *Amazing Stories, Fantastic Adventures*, and *The American Weekly*. The assignments were finally at hand to make a decent living possible.

Rates were better, too. *Famous Fantastic Mysteries* paid him $150 for a cover, $45 for a full page, $30 for a half-page, and $55 for a two-page spread. *Thrilling Wonder Stories* and its companion *Startling Stories* offered $125 for covers, $35 for full pages, $25 for a half, and $40 for a two-page spread. *Amazing Stories* and *Fantastic Adventures* paid $150 for covers, $50 for full pages, $35 for half-pages, and $60 for a two-page spread. *The American Weekly* was good for $35 for a one-column and $75 for a two-column drawing. He did not sell *covers* to the *Thrilling Wonder Stories* and the *Amazing Stories* group, but did sell them many interiors of all sizes.

His return did not crowd out Lawrence. To the contrary, the old man followed Finlay into *Thrilling Wonder Stories* and eventually into many other magazines, attaining a popularity as an interior artist second only to Finlay himself.

Virgil Finlay's illustrating techniques sharpened magnificently after World War II, and readers of the fantasy and science fiction pulps were given a display of inspired symbolism, breathtaking imagery, along with a glorification of the human figure, chilling closeups of evil incarnate, and dazzling visions of a scientific future, all executed in a meticulous style that made even the black and white tones appear to possess infinite gradations of light and dark.

When the paper shortage eased, his primary markets began to add companion magazines. Standard Magazines issued *Fantastic Story Magazine,* Popular Publications reissued *Super Science Stories, Fantastic Novels,* and added *A. Merritt's Magazine of Fantasy.* For a while it seemed that the demand for Finlay illustrations was insatiable. During the years 1947 to 1951, Virgil Finlay did much of his very finest black-and-white work, frequently better than his portfolio material, but not reprinted because they were often broken-paged spreads.

The proliferation of science fiction titles could not go on endlessly. Many of them began to fold, among them some of Finlay's markets. *A. Merritt's Fantasy Magazine* ceased publication in 1950. Far more serious in quantity of Finlay work used was the demise of *Fantastic Novels* in 1951 and *Super Science Stories* the same year. *Famous Fantastic Mysteries* eliminated all interior illustration in early 1951 as they went to a more compact format. All of these magazines were published by Popular Publications, and they made up the largest part of Finlay's income. He was devastated by the loss.

There were strong, new magazines entering the science fiction field but they were digest-sized. The pulp magazines had gone into disfavor and the smaller publications survived by getting display in front of the large, flat magazines. Among the new entries were Lawrence Spivak's *The Magazine of Fantasy and Science Fiction,* but it used no illustrations at all. *Galaxy,* Horace Gold's monthly, which quickly became one of the leaders, bought illustrations for as little as $5 or $10 apiece in special package deals. Most of the other magazines paid very little for drawings.

An exception was Blue Ribbon Publications, who reissued a pulp they had suspended back in 1943, titled *Future Combined with Science Fiction Stories,* under the editorship of veteran Robert A. W. Lowndes. The magazine resumed with the May-June 1950 issue, and Virgil Finlay, aware of the approaching debacle and looking for markets, spotted the magazine on the newsstand.

He called up Lowndes and was told that while they would be delighted to have his work, they could pay no more than $25 for a full-page drawing. He accepted and with the July-August 1950 issue they began to run one Finlay most issues up through March 1952, when they cut off in a blaze of glory, running a Finlay cover.

Finlay, who had curtailed his work for the Standard Magazine group in his emphasis on Popular Publications, now stepped up his efforts there. In desperation he also approached *Weird Tales,* and at rates of half or less than what he was getting elsewhere began to appear on their covers and interiors with the May 1952 number.

For a short while it looked as if he might be able to restore contact on a profitable basis with Ziff-Davis Publications, when that company, under the editorship of Howard Browne, decided to drop *Fantastic Adventures* and revive it as a "quality" digest-sized magazine titled *Fantastic.* The first of the new series, dated Summer 1952, carried three Finlay illustrations for "Six and Ten Are Johnny," the lead story by Walter M. Miller, Jr., but there were no other assignments.

Hugo Gernsback's return to the science fiction field with *Science-Fiction Plus,* an all slick-paper magazine, in 1953, found Finlay approached by editor Sam Moskowitz for drawings. He was delighted to work for the magazine at rates of $50 for a full page, $35 for a half page, $20 for spot drawings, and $55 for a two-page spread. These rates were actually better than he was receiving anywhere else at the time. He turned in six superb drawings for Philip José Farmer's novella *Strange Compulsion* in the October 1953 issue and seven more, including five for Harry Bates's *The Triggered Dimension* in the December 1953 number. The magazine folded, and Finlay found himself out of a good market before he had reaped too much benefit.

During 1953, *Famous Fantastic Mysteries*, which had resumed using illustrations after its initial experiment without them, also gasped its last. Even the low-paying market, *Weird Tales*, threw in the sponge after twenty-nine years with its September 1954 issue.

Straining to stay afloat financially, it was small comfort to Virgil Finlay that he would win a national science fiction art award in 1953, presented by the Eleventh World Science Fiction Convention in Philadelphia on September 6. This was actually the first of the Hugo Awards (though they had not been given that name yet) and Finlay's was for the best "Interior Artist." Ed Emschwiller and Hannes Bok had tied for the best cover artist.

Virgil Finlay had been winning awards in lesser-known science fiction polls since 1940. He took first place as the best all-around artist, first place as the best interior illustrator, and third place for covers in Arthur L. Widner's poll, the largest ever taken up to that time, and released December 1, 1940.

The results of the Beowulf Poll published by Gerry de la Ree on February 21, 1944, showed Finlay voted the best fantasy artist. He repeated this performance in the Beowulf Poll of the following year, published in the Spring 1945 issue of *Sun-Spots*. Finlay again won first place as the best fantasy illustrator in a poll taken for *Fantasy Annual-1948*, published by Forrest J. Ackerman and edited by Redd Boggs.

Virgil Finlay took a full-time job out on Long Island for $75 a week repairing paintings, designing lampshades, retouching antique frames, and anything else they wanted him to do. Evenings he worked late hours to complete whatever assignments he could get. His life-style completely destroyed the public image of the artist as temperamental, self-indulgent, amoral, and undependable. Even when burdened with the heaviest load, Finlay rarely ever missed a magazine deadline. He was always willing to make suggested changes in the artwork, when the editor felt it was necessary. There was no limit to the hours he was willing to work to make a living for his family, and when art failed he was not too proud to go out and repair lampbases. Once married, he remained a devoted husband and father his entire life.

In 1955, Standard Magazines packed in *Thrilling Wonder Stories, Startling Stories*, and *Fantastic Story Magazine*, the largest single remaining source of income from artwork Finlay had. It was not that there were no other markets, but rates were sliding back towards those paid before World War I.

Finlay's semiseclusion in the suburbs and the rarity with which he ever came in to see editors—part of the reason was his lack of clothes and train fare—worked against him. It also meant there was no group of professional friends closely connected to tip Finlay off to new markets or to recommend him to editors looking for artists.

One of the few who did so was Sam Moskowitz, who secured Finlay an occasional assignment in *Radio Electronics* or for Gernsback's annual Christmas booklets. When Virgil Finlay received the commission for *The Complete Book of Space Travel* by Albro Gaul from the World Publishing Company, he returned the favor by suggesting to the editors, Donald Friede and Jerome Fried, that they employ the services of Sam Moskowitz to compile *An Album of Historical Space Travel Art* to supplement the book. It appeared in 1956, containing twenty interiors, many of them two-page spreads, and a cover jacket by Virgil Finlay. The book was an attempt to duplicate for the juvenile audience the success of Chesley Bonestell and Willy Ley's bestselling *The Conquest of Space* issued by Viking in 1949, and which was eventually to market better than 80,000 copies. It was also Finlay's opportunity to get a large sampling of his work reproduced on fine bookpaper and his name featured on the jacket as prominently as the authors'. The hope was that this book might do for Finlay what Willy Ley's had done for Bonestell. Finlay did a splendid job, and the book did go into a second printing, but because it was a juvenile, received little critical attention and made virtually no impact.

The severance by Leo Margulies of relations with King-Size Publications, which he had started in partnership with Larry Herbert in 1953 and which issued a monthly digest-sized science fiction magazine titled *Fantastic Universe Science Fiction*, gave Hans Stefan Santesson, former editor of The Unicorn Mystery Book Club, who had been doing book reviews for the magazine, a chance at the editorial seat with the September 1956 issue.

The only artwork that *Fantastic Universe Science Fiction* bought was for its covers, and Santesson had succeeded in getting four from Hannes Bok, but three of them had been previously painted and Bok did not wish to re-establish himself as a commercial artist. Santesson, seeking a replacement, had Sam Moskowitz act as his intermediary in an arrangement whereby Virgil Finlay would do a cover a month for $150.

This monthly assignment was a godsend to Finlay, and his first cover appeared on the March 1957 issue depicting the goddess of Justice with a cowboy hat, gun, and holster, holding in balance scales on which two groups of men in western garb were shooting at one another while a spaceship blasted off to the stars. Finlay did all but two covers through November 1959. The covers were of uneven quality, but some of them have since become "classics." The April 1957 picture of aliens casting the map of earth in green sand was reproduced by *Newsweek* magazine. Several flying saucer covers of extraordinary beauty and effectiveness were June 1957, where a tiny naked alien staggers away from a crashed and burning ship, and May 1958, where a great eagle swoops down to attack a small alien keeping a lookout while his saucer prepares to launch a missile from the Rocky Mountains. Justly famed is the March 1958 depiction of a couple removing their masks at a masquerade ball; the face behind the man is revealed to be a robot. When first published, the July 1958 cover showing the first American landing on the moon was ridiculed because the flag appeared to be flying in the breeze. When the *actual* first landing occurred, a flag was deliberately given that appearance with the aid of wires.

When the magazine briefly went pulp-size beginning with the October 1959 issue, Virgil Finlay was given considerable interior illustrating work, and virtually all he did was of good quality. This bread-and-butter account disappeared when the magazine folded with its March 1960 issue.

Actually, the best-paying market for him was the astrology magazines which were part of the Standard chain, *Everyday Astrology* and *Astrology—Your Daily Horoscope,* whose editors were familiar with Virgil Finlay's illustrations on their science fiction magazines and in 1956 gave him interior work to do. When he lost his cover assignments on *Fantastic Universe Science Fiction* in 1959, he was given a chance to do covers for the astrology publications. For them he drew black-and-whites in his best style and color was added in printing. These were among the finest commercial productions of his later period.

If Virgil Finlay had confined himself to the production of low-paying illustrations for magazines that had begun to regard art as nothing more than a decorative gap in solid banks of type, he would have been through as an artist.

Every spare moment he had, he painted, and long-term adherents of Virgil Finlay would have been astonished at *what* he painted. He was in the throes of experimentalism and renewed learning, doing abstract, Impressionistic, Surrealistic paintings of every type, playing with water colors, oils, colored glues, ceramic finishes, and anything else he could find which seemed to strike a fresh path.

Literally hundreds of paintings were executed. Visitors to the house occasionally became patrons for his new type of paintings and gradually a large selection moved into private art collections. Giant canvases had titles like *Voyager, Icarus, Jacob Wrestling the Angel, Hello from Bertha, The Prophet, Metzengerstein, Flying Dutchman, Still Life with Zinnias, Walker in the Storm, Dybbuk Dance, King Creon, The White Bull, Tiger, Tiger,* and innumerable others.

Virgil Finlay made only a single public appearance at a science fiction event in his life and that was at The Eastern Science Fiction Association Annual Expanded Meeting of March 1, 1964, held in Newark, New Jersey. At that meeting there was a slide showing of the forty-year career of the late science fiction artist Frank R. Paul. It was also at this meeting that The Eastern Science Fiction Association presented Virgil Finlay with a plaque as the "Dean of Science-Fiction Art for unexcelled imagery and technique." It was quite evident why Finlay had not made previous public appearances. Perspiration poured from him in a cascade and he trembled in every member as he rallied himself to give a talk and express appreciation of the honor bestowed upon him.

There was a moment when it appeared that Virgil Finlay might illustrate a new edition of *The Hobbit* by J. R. R. Tolkien for Houghton Mifflin. He had been asked for and submitted a sample drawing, but Tolkien was furious at the art, claiming that it was mockingly satirical, and it was returned on July 24, 1964, by Walter Lorraine of Houghton Mifflin, who said, "Unfortunately, after much discussion between ourselves and the English publisher, we have decided to keep the existing edition in print and later perhaps bring out a deluxe edition of a somewhat different nature."

During his last years, Virgil Finlay's major sources of income were the astrology magazines *Astrology—Your Daily Horoscope* and *Everywoman's Daily Horoscope*, which each paid him $150 for black-and-white illustrations, using one a month each on their covers. His work for them was of consistently fine quality. Occasionally he got calls for promotion pieces from the Doubleday Book Club, and these were always well paid-for.

He sold some of his paintings to visitors and through such gallerys as the Vera Luzuk Gallery, the Hitch Horse Gallery, and the Gallery Beyond the Blue Door. He had five one-man shows, and for a while the gallery outlets seemed to offer the dual hope of income and the latitude to paint the way he wanted to. This proved illusionary, because he found that in order to generate sales he had to paint what sold best, and this was constricting both in subject matter and technique.

Early 1970 found him ill, and a medical examination indicated cancer, requiring extensive surgery involving his tongue, gums, and lymph glands. His recovery was slow, but he continued to do his two monthly covers for the astrology magazines. There were periods when he was too ill to work and they reprinted an old cover. He experienced a great deal of pain and finally returned to the hospital for further tests. It was determined that he had serious liver trouble. He died January 18, 1971, at the age of fifty-six. The cause of his death was given as cirrhosis of the liver, but when an autopsy was taken, he was found also to have lung cancer in an advanced stage.

It was ironic, but the best year of his life financially was his last year, because he had begun to sell off in large quantities some of the several thousand originals in his possession. In the final analysis, it was the rabid, letter-writing science fiction and fantasy fans who had filled the readers' columns of the magazines with their praise of him for so many years who put their money where their mouths were.

Virgil Finlay's reputation will live on and may even form the basis of a cult. Hundreds of his unique stipple and crosshatch masterpieces exist in collections in the United States and abroad. Because of the superb symbolism in so many of them, they will be suitable to illustrate stories, articles, poems, and bits of philosophy for generations to come. There will be portfolios and collections of his work in the future. Virgil Finlay is destined to become a "classic."

Time may bring some of his gallery art to the fore and give him a new sort of reputation, but that is not predictable. Within the fantasy world where he did most of his work he was a once-in-a-lifetime phenomenon.

It is unlikely that anyone in the foreseeable future will possess the talent and dedication to surpass him in the specialization which he made his life's work.

INDEX